A HISTORY

OF THE

HOLY EASTERN CHURCH.

The Patriarchate of Antioch.

A HISTORY

OF THE

HOLY EASTERN CHURCH.

The Patriarchate of Antioch.

BY THE

REV. JOHN MASON NEALE, D.D.

Late Warden of Sackville College, East Grinsted,

(*A POSTHUMOUS FRAGMENT*);

TOGETHER WITH

MEMOIRS OF THE PATRIARCHS OF ANTIOCH

By CONSTANTIUS,
PATRIARCH OF CONSTANTINOPLE,

TRANSLATED FROM THE GREEK

AND

THREE APPENDICES,

EDITED WITH AN INTRODUCTION

BY THE

REV. GEORGE WILLIAMS, B.D.
VICAR OF RINGWOOD, LATE FELLOW OF KING'S COLLEGE CAMBRIDGE

WIPF & STOCK · Eugene, Oregon

Wipf and Stock Publishers
199 W 8th Ave, Suite 3
Eugene, OR 97401

A History of the Holy Eastern Church: The Patriarchate of Antioch
By Neale, John Mason
ISBN 13: 978-1-60608-330-7
Publication date 01/2/2009
Previously published by Rivingtons, 1873

TO THE RIGHT REVEREND

EDWARD HAROLD,

LORD BISHOP OF WINCHESTER,

IN GRATEFUL REMEMBRANCE OF HIS

UNDEVIATING KINDNESS

FOR MANY YEARS PAST,

AND AS

A PLEDGE OF FILIAL DUTY AND REVERENCE

FOR THE TIME TO COME;

THIS VOLUME IS, WITH HIS PERMISSION,

INSCRIBED

BY HIS FAITHFUL AND AFFECTIONATE SERVANT

THE EDITOR.

ADVERTISEMENT.

I HAVE to acknowledge with gratitude the kind assistance of the following friends in preparing this Volume for publication, and in passing it through the Press.

First of these is Gregory, the very learned and Most Reverend Metropolitan of Chios, who may be regarded as having contributed to the Volume, not only the documents contained in the first Appendix from the Archives of the Patriarchate of Constantinople, of which he was once Chief Secretary, but also the continuous Catalogue of the Patriarchs of Antioch, by Constantius Patriarch of Constantinople, which forms the sequel to Dr Neale's Historical Fragment.

These documents and the Third Appendix were translated for me—the former from the Greek, the latter from the Russ—by Olga, the eldest daughter of my old and valued friend Admiral Count Poutiatine.

The Second Appendix was carefully revised and compared with the original Russ by the Deacon Basil Popoff, son of the Very Reverend Arch-Priest, whose name is so well known by all interested in the Russo-Greek Church.

The Rev. Dr Lightfoot, Hulsean Professor in the University of Cambridge, and Canon of S. Paul's, was so good as to read the proofs of the fragment of Dr Neale's Work, and to verify the quotations and references—often, I fear, at the sacrifice of much of his valuable time, so fully employed in the service of the Church, and in the promotion of theological learning.

CONTENTS.

INTRODUCTION.

	PAGE
Dr Neale's Historical Works	ix
Discovery of this Fragment	xi
Other materials for the Volume	xiv
Ecclesiology of Central Syria	xix
Ruined Cities and Churches	xxi
Church of S. Symeon Stylites	xlix
Modern Antioch	lvii

HISTORY OF THE PATRIARCHATE OF ANTIOCH,
BY THE REV. JOHN MASON NEALE, D.D.

BOOK I.

A.D.		
	S. James, Bishop of Jerusalem	2
33	S. Peter, Founder of the Church of Antioch	3
40	Succeeded by Euodius	4
	S. Thomas evangelises Persia and India	5
	S. Thaddæus, one of the Seventy	7
	His disciples Achi and Mari	8
	The Martyrdom of S. James the Just	10
	S. Symeon succeeds him as Bishop of Jerusalem	11
	S. Ignatius, Bishop of Antioch	ib.
	Trajan's Expedition to Parthia	13
	Martyrdom of S. Symeon	14
	Martyrdom of S. Ignatius	15

CONTENTS.

A.D.		PAGE
	His Epistles, and their teaching	17
	Episcopal Succession at Antioch and Jerusalem	21
	Revolt of the Jews under Hadrian	23
	Theophilus of Antioch, and his Writings	25
	Episcopal Succession in Seleucia	29
	Episcopal Succession in Jerusalem	30
	The Paschal Controversy	31
198	The Council of Cæsareia	32
	Narcissus, Bishop of Jerusalem	34
199	Serapion, Bishop of Antioch	35
212	S. Alexander, Bishop of Jerusalem	37
	Episcopal Succession in Seleucia	38
	Pantænus, his Mission to India	40
249	Martyrdom of S. Alexander of Jerusalem	41
251	Martyrdom of S. Babylas of Antioch	42
252	Council of Antioch against Novatus	44
260	Paul of Samosata—his Heresy	46
	Condemned in a Council at Antioch	49
269	Deposed in a second Council	52
	Supported by Zenobia	53
	Eusebius and Anatolius of Laodiceia	54
266—298	Episcopal Succession in Jerusalem	56
303	The Tenth Persecution	57
	Martyrs of Syria	58
	The Crimea evangelized	61
	Martyrs of Tarsus and Palestine	62
	S. Pamphilus, Bishop of Cæsareia	69
311	Martyrdom of S. Lucian of Antioch	71
	The Conversion of Armenia	74
	Eusebius of Cæsareia—his Writings	78
	S. Helena, the Mother of Constantine, in the East	81
	Persecution under Licinius	83
319—325	Episcopal Succession in Antioch	84
325	The Council of Nicæa	85
	The Arians persecute the Church	87
331	Sufferings of S. Eustathius of Antioch	88
	Maximus II. succeeds Macarius at Jerusalem	91

BOOK II.

A.D.		PAGE
	Episcopal Succession in Antioch	95
	Dedication of the Church at Jerusalem	97
341	Council of Antioch	99
	The New Creed of the Arian Party	103
	Marcellus of Ancyra	105
	The Canons of Antioch	107
329	S. Hilarion of Palestine—his Miracles	111
340	Persecution in Persia under Sapor	114
	The Acts of the Martyrs	121
338—350	Three Sieges of Nisibis	131
	Arian Mission to Arabia	132
	S. Gregory, the Illuminator, in Armenia	133
	Episcopal Succession in Antioch	ib.
345	Stephen, the Arian—his vile plots	134
	The Catholic Leaders, Flavian and Diodorus	137
349	S. Athanasius at Antioch and Jerusalem	138
351	S. Cyril, of Jerusalem, succeeds Maximus	141
	The luminous Cross	142
	The Progress of Arianism	143
c. 355	S. Cyril tried and deposed at Antioch	145
354	Persecution still raging in Persia	146
	Sapor invades the Roman Empire	147
	Besieges Amida	149

THE PATRIARCHS OF ANTIOCH,

By Constantius, Patriarch of Constantinople . . 153—190

APPENDIX I.

Extracts from the Archives of the Patriarchate of Constantinople, relating to the Sees of Antioch and Aleppo . . . . 193—198

APPENDIX II.

Memoir concerning the Patriarchate of Antioch, published at Moscow in A.D. 1845. (Translated from the Russ)   199—212

APPENDIX III.

State of the Patriarchate of Antioch in 1850. (Translated from the Russ.)

Sketch of its History	213
Power of the Patriarch	215
The Bishops	216
The Monasteries	218
The Parochial Clergy	222
The Schools	224
The Orthodox people in Syria	226
Their Number	228

INTRODUCTION.

By all who are interested in the fortunes of the much-enduring portion of the Church of Christ comprehended within the limits of the four Eastern Patriarchates, the death of the gifted author of the great Work, under the general title of which this present volume appears, was regarded as an irreparable loss to this branch of Sacred Literature; at least so far as this generation is concerned.

Dr Neale had devoted the best years of his laborious life to the accumulation of materials for this, which he evidently designed to be the chief monument of his industry, and a $\kappa\tau\hat{\eta}\mu a$ $\dot{\epsilon}s$ $\dot{a}\epsilon\acute{\iota}$ to the Church; specially to that cause which had early engaged his warmest sympathies, and to which he consecrated his matured powers with an enthusiasm thoroughly characteristic of the man.

That sacred cause was, the gradual approximation and ultimate reconciliation of the long-estranged families of Catholic Christendom, on the basis of a better mutual understanding; which he hoped might result in a more just appreciation of the comparative unimportance of the points of difference, when viewed in relation to the vast heritage of Divine Truth which all hold in common. And although he was not permitted to see the consummation of his ardent desires, yet his latter years were gladdened by the unmistakeable evidences of a wider and constantly-increasing interest—both at home and abroad—in the cause of a reunited Christendom, which had been for many years the day-dream of a small and un-influential section of Anglican Churchmen. How largely his indefatigable industry had contributed to this hopeful progress of opinion, was known to others better than to himself; and I can myself bear witness to the fact that, while his zeal provoked very many in our own Communion, the exhibition of it in its results, in Russia and the East, was effectual in stimulating a reciprocal interest in various parts of the Orthodox Church.

His chief contribution to this cause, and to that of Sacred Literature, was undoubtedly the great Historical Work above referred to; two instalments of which he was permitted to complete; the first, in the History of the Patriarchate of Alexandria, published in 1847, the second in the General Introduction, published in 1850. In both these works the most striking features to those who had known the author as a writer of life-like fiction, and the uncompromising champion of distinctive Catholic teaching, were, first, the complete subordination of his exuberant poetical imagination to the strict requirements of historical accuracy; and then the rigid impartiality of his estimate of moral worth, unbiassed by theological prejudices and predilections:—a rare quality it will be admitted, whether in ecclesiastical or civil historians, within the domains of religious or political controversy; but indispensable in one who would fairly represent the various phases of thought that have been developed within the Church during the long centuries of her chequered history.

It was, therefore, with no ordinary satisfaction that I learnt, some two years after the death of the author, that his literary executor had discovered among his papers a considerable fragment of what appeared to be a continuation of the "History of the Holy Eastern Church." This pleasing intimation was accompanied with the gratifying request that I would examine, and (if I thought it worth publishing), undertake the editorship of the manuscript; which was accordingly submitted to me for that purpose. A cursory glance at the sheets sufficed to convince me that the "History of the Patriarchate of Antioch" had been undertaken with the same conscientious care that had distinguished the preceding volumes; while it was natural to conclude that the experience obtained in the progress of the work would give additional value to the later production of the author. Unfortunately, however, there was no opportunity of testing the authority of the work; for, while the text was largely interspersed with numerals of reference, the corresponding notes were not forthcoming. On pointing out this fatal defect to Mr Haskoll, I was informed that the missing notes could nowhere be found; and it was feared that this must have been the manuscript, the accidental destruction of which Dr Neale had deplored some years before his death.

As I felt that it would be impossible for anyone but the author himself to supply the verifications and references to authorities, and that the absence of these would detract seriously from the historical value of the work, I was reluctantly obliged to decline the responsibility of editing it.

Many months after this unsatisfactory termination of our first negotiations, the correspondence was re-opened by Mr Haskoll, informing me that he had reason to believe that the missing Notes were at last discovered, and renewing his previous request; with which I could no longer hesitate to comply.

True indeed it is that any posthumous work must appear at a disadvantage; as the "limæ labor" can never be regarded as complete until the last revise has left the writer's hand, and consequently the composition must not be too severely criticised. I have not felt at liberty to depart a hair's breadth from the manuscript, except where it was hopelessly illegible. Happily these exceptional instances are very rare, and are confined to a few words or phrases, which it was not difficult to supply conjecturally from the context.

The fragmentary character of the work was not, in my opinion, any serious objection to its publication: for nothing is more common than for writers—whether of civil or ecclesiastical history—to select some portion of the wide field of study for special illustration; as, notably, the periods of the First Three Centuries of the Church, and of the Reformation, have been frequently handled by writers of various schools. This fragment then may be regarded as a monograph of the History of the Church of Antioch during the first four centuries of its existence; and when it is considered how very important a rôle that Church was called upon to play in the Ecclesiastical History of the early ages; how prominently the names of some of the most distinguished Martyrs and champions of the Faith, as well as of some of its most notorious heretical impugners, are exhibited in its annals; particularly while it comprehended within its limits the Churches of Palestine, subsequently to be formed into a distinct patriarchate; it will be seen that the History of the Patriarchate of Antioch is in fact the History of Eastern Christianity; and however we may regret that the author was not spared to complete what was to him indeed a labour of love, we shall congratulate ourselves that his masterly hand was permitted to strike off the life-like portraits of some of the most renowned of the Church's worthies, which will be found in the following pages.

Having thus narrated the circumstances under which this work is now published, and the causes which have delayed its publication, I may be permitted to mention some motives which strongly influenced me to accept the office which Mr Haskoll was so good as to press upon me,—independently of the deep interest which I have long taken in the fortunes of the great Eastern Church, and of my high appreciation of the value of Dr Neale's Historical Researches. That interest has naturally led me to avail myself of such opportunities as have presented themselves to me of procuring information on subjects connected with the Christian East; and two visits to Russia and two to Syria, at different times and at long intervals, have placed in my hands materials which I hoped might prove serviceable for the illustration of the "History of the Patriarchate of Antioch." It has also been my good fortune to make the acquaintance of some of the best learned of the ecclesiastics of the Orthodox Church, whose aid has been very valuable in the production of the supplementary portion of this Volume; and although this cannot be said of the present Patriarch of Antioch, yet the fact that I have had a personal knowledge of him for some thirty years has given me an additional interest in the fortunes of his Church, which ought to be reflected in these pages.

When I first became acquainted with Hierotheus in 1842 he was Bishop of Mount Tabor, but was better known by the title of ὁ Διάδοχος—"the successor" i.e. of the Patriarch of Jerusalem; having been nominated to that dignity by the then occupant of the see, in accordance with the prevailing practice. On the death of the Patriarch, however, in 1845, the Porte refused to confirm the nomination of Hierotheus, who was suspected of Russian proclivities ('Ρωσσόφρων); and Cyril, Metropolitan of Lydda, was chosen by a free election of the Council of Hagiotaphitæ. When, however, the Patriarchal See of Antioch became vacant some few years later, Hierotheus was elected to that dignity; and the Porte confirmed the appointment. I have twice seen the Patriarch since his elevation, the last time on August 10th, 1866, when I passed a night in his Monastery of Mar Elias, in the Lebanon, some four hours distant from Beyrout. On that occasion I made enquiries of him concerning any materials that might exist in the Archives of the Patriarchate for a history of his Church, and was disappointed to learn that nothing of the kind was to be found in his house at Damascus; which had then been recently destroyed by fire—not for the first time within recent memory. This may account for the disappearance of all documentary annals of the Church of Antioch. When I made that enquiry, I little expected that it would ever devolve upon me to edit a history of the Patriarchate. It was made solely in the interests of Dr Neale, and, as I discovered afterwards, within a very few days after his death, on the Festival of the Transfiguration, August 6th.

But although I thus signally failed in my endeavours to procure information concerning the Patriarchate of Antioch at the fountain-head, my disappointment was partially compensated by obtaining valuable assistance from a most unexpected quarter. Soon after I had undertaken the editorship of Dr Neale's fragment at Mr Haskoll's request, I received from my revered friend, the Metropolitan of Chios, a collection of Greek books and pamphlets bearing chiefly upon the recent history of the Orthodox Church. Among these were two volumes of the Minor Works of Constantius, Patriarch of Constantinople; an author well known and highly esteemed in the East for his learned historical, archæological, and topographical works on Constantinople, and on Egypt. This learned man, born in 1770, was educated in the Patriarchal School of Constantinople, from which he passed first to Jassy in Moldavia, and afterwards to Kieff in Russia. Having been elected Archbishop of Mount Sinai in 1805, he was raised to the Œcumenical Throne of Constantinople in 1830. He occupied it only four years, when he was deposed, and joyfully returned to his literary pursuits in the island of Antigonus; where he survived his fall twenty-five years. The collection of his Minor Works was published in Constantinople in 1866. Among the interesting contents of these volumes I was not a little gratified to find a Treatise entitled, "Concerning the Patriarchs of Antioch until this day," i. e. "until Methodius, the immediate predecessor of Hierotheus, the present Patriarch." This very opportune contribution to my subject enabled me to append to the original fragment of Dr Neale's work a continuous Catalogue of the Patriarchs; and, in some places, something more than a bare Catalogue; for the incidents connected with some of the Patriarchs are full of interest, and narrated in a very graphic style.

I am further indebted to the Metropolitan of Chios for some extracts from the Archives of the Patriarchate of Constantinople (of which he was formerly Secretary), in illustration of the aggressions of the Latin Missionaries in the East, frequently mentioned by Constantius in the biographical notices of later Patriarchs of Antioch.

But besides these unexpected and most opportune contributions to my Volume, I found that I had been unconsciously collecting materials for my unforeseen and unsought-for task, in two Russian Pamphlets, which I have had by me for so many years, that I had actually forgotten the existence of one of them until it came to the surface in the surge of an accumulation of papers, at the very time that it was wanted. These two pamphlets, which are given in the Appendix, furnish a very excellent conspectus of the present condition of the Orthodox Church in Syria; for little change has taken place in it during the last thirty years.

Such is a brief account of the Supplementary portion of this Volume. It remains to offer some explanation, or apology, for the Introduction; and to bring it into harmony with Dr Neale's monograph; the nucleus round which so much apparently extraneous matter has formed. That it is not really irrelevant, it will not be difficult to show. A very considerable portion of that marvellous Repertory of Oriental Ecclesiology which his unwearied industry accumulated in the "General Introduction," is devoted to the Church Architecture of the Orthodox Communion and its offshoots. It was many years subsequent to the publication of that work that the enterprize of a French nobleman—whose name, after having been long before the public as a Christian *savant*, has lately obtained a wider and nobler celebrity in connection with his devoted services as Head of the Ambulance Department on the bloody field of Wörth, where his brother met a soldier's death—the Count Melchior de Vogüé, now French Ambassador at the Porte, discovered and explored a mine of Christian antiquities within the Jurisdiction of the Patriarchate of Antioch, which would have furnished Dr Neale with materials for another important and interesting Chapter on the Eastern Ecclesiology.

Very inadequate as I am to the task of expanding his work, I feel that I ought not to let slip this opportunity of introducing to the notice of the English reader those very large remains of piety and civilization which illustrate in so remarkable a manner the religious life of the Asiatic Christians in the palmy days of the Church of Antioch, during the lifetime of S. John Chrysostom and other eminent lights of the Christian East; particularly as I can do this from my own actual observation: for shortly after I had heard from the Count de Vogüé of the discovery of these Christian cities, I was presented with an opportunity of visiting them, of which I gladly availed myself.

That visit too is closely associated in my mind with the memory of the lamented Dr Neale; for it was in the midst of these noble memorials of the Orthodox Faith, and on the eve of our visit to the grandest monument of one of its most remarkable phases, that the intelligence of his death reached us; and his name was uppermost in our thoughts on the following day, as, amid the ruins of the magnificent Church of Symeon the Stylite, we commemorated, in the Scottish Liturgy, all those "lights of the world in their several generations," who, "having finished their course in faith, do now rest from their labours."

Neither is the subject irrelevant to the History contained in the following pages; for the vast expanse of ruins of which I am to speak is situated in the very centre of the Patriarchate of Antioch, and most of the towns represented by them were, doubtless, subject to the episcopal jurisdiction of the Patriarch himself; and, further, it is highly probable that they were standing in their integrity at a time covered by the narrative contained in Dr Neale's Memorials; for the dated monuments range from the 3rd to the 6th century; and it is almost certain that they were abandoned by their Christian inhabitants early in the following century; if not on the irruption of the Persians under Chosroes I. in A.D. 574, or under Chosroes II. A.D. 611, or, at the latest, on the Saracenic invasion of Syria under Abu Bekr, A.D. 632.

Then there is a melancholy interest in contrasting the ancient dignity and grandeur of the Church in Syria as witnessed to by these stately ruins, with its present deep decline and degradation as exhibited among the scattered remnants of the flock of Christ which still exist in the city where the disciples were first called Christians, and in the Eparchy once subject to the fourth See in Christendom: and I am in a position to exhibit both sides of the picture from my own actual observation.

This perhaps will best be done by extracting a few leaves from my Journal of a visit to Syria in the autumn of 1866, when I have first given a general view of this rich field of ecclesiological research in a graphic summary of my friend the Count de Vogüé, whose general description of these ruins, which he has fully delineated in his great work on the "Civil and Religious Architecture of Syria," first inspired me with a longing desire to follow in his wake.

They are situated "in the mountains which lie between Antioch, Aleppo, and Apameia, on the right bank of the Orontes, and which are known in the country under the names of Jebel Riha, Jebel Ala, Jebel Alaqua and Jebel Semáan. I am almost tempted to refuse the name of ruins to a series of towns almost untouched, or, of which, at least, all the elements are found; sometimes overthrown, never dispersed; the sight of which transports the traveller into the midst of a civilization now lost, and reveals to him, so to say, all its secrets. In passing through these deserted streets and forsaken courts, these porticos where the vine entwines itself round mutilated columns, one experiences an impression analogous to that which is felt at Pompeii—less complete, perhaps, for the climate of Syria has not preserved its treasures as the cinders of Vesuvius; but more novel; for the civilization which one contemplates here is less known than that of the Augustan age. In fact, all these cities, which exist to the number of more than a hundred and fifty in a space of thirty or forty leagues, form a whole from which it is impossible to detach any part; where all is bound and chained together; belonging to the same style, and to the same system; in short, to the same epoch; and that the epoch of primitive Christianity; which is hitherto least known in an artistic point of view, viz. that which extends from the fourth to the seventh century of our era. We are here transported into the middle of the Christian society; we come upon its life—a life not hid in the catacombs; an existence not of depression, timidity, suffering, as it is commonly pictured; but a liberal, opulent, artistic life;—in large houses, built of huge blocks of squared stone; perfectly arranged, with covered galleries and balconies; beautiful gardens, planted with vines; wine-presses, cellars, and stone jars for preserving wine; large subterranean kitchens, and stables for horses; in squares surrounded by porticos; elegant baths, magnificent churches supported by columns, flanked with towers, surrounded by splendid tombs. Crosses, and monograms of Christ are sculptured on most of the doors; numerous inscriptions may be read on the monuments. These, through a sentiment of Christian humility which contrasts with the boastful emphasis of pagan inscriptions, contain no proper names. Pious sentences, passages of Holy Scripture, monograms, dates—that is all: but the tone of these inscriptions marks an epoch not far removed from the triumph of the Church; for there reigns throughout an accent of victory, which sets off still more the humility of the individual; and which animates the least line, from the verse of the Psalmist engraven in beautiful red letters on a lintel covered with sculpture, to the scribbling of an obscure painter, who, while engaged on decorating a tomb, in order to try his chisel traced on the wall of rock some monograms of Christ, and, in his enthusiasm as an emancipated Christian, paraphrasing the Labarum, wrote—Τοῦτο νικᾷ—'THIS CONQUERS!'

"By one of those phenomena of which the East offers frequent examples, all these Christian towns were abandoned on the same day, probably at the time of the Mussulman invasion; since which time they have not been touched. But for the earthquakes, which have thrown down many walls and columns, nothing would be wanting but the roofs and floors of the buildings."

If this description should appear highly coloured, it will be found from the more detailed descriptions which follow, that it is not at all exaggerated.

By commencing my Ecclesiastical and Ecclesiological Survey of Syria at Homs, and continuing it to Antioch, we shall pass over the whole district indicated in the foregoing summary, and shall be presented with some remarkable examples of those contrasts between the ancient and modern phases of its Christianity, of which I have already spoken.

HOMS, the ancient Emesa, reckoned the metropolis of Phœnicia Secunda, in the *Notitia* of Hierocles, is situated near the river Orontes, on its right, or eastern bank. It was noted in pagan times for its magnificent Temple of the Sun; the youthful priest of which, Bassianus, at the early age of fourteen, was raised to the imperial purple by the Roman legionaries in Syria (A.D. 218), which he wore under the name of Heliogabalus for less than four years. It was, perhaps, in rivalry of this temple of the Syrian Sun-god that, under the Emperor Constantinus, a splendid Church, renowned for its beauty, was erected in this city[1].

This church, there can be no doubt, occupied the present site of the great mosk of Homs; so that here, as at Damascus, Jerusalem, and in so many other places in the East, the Christian edifice was adapted to the worship of the followers of Islam. Indeed, it retained, until within three years of my visit, a character that admitted of its being identified with the grand Church mentioned by Sozomen: for it was described to me as having been divided longitudinally by a double row of columns; and this account is confirmed in a very interesting manner by a large fragment of the original building excluded from the modern mosk, because happily the funds were insufficient to assimilate the whole to the modern style. This fragment is, in fact, the east end of a noble Basilica; consisting of five bays divided by double columns in the side walls, and

[1] Sozomen singles it out for special mention, *H. E.* Lib. III. cap. 17: ἀξιοθέατος καὶ κάλλει ἀοίδιμος Ἐμέσης Ἐκκλησία.

distributed into three walks, of which the middle is 32 feet 9 inches wide, and the side aisles 15 feet 8 inches each; giving a total width of 64 feet. The columns, of which some few are *in situ*, are all of red granite, about 16 feet in height, exclusive of the capitals, which are of a very debased classical, or early Byzantine, type. Besides the 5 bays in the old church, I counted in the north wall of the modernized mosk, which is built into the ancient arcading, 16 other bays; and, as each bay was 11 ft. 2 in. wide, this gives a total length of 276 feet—about the interior length of King's College Chapel; nor is it at all certain that this was the extreme length; for there is nothing to mark its termination either to the east or to the west. This noble church is said to have been dedicated to S. John Baptist, whose head was found here in the time of Theodosius[1]; as was the grand Basilica now forming the mosk at Damascus—for the same reason!

And now for the present condition of the Church of Emesa. Dionysius the Bishop had only been two or three months at his post, at the time of my visit. He was advanced in years, and had been a parish priest in the church of S. Nicolas at Constantinople, until he was appointed to this See; which he accepted only at the earnest solicitation of the Patriarch of Antioch. He presides over a small flock, and the Church is a poor and mean building.

[1] Pococke, *Description of the East*, Vol. II. Pt. 1, p. 141.

RESTEN.—About three hours north of Homs are the ruins of a large Church, originally built in the form of a Greek Cross, with a semicircular apse to the east. A story connected with this Church, which fills a bloody page of the annals of Islam, and of the Church of Syria,—may here be told. When Abu Obeideh was subjugating the Valley of the Orontes from the south, he arrived before Resten, which was so well fortified and garrisoned that it refused his summons to surrender. The General promised not to attack it, on condition that he was permitted to deposit there some of his heavy baggage, which impeded his march. Having obtained the governor's consent, Abu-Obeideh chose twenty of his bravest soldiers, whom he shut up in twenty large cases, which opened from within, and had them conveyed into the citadel. Then leaving Khaled, with some armed troops, in a wood near the town, he continued his march to the north. Scarcely was he out of sight, with the bulk of his army, when the inhabitants of Resten congregated in their Church, to return thanks to God for their deliverance. The Arabs, emerging from their concealment, took advantage of this opportunity to seize the wife of the governor, whom they forced to deliver up the keys of the town. Thus they opened the gates to Khaled, and fell upon the unhappy townsmen in their Church, still singing praises to God for their deliverance; whom they butchered in an indiscriminate massacre at the very altar! This place is called Restam by Pococke[1], who notices these ruins of the Church under the description of a "very large convent," and thought the place might represent "the Arethusa of the Itinerary of Antoninus and the Peutinger Tables; though the distances do not well correspond."

HAMAH is the Hamath of the Bible; afterwards named Epiphaneia from Antiochus Epiphanes, and known under that description in the Ecclesiastical annals; which represent its bishop as subject to the jurisdiction of the metropolitan of Apameia. Its bishop, Maurice, sat in the council of Nicæa; and several of his successors appear in Ecclesiastical history[2]. Here, as at Homs, was a noble Church, now converted into a mosk; from the interior of which all traces of its Christian origin and use have been obliterated, with the exception of two columns in its eastern wall. Externally, on the west, a large central gate and two side portals, all with semicircular arches, still retain their original character; and a Greek inscription over a window in the south wall, unhappily illegible from the ground, affords further evidence of its original designation. Tradition says that this Church also was dedicated to S. John Baptist.

The Christians of Hamah are, with very few

[1] *Description of the East*, Vol. II. p. 145.
[2] Le Quien, *Oriens Christianus*, Tom. II. col. 915—918.

exceptions, of the orthodox Greek rite, and number about 1500 souls; with a church, a school, four priests and a bishop, of whom more presently. There are about 6000 orthodox in the diocese, of whom Edlip (to be noticed below) contains about the same number as Hamah.

The worthy Bishop Germanus has a melancholy history, which may be recorded as a specimen of the life of an Eastern Prelate, which it is often thought must be very monotonous and uneventful. He is a native of Damascus, where his family has resided for several generations. Having passed through the inferior grades of the ministry, he was ordained priest, and in due time became Archimandrite at Tyre. His father and brother were murdered in the massacre of the Damascene Christians in 1860. He was at Jerusalem at the time, and only learnt of this domestic bereavement on his return to Beirout some time after. His grief was so intense that his health became seriously affected, and he procured the permission of the Patriarch to absent himself from his post and to travel for a twelvemonth; which he passed chiefly at Athens. At this time the See of Epiphaneia became vacant, and was so strongly urged upon his acceptance by the patriarch, that, unwilling as he was to settle again in Syria, he felt that he must not refuse this providential call; and here he had been for four or five years, far removed from the sympathies of civilized society, to which he had been accustomed; living in the midst of a semi-barbarous people; but having this inestimable advantage over his episcopal brother at Homs, that, as a native Syrian, he is familiar with the language and manners of his people. The church at Hamah is but a poor modern building; also dedicated to the Forerunner.

About six hours north of Hamah is a large Moslem village named Khan Sheikhûr, which I am unable to identify with any ancient site, although a remarkable mound outside the village, apparently in great part artificial, would seem to indicate here, as elsewhere in this part of Syria, that it was formerly occupied by a town. This village is just on the confines of the district occupied by the ruined Christian towns, to the description of which I now proceed.

EL-HASS is situated about four hours north of Khan Sheikhûr, on the left of the direct road to Aleppo. It consists of a vast expanse of ruins, which gives promise of the architectural treasures beyond. Most conspicuous among these ruins is the Church, of a design which we afterwards found to be typical of the general character of the ecclesiastical buildings of central Syria; while the variations in detail are infinite. The south wall and the southeast tower were well preserved; and enough remained of the rest of the building to shew what was its original plan. It was built of stone quarried on the spot, beautifully squared and fitted. It was of an oblong form, with a porch between two towers at the west, and a semicircular apse, also flanked by two towers on the east. It had been divided by columns into a nave and side aisles, over which latter was the gynicæum or women's gallery. The entrance to the porch was by two doors, and from the porch was an ascent on either side, by the towers, into the galleries, which were also connected by a western gallery. The purpose of the eastern towers, flanking the apse, was also well defined. On the ground-floor was the *diaconicon* on the South side, and the *prothesis* on the North; the latter communicating both with the apse and the aisle, the former with the aisle only. The Church had two side doors to either aisle, besides the great west door opening from the porch; and these doors, as well as the windows, present that combination of the arcuate and trabeate construction which may be said to be the distinctive characteristic of the Syrian school of architecture, though by no means confined to that country. I have given a full description of this first Church, which I explored, in order to be able to refer to it hereafter, and to obviate the necessity of frequent repetition.

Next to this Church, which the natives dignify by the name of "Ed-deir," the Convent, the most striking objects in the extensive ruins of El-Hass are the tombs. They vary very much in character, and many of them are exceedingly handsome. Some have been excavated in the live rock, in the walls of the quarries out of which the buildings have been erected. Others are solid square structures, sometimes in two stories, covered in some instances with massive semicircular covers, in others with pyramidal roofs, very similar to Absalom's pillar at Jerusalem. On one of these latter is a long Greek inscription, beautifully carved, running along the cornice; part of which I deciphered[1], and found it to contain passages from Psalms cxvii. ver. 26, 27, and lxiv. 10 (Sept.)—"Blessed be he that cometh in the name of the Lord. God is the Lord, and hath appeared unto us. Thou hast visited the earth, and watered it abundantly," &c.

To the north of the modern village and the tombs just described, are very extensive ruins of the ancient town, situated in a rocky district; so that the building materials were close at hand. This is called *Khirbet-el-Hass*, "the Ruins of Hass;" and conspicuous among them are two large public buildings, one of which may have been a civil Basilica, the other was undoubtedly a church, similar in plan to the one called Ed-Deir, which has been already described.

EL-BARA is about an hour north of El-Hass, and there the ruins are even more extensive than at Hass, and not less important; for although the prin-

---

[1] More fully given in Capt. Burton and Mr T. Drake's *Unexplored Syria* (Vol. II. p. 2 of the plates), the decipherments in which (p. 380) are, however, frequently very unfortunate.

cipal Church is not so well preserved, the streets of the town, and the dwelling-houses, with their courts and offices and wine-presses, are more clearly defined, and reveal more of the domestic life of the ancient Syrian Christians. This is the Elbarraw of Pococke[1], to which he seems to have paid only a hasty visit, and dismisses the description of it in very few words: " Here there is a ruinous well-built castle and some decayed houses, which are of no mean structure; there is likewise a well cut down through the rock." This was, Count de Vogüé informed me, the only place, of all the ruined sites in the district, of which he had been able to identify the name in any historical monument; and that was in one of the chronicles of the Crusades, to which period the fine mediæval castle mentioned by Pococke probably belonged. Its name among the natives is Kala'at Saphian. Many masons' marks chiselled on the walls are in excellent preservation, and might possibly throw light on the date and origin of this building.

In this place we noticed for the first time those sacred inscriptions upon the houses, which no doubt suggested to Symeon Stylites the talisman that he recommended the inhabitants to adopt as a preservative against earthquakes: "Christ is with us. Stand!" We did not discover any copy of that identical inscription; but many were precisely to that effect. A few examples from El-Bara and elsewhere

---

[1] *Description of the East*, Syria, p. 147.

may be given, as they are curious, not only as illustrating the pious practice of the age to which they belong, but also as throwing additional light upon the question of the pronunciation of the ancient Greek. The first carried my thoughts to Castle Ashby, where the Latin version of the same inscription, wrought in the open battlement, "welcomes the coming, and speeds the parting, guest."

✣ ΚΥΡΦΥΛΑΞΗΤΗΝΙϹΟΔΟΝϹΟΥΚΑΙΕΞΟΔΟΝ
ΑΠΟΤΟΥΝΥΝΚΑΙΕШϹ...ΑΙШΝ...

"The Lord preserve thy coming in and thy going out from this time forth and for evermore."

This was on the lintel of a small house.

At El-Bara was the only Latin inscription which we discovered throughout this region. It was well carved on the wall of a wine-press, over the aperture —much resembling a gigantic letter-box—through which the grapes were emptied into the cellar. It read as follows:

✣ ...AREOSSUCCOSBACCHEIAMONERACEMIS
...BITISCENUITAPRICOSOLEREFECTA

Not the least striking feature in the ruins, here as at Hass, are the sepulchral monuments, exhibiting, as they do, a vast variety of plan and detail, some of very beautiful design and execution in the elaborate carvings of the cornices, and doors, and windows. Some of these tombs are excavated in the rock and have a descent by steps into the subterranean chambers; others are sunk in the perpendicular side of a smooth wall of live rock, on a level with the soil; others, again, are massive stone erections, generally square in plan, arranged in two stories and covered with a pyramidal roof of great elevation. One striking fact in connection with these sepulchral monuments deserves special notice for its bearing upon ancient Syrian Christianity. It is the absence of anything like a necropolis. These tombs are not all grouped together in any particular quarter of the city or its suburbs; nor are they gathered round the Churches. They are scattered all about the town, sometimes in vineyards and olive-yards; sometimes in the courts and gardens of the larger houses, with which they were connected by terraced walks. Thus the tombs themselves and their positions strikingly illustrate the remarks of the Count de Vogüé touching the type of Syrian Faith prevalent at the time when this district was teeming with civilized life. He, indeed, dwells on the triumphant tone of the inscriptions and emblems carved on the civil, ecclesiastical and sepulchral buildings, and contrasts the Christian humility of these nameless monuments with the vainglorious emphasis of pagan inscriptions. But the contrast is most striking between the different aspect which death wears in these days and that in which it was regarded when these cities were inhabited; and a most striking illustration is thus obtained of much of the language of S. Chrysostom and other Greek and Latin Fathers concerning the faithful departed: for that language is here seen not to have been rhetorical and unreal, as is sometimes supposed, but the genuine expression of the practical belief of the time—breathing "a hope full of immortality." For here was no attempt to hide the memorials of the departed out of sight, or to associate those memorials with all that was gloomy and repulsive. The "coverlids"—(some of these tombs were called *calybes* from καλύπτω *to cover*)—of those who slept in the Lord were bright and cheerful as art could make them; and conveniently placed, where the survivors might often resort to them, to cherish the fond memories of their beloved ones, and to continue their pious offices to the mortal remains of those whom they considered as "not lost, but gone before,"—regarding them still as members of the same family and household of the faith.

On the outskirts of the town of Bara are the remains of a large villa, in so complete a state of preservation as to admit of an accurate architectural restoration, which is given in M. de Vogüé's great work. To this the inhabitants still give the name of "the House of the Lady Elizabeth," and we liked to believe this to be the name of its last Christian inhabitant. In the neighbourhood of El-Bara are the following:

MOUDJLEYEH is not more than half an hour distant to the South-East. It contained a great number of private houses, surrounding the Church, of which large ruins still remain. But here again the most striking and impressive of the Christian remains is a fine sarcophagus in excellent preservation, with an inscription boldly carved on its side from Psalm xci. 9, 10; a most convincing evidence that for the Christians of those days death had lost its sting, the grave its victory. For thus it speaks of the departed, and to the survivors:

TΟΝΥΨΙCΤΟΝΕΘΟΥΚΑΤΑΦΥΓΗΝCΟ
ΥΟΥΠΡΟCΕΛΕΥ   ✝   CΕΤΕΠΡΟCΕΚΑ
ΚΑΙΜΑCΤΙ   ✝   ΞΟΥΚΕΝΤΙΙΕΝΤ
ШCΚΗΝШΜΑΤΙCΟ   ✝   Υ

"Thou hast made the Most High thy Refuge—no evil shall approach thee—no plague come nigh thy dwelling."

Another sepulchral epitaph roughly carved on the side of a rock-hewn cave, and which had escaped the notice of Count de Vogüé, was not less striking. It was surmounted by the cross, with the **XP.** and **A.Ω.** so universally prevalent in these towns; and read as follows:

ΚΕΧΕΒΟΗΟΙ
ΙΟΥΛΙΑΝΟΝ ΚΑΙ
ΔΗΜΗΤΡΙΟΝ ΟΤΙ
ΕΤΕΛΕCΑΝ

"Lord Christ, succour Julian and Demetrius; for they are dead."

BETEYRSEH is half a mile south of Moudjleyah, with a small Church very much ruined, and at the same distance is *Rubeyah*, where was the only example of a secular monument to be found among these ruins. It was an equestrian figure carved in deep relief on a large slab of stone, almost the size of life. The rider carried a wreath in his hand, but the carving was too much decayed by exposure to allow us to judge of the execution, though it appeared not to be devoid of spirit.

SERJILLIA, about half an hour to the east. Here the buildings are better preserved than in most of the other towns, some of the private houses having their porticos and balconies perfect, with the steps leading up to them. Here too is a large bath-house, and a Church of the normal type; all carefully figured by Count de Vogüé.

DELL LOUZEH is a ruined town about one hour east of El-Bara, where are the remains of a fine Church, and several houses in fair preservation, with their colonnades of debased Corinthian columns still standing. From one such portico I copied the two following inscriptions:

✣ ΕΙΘΕΟΣΥΠΕΡΥΜШΝΤΙΣΟΚΑΘΥΜШΝ
ΔΟΞΑΑΥΤШΠΑΝΤΟΤΕ.

"If God be for you who can be against you? Glory to Him always."

DEIR SAMBIR.

✢ ΚΥΡΙΕΒΟΗΘΙΤШΟΙΚШΤΟΥΤШΚΑΙΤΟΙ
ΣΥΚΟΥΣΙΝΕΝΑΥΤШΑΜΗΝ.

"Lord, succour this house, and those who dwell therein. Amen."

On a smaller house was an abbreviated and debased repetition of the former of these two inscriptions, with the date, thus:

✢ ΕΙΘΕШCΥΠΕΡΗΜΟΝΤΙCΚΑΘΗΜΟΧΜΓ ✢

"If God be for us, who can be against us? 643."

The date indicated by the last three letters, whose numerical value is equivalent to 643, is probably to be reckoned by the æra of Antioch, and would so correspond with A.D. 595, for the æra of the Seleucidæ, which would give A.D. 331, is too early a date to assign to these buildings.

DEIR SAMBIR is about half an hour east of Dell Louzeh, and contains a Church of which the three west doors remain, but all vestiges of the portico—if ever it had one—have disappeared. Here we observed on the wall of a house, sculptured on a large stone, the Agnus, bearing a Cross on its back, figured by the Count de Vogüé; and a handsome tomb, well preserved, with the following Inscription running round a semi-circular arch[1],

---

[1] On the side wall, in the porch of this tomb, is a device of the *labarum* with Α and Ω, twice repeated, and the paraphrase (as M. de Vogüé happily calls it) of its motto—Τοῦτο νικᾷ, *This conquers.*

Ι ΤΟΥΚΥΡΙΟΥΗΓΗΚΑΙΤΟΠΛΗΡШΜΑΑΥΤΗĊΚΑΙ
ΠΑΝΤΕϹΟΙΚΑΤΟΙΚΥΝΤΕϹΕΝΑΥΤΗ ✣ ΧΜΓ Ι

"The earth is the Lord's and the fulness thereof and all that dwell therein. + 643"—

the same date, be it observed, as that on the house above copied. Another remark of some interest occurs in connection with this epitaph: this opening verse of the 24th Psalm is the Stichos peculiar to the Burial Service of a priest in the Greek Church, introduced near the beginning of the office.

ROUEIA is situated about two hours from Deir Sambir, in a south easterly direction, and covers as large an area as El-Bara. This important ruin is the only one described in any detail by Pococke, whose account it may be well to transcribe. "Rouiah is near the plain that leads from Marrah to Aleppo. This is a more magnificent place than the others: there are in it about six or seven fine palaces, some of which are almost entire, and there are almost as many Churches. The houses are built round courts with porticos all round within, supporting a gallery, which communicates with the rooms above, there being a door from it to every room. The capitals of the pillars, which are no bad work, are of the Corinthian and Ionic orders. The Churches seem to have been more magnificent than the houses, especially three or four, which are built with three naves [i.e. a nave and side aisles], the arches of which are supported by pillars, and the largest has great pillars in it of an oblong square figure, and a portico before it; on one side there is an open building with a dome supported by columns, which seems to have been a baptistery: on the north side of the Church there is a building like a small ancient temple, with an angular pediment at each end; the corners are adorned with Corinthian pilasters, not of the best workmanship. The whole building is raised on a fine basement, and before it there is a portico, consisting only of two pillars, which are in the front between the side walls that support the pediment: *this seemed to have been a family Chapel, and under it is a vault with stone-coffins or graves cut in the rock. There is another of the same kind near one of the palaces, with an unintelligible Greek inscription on the pediment*. There are ruins of great buildings all round the large Church, where probably many persons might live in a sort of community; and this possibly might be the first beginning of that sort of retirement in these parts, which was afterwards introduced and settled in public communities in the monastic life. One of these Churches was dedicated to St Peter and Paul, and has on it this inscription:

$$\text{ΠΕΤΡΟC} \quad \boxed{\text{A} \; \overset{\text{P}}{⳨} \; \Omega} \quad \text{ΠΑΥΛΟC}$$

* The passage between asterisks has evidently got transposed. It belongs, not to the great Church, but to the small building similar to a pagan temple on the north side of it, described just above.

"There is one sepulchre here of a very particular kind; two arches are turned at proper distances, and about six or seven feet above the ground a very large stone coffin is placed on them, which is nine feet long, four feet ten inches wide, and five feet ten inches deep; the part below, which is enclosed, has in it two graves cut down in the rock[1]."

Thus far Pococke, whose description answers very well at this day, except that another century of exposure to climate and earthquakes have brought down more of the stately buildings of Roueia. The domical building on the south, and the small pagan-like temple on the north side of the great Church—both which I take to have been sepulchral monuments—remain in their integrity, as does also the second temple of the same kind mentioned by Pococke. The Church deserves some further notice, as it varies somewhat from the normal type already described at El-Hass, of which also a fine example is found among the ruins of Roueia. This is a more unusual type, having the aisles separated from the nave—not by rows of columns, but by massive piers, carrying arches of wide span, dividing the Church lengthways into three bays. The aisles are much wider than in the columnar Churches. The west end of this Church is very fine, with its portico between the flanking towers, and the west wall of the Church rising into a

---

[1] *Description of Syria*, p. 148.

lofty gable pierced by a circular window, with mullions forming a bold cross.

To the east of *Roueia* are the important remains of *Dana;* and half an hour to the west are large heaps of ruins, named *Jeradi,* neither of which have yet been properly explored.

The region in which the ancient towns hitherto described are situated, is named Jebel Riha, from a large village of that name on the road northward from El-Bara to EDLIB, about an hour south of the latter place, which must now be described, in the pitiful contrast which the Church there exhibits to its ancient condition, in the palmy days of which the massive monuments of the past, above enumerated, still bear witness. The Christians of EDLIB number about 400 souls, and have one Priest, a Church and a School of some 50 boys and as many girls. The priest is a dyer by trade, and still pursues his avocation as a means of livelihood. The Church is a miserably poor building, and the iconostasis and all the appointments are in keeping with the fabric. The Christians, however, had for a few months past enjoyed unwonted peace and security under the protection of an Armenian Catholic from Aleppo, named Ouanes Effendi, who held the important office of District Collector for the Turkish Government, in whose service he has been for forty years. The Orthodox Christians were loud in his praises, and through his influence their condition was much ameliorated from what it was in the year 1845, when the place was visited by Dr Thompson, the American Missionary from Beirout[1]. Before the appointment of this worthy man there was no justice to be had by the Christians in any suit against a Moslem: but now a Council of Ten has been established—five for the town, and as many for the country—in which the Christian community is represented by a brother of the priest. But, besides this, the shameful extortions to which the members of the tolerated creeds are subjected in Turkey, have been put an end to by this righteous publican. Not one para in excess of the legal contribution of one-tenth can now be demanded, and altogether this excellent officer's appointment is hailed as a blessing by the poor Christians. They spoke gratefully also of the help they had received from the former bishop of Aleppo; but the present bishop of Hamah, in whose diocese they are, is not able to do much for them.

Edlib appears not to have any Christian, or other, remains of antiquity: but it is remarkable as forming a kind of boundary line between two styles of domestic architecture—in one striking particular. All the columns supporting the porticoes in the towns south of Edlib have a marked architectural type, approximating to the Doric. North of that, this column disappears altogether, and is replaced by plain square blocks, without either base or capital,

[1] *Bibliotheca Sacra*, Vol. v. p. 671, 2, A.D. 1848.

carried to the requisite height. This deterioration is confined to the secular buildings; the northern Churches are perhaps richer in architectural detail than the southern.

Jebel Riha, which has now been described, is separated from Jebel A'ala by a wide plain called Saal-er-Rouj, and Jebel A'ala is continued northward by Jebel Semân. The following Ecclesiological Notes relate to Jebel A'ala.

ARSHIN is situated in a hill above the modern village of Harbanoush—a stiff climb of half an hour—and has a very handsome Church in a good state of preservation. The vaulted apse at the east is still perfect, with a very massive parapet, supported by heavy corbels, carried round it and its two invariable accessories, the diaconicon (with its upper floor entire) on the south, and the prothesis on the north of the apse. The west end is also complete, having its entrance porch flanked by two massive towers, with some very handsome carving over the door which opens from the porch into the Church. A feature peculiar—so far as I know—to this Syrian style, is exhibited in such profusion here, that this seems to be the proper place to describe it. It consists of a broad band of moulding running continuously round the windows externally; so as to embrace the sills, the jambs and arches in one flowing line from one end of the Church to the other; as likewise round the windows of the apse. It is not elegant in effect, but decidedly original, and therefore worthy of remark.

DEIR ZEITA, about an hour north-east of Arshin, has the remains of a large Church, of which the north wall was entire, and the lower part of an apse of noble proportions. This Church was connected, towards the west, by a paved court, with an octagonal building, which may have been a baptistery.

KOKANAYA, about one hour and a half north of Deir Zeita, is a large heap of ruins, with two wide streets, very well defined, leading to the principal gate; great part of which is still preserved. The only Church we saw was small and insignificant for so important a town. A dated sepulchral inscription, however, is deserving of notice, for its eloquent simplicity. It is carved in the rock over a semicircular loculus, in a subterranean tomb:

+ ΕΥϹΕΒΙѠ + ΧΡΙϹΤΙΑΝѠ +
ΔΟΣΑΠΑΤΡΙΚΑΙΥΙѠΚΑΙΑΓΙѠΠΝΕΥ
ΤΙΕΤΟΥϹΖΙΥΜΗΝΙΛѠΟΥΚΖ i.e. Aug. 27, 369.

DOWAR is twenty minutes distant south-east of Kokanaya, across a valley; and ten minutes east of that *Kusr-el-Benát*, probably a nunnery; and ten minutes east of that the large remains of *Bakousa*, with a noble Church, situated on a hill, the apse of which, and the north wall, are in excellent preservation. It is of the usual type, and presents nothing remarkable except its very superior and massive masonry.

e

Proceeding northward by the modern village of *Maaret esh-Shilf* we come to another village named *Sardin*, above which rises a hill surmounted by a ruined site and church named *Bahaku*, but formerly —the inhabitants told us—*Miliêh*. Here the Church presents the rare exception of a square east end, both in its external and internal plan. On the top of the same range of hills, and at no great distance to the north, is *Kulb Louzeh*, commanding a fine view of the Lake of Antioch and all the surrounding country. Here is a grand Church, in a remarkably perfect state, even to the vault over the noble apse. It was dedicated to the Archangels, as is indicated by their names over the easternmost door on the south side + ΜΙΧΑΗΛΓΑΒΡ...This Church is divided into three bays by massive square piers, supporting round-headed arches of very wide span. The faces of these arches are carved with bands of rich mouldings, but that of the apse is most profusely ornamented. The wall-space above the arches is pierced with twelve clerestory windows.

Leaving now a large number of ruined sites unexplored, I proceed to the most important of all these Ecclesiastical remains, when I have briefly noticed an ancient nunnery which I visited at the special request of the Count de Vogüé, as he had not had time to do so. This is *Kusr el-Benât*, on the old Roman road between Aleppo and Antioch, which is here very well defined; but is not that now usually followed. The ruins are situated at the west end of a pass cut through the rock, and are very extensive. The Church, however, is a complete ruin, with the exception of the lower part of the apse, which was carved in the live rock, and some few courses of stone above it. The convent stood on the north side of the Church, and formed three sides of an irregular quadrangle. The building was three stories high, and the massive character of the masonry gives it an imposing appearance, as in many parts the façade remains entire. In the court stands a tower still six stories high, although from the present appearance of the summit, as well as from the débris at the base, it would seem to have been carried higher. This is probably of later date than the Church and Convent; added, perhaps, when the buildings were converted into a fortress, as its name intimates that it was, probably during the time of the Crusades.

TOURMANIN is situated at the southern base of Jebel Simân, and through it lies the road from Antioch to Aleppo, now usually followed. Here is a noble building, which seems formerly to have served as a caravanserai; but its architecture claims for it a date anterior to the Mohammedan occupation of Syria.

We probably have in it an example of the guest-houses ($\xi\epsilon\nu o\delta o\chi\epsilon\hat{\iota}a$) of which we read e.g. in Procopius's account of the buildings of Justinian, which were built on a very large scale, particularly at places of pilgrimage; and as Tourmanin must have been always the junction—so to speak—on the main line of commerce, for pilgrims to the shrine of the popular saint, this building was erected for their accommodation. It is indeed called *Deir*—i.e. Convent, but this name does not necessarily imply that it was a religious house. It consisted of a large hall, with other buildings and offices attached to it; well supplied with cisterns for rain-water, formed in the rock out of which the stones for the buildings were quarried,—a method very usually adopted in this country for economising both labour and materials But here a sad disappointment awaited us. One of the most imposing churches in Count de Vogüé's collection of drawings was that of Tourmanin, the façade of which was complete only three years before our visit. Now, not a vestige of that stately elevation was to be seen, and the explanation of the utter ruin which had been wrought in so short a time was to be found in the fresh chips of stone around the spot; indicating that the Church had been converted into a quarry for the citizens of Aleppo; from which it is some six miles distant. And thus these noble monuments of ancient Christian piety, which have resisted the shocks of earthquake and tempest for fourteen hundred years, are disappearing under the axes and hammers of modern civilization.

KULAÁT ES-SIMÂN, is situated on the top of a hill of the same name, and is reached by a steep rocky path, in about two hours from Tourmanin. It is, even in its deep decay, a most imposing pile, and in its palmy days might vie with any ecclesiastical establishment of East or West for the extent and grandeur of its buildings, the ruins of which cover many acres. It consists of a large transeptal Church, built round an octagonal hypæthral court, in the centre of which once rose the pillar of S. Symeon of the Column; whose eccentric piety and devotion this Church was built to commemorate, very shortly after his death. And it is a happy fact for the ecclesiology of this building that we have preserved to us a particular description of it, by one who may have visited it only a few years after its erection; as may be inferred from the following facts. Symeon Stylites died under the Emperor Leo, while Martyrius was Bishop of Antioch, i.e. between 461 and 465. Evagrius Scholasticus was born A.D. 536, and he describes the Church precisely as it may be seen (in ruins) at this day. A very good idea may be formed of its general plan from a comparison with Ely Cathedral, which I refer to as an illustration in preference to any other transeptal Church, on account of its octagonal lantern, in which it resembles its Syrian prototype; except that we learn from Evagrius that the central court of Symeon Stylites was open to the heavens, with the column rising in the middle; the rocky base of which, rudely shaped, is still remaining. This octagonal court was encircled by eight noble arches, of which five still remain, supported by massive piers with detached columns of the Corinthian order; and wonderfully pure in architectural detail considering the time when they were executed. The alternate arches of this arcade—those i.e. facing the cardinal points—open into the middle walk of the four arms of this transeptal Church; the intermediate arches into the side aisles, and into semicircular apses formed in the angles of the outer walls (a very beautiful and novel feature of this most interesting Church), probably presenting a specimen of the *exedræ* of the basilican churches, such as are described by Eusebius in his account of the Sepulchre Church at Jerusalem. The purpose which these alcoves were designed to serve may be gathered with great probability from the description of Evagrius Scholasticus, who speaks of the pilgrims encircling the pillar in a continuous procession, some on foot, others mounted on horses and mules, in order to do honour to the memory of the saint; whose visible shade, according to the same authority, continued to flit about his accustomed column. These apsidal recesses would form a secure retreat from which to witness the stream of pilgrims, or a quiet resting-place for the pilgrims themselves when wearied with their gyrations round the pillar.

Whether the four arms of the cross were separated from the octagonal court—or, if so, how—there remains nothing to shew: a solid stone wall built into the eastern arch, so as to isolate the choir, is evidently modern. The apse of the choir is very fine; its vault remains almost complete, the face of the arch being richly carved. It has its two invariable adjuncts on either side, also apsidal,—the prothesis and diaconicon. The west member of this cruciform Church, which would be represented by the nave of an English cathedral, is a perfect triumph of engineering skill as well as of architectural ingenuity. In this direction the rocky ridge on which the Church is built falls away in a steep declivity, so the building could only be extended in this direction by supporting it on solid substructions. This was accordingly done, and the crypt of S. Symeon Stylites far surpasses in solidity and grandeur any of our cathedral crypts of the middle ages; and so solid was its structure that nearly all the arches remain entire, notwithstanding the frequent earthquakes to which this region has been subjected. A grand doorway with side portals opening on an elevated terrace terminated the Church in this direction. The main entrance to the Church was, however, through the south transept, the south front of which is covered with a stately porch, in a wonderful state of preservation. The northern transept calls for no special remark; but it may be observed that the four members of this Church were treated as so many separate churches; each of them having the two doors on either side, covered by porches, which has been noticed as a normal feature of these Syrian churches. The side aisles are divided from the middle walk by rows of columns; of which there were nine on a side in the choir, and six on a side in the nave and transepts. In the side walls the mixture of trabeate and arcuate construction is here found in its fullest development.

Such is a brief description of the interior of this great Church. The exterior calls for no special remark, except at its east end, where the wall is ornamented with two tiers of columns of the Corinthian order, supporting a bold corbel table, and is an exquisite architectural composition.

The Church is surrounded on three sides by courts; and large remains, which at first suggest the idea of conventual buildings, are to be seen to the south-east. Possibly, however, it was nothing but a huge caravanserai, built for the accommodation of the pilgrims who flocked hither from all quarters; though a small chapel, communicating with the south-eastern apse of the great Church, rather countenances the former notion of a monastery of Regulars, whose oratory this may have been.

The ground-plan of the Church and contiguous buildings contained in the work of the Count de Vogüé will best serve to illustrate the preceding description.

We have not yet exhausted the marvels of this fertile field of architectural and ecclesiological research. A hundred yards or so to the south of the main pile of buildings, with which it is now connected only by heaps of less considerable ruins, is a Church of peculiar design, very richly ornamented, which demands a brief notice. It is in fact a double Church. On the north is a small Church on a square plan, rising into an octagonal lantern, with a narthex and side aisles. On the south of this is a small Church of the more usual type; the middle walk being divided from the side aisles by five columns; the east end distributed into a semicircular apse and rectangular side chambers. The north and west fronts of these churches were covered by a portico, and to the east were a series of chambers covered by a cloister. It is difficult to conjecture what purpose these twin churches were designed to serve; but this is only part of the puzzle presented by these complicated ruins, in the absence of all monumental records of the site—with the exception of the notice of Evagrius Scholasticus, which, however, refers only to the transeptal Church.

The absence of all inscriptions from this Church and its surrounding buildings is a noteworthy fact, contrasting, as it does, with the usual practice which, as we have seen, prevailed at the period, both in ecclesiastical and civil buildings. We only discovered indications of one inscription in all this vast expanse of buildings. That was carved over the western portal of the south transept, within the porch; but it was so damaged by exposure as to be illegible.

To the south of the octagonal Church is a handsome gateway with its side portals, which seems to have been the main entrance to the Precinct or Close; evidently designed by the architect of the great Church; for it has detached columns of precisely similar design to those which have been noticed as flanking the piers round the octagonal court of the great Church.

Outside this gate are extensive ruins of a large town, built on the two sides of the rocky valley which has been noticed as bounding the ridge on the west. Among these are the remains of two churches, the roof of one of which, and the mosaic pavement, still exist; some fine tombs; and a large Pandocheion, or hostelry, with a solidly constructed stone viaduct across the valley, connecting it with a court surrounded by handsome tombs and a kind of mortuary chapel. This hostelry is dated, and the date is interpreted by Count de Vogüé as equivalent to A.D. 477; when the building was completed by Simeon, on the 12th of July. This town bears the name of Deir Simân—the Convent of Symeon, and no doubt owed its origin to the devotion which the Stylite attracted: so that here, as in so many cases in western Christendom, the shrine of a saint became the nucleus of a large town and the centre of a busy population.

This was eminently the case in this instance, for

the hills for many miles around are covered with ruins, and the sole denizen of Kulaát Simân gave me the names of some twenty sites in its immediate neighbourhood, which would, I have no doubt, well repay the labours of the ecclesiologist and the antiquarian.

I must now quit the precincts of the Church of S. Symeon Stylites, to which I have devoted so much space; for this is not the place to discuss either the religious or the historical bearings of that very curious phase of Eastern Christianity of which it presents the most remarkable, but not the only surviving memorial: for I afterwards visited the ruins of another large Church celebrated for the asceticism of another Symeon Stylites (the Younger), a contemporary of Evagrius Scholasticus, who has recorded some particulars of his personal intercourse with "this admirable man." This Church is situated between three and four hours north-east of Antioch, on the summit of a mountain, synonymous with this—"Jebel es-Simân;" which rises abruptly from the narrow plain which here skirts the Mediterranean, and in which the modern village of Souadieh is situated. The ruins are inconsiderable in comparison with those which have been above described, but the remains of the pillar, cut out of the live rock, with rude base-mouldings, are much more pronounced; while the ground-plan of the Church is peculiar, and would repay the outlay of much more time than I was able to devote to it.

*

With regard to the state of Christianity which could not only produce, but admire and repeat, such a type of sanctity as Symeon of the Column, it is not without interest to find a kind of anticipatory condemnation of it, in the language of one of the most eminent of the Greek Fathers, whose life and character, not less truly ascetic than that of his eccentric countryman, presents a marked contrast to it; while the Church has tacitly disallowed it; for, although she canonised the Syrian *Fakeer*, the example of his peculiar form of devotion was soon suffered to fall into disuse, nor have any attempts been since made to revive it.

It were an anachronism to suppose that the following passage from a Homily of S. Chrysostom, delivered probably at Antioch, could have any personal reference to the eccentric hermit of the Mandra in the neighbouring mountains: but it certainly has a close, and even literal, bearing on his case. The preacher is deploring the general decay of ancient piety among the Christians of his day; which he ascribes to the relaxation of the wholesome discipline of former times, and the consequent enervation of Christian energy, through the love of money and worldly conformity. He adds: "And if one be found having a vestige of the ancient philosophy, leaving the cities, and the market-places, and the society of his fellows, and the direction of others, he betakes him to the mountains: and if asked the reason of this retirement, he invents a pretext which cannot be allowed. 'For,' he says, 'I start aside lest I also perish, and my virtue lose its edge.' But how much better were it for thee to lose the edge, and gain others, rather than remaining on high to neglect thy perishing brethren[1]!"

But I must proceed with my contrasts; and turn from the vision of the Church in the zenith of its power, which has been conjured up by these ruins, to its actual material degradation as witnessed by the present aspect of the once proud capital of the East, which claimed for itself the somewhat presumptuous designation of "the City of God," but is ever glorious for the memories of the apostolic and early Christian ages with which it is associated.

No ancient city of any consideration has more utterly perished than Antioch. It once boasted a population of little short of half a million; and its public buildings, civil and sacred, vied with those of imperial Rome herself in their magnificence; and though frequently desolated by earthquakes, yet under the fostering care of successive Emperors it rose again and again phœnix-like from its ruins. Now not a single vestige of its ancient magnificence is to be seen in its squalid streets. Not even the fragments of a column or capital or cornice or frieze are to be seen built into modern hovels, as in most other ancient cities; even the mediæval castle,

[1] St Chrysost. in 1 Ep. ad Cor. Cap. I. Hom. VI. ap. fin.

crowning the height, preserves but scanty traces of the Crusaders' or of Saracenic architecture.

As regards the present condition of the Orthodox community in Antioch it is somewhat ameliorated from what it was thirty years ago, as described in the second Appendix to this volume, when their only place of worship was a natural cave in the rock, which they shared with the flocks and herds of the Moslem shepherds. This cave they disposed of, about ten years since, to the Latins, and an inscription records that the present Pope has restored it to public worship[1]. The marble columns of this old church were used in the construction of the handsome and spacious Church in which the Greeks now worship, erected on the site of an old one, after centuries of desecration. The permission to restore the building was obtained from Ibrahim Pasha, during his temporary occupation of Syria,— that golden era for the Christians and other oppressed nationalities of this part of the Turkish Empire—but it was not completed until some twenty years ago, under the present Patriarch. The icons, lamps, church-books and vessels are the gifts of the Emperor of Russia. A handsome throne is provided for the Patriarch in the middle of the apse,

---

[1] This inscription runs as follows: "Honori S. Petri, Quod Antiochiæ ministerium gerens, illic sacra officia obivit, Ecclesiam, loco a dominis redempto, Pius IX., P.M. sua munificentia reparavit, et cultui publico restituit, Anno MDCCCLXII."

and another at the side of the iconostasis, likewise facing west, but neither of them had been occupied by Hierotheus for more than ten years before our visit, although the numbers of the believers of the Orthodox Greek rite in and about Antioch might justly claim more frequent visits from their chief Pastor, even if the greater importance of Damascus makes that modern capital of Syria more eligible for his permanent official residence. By a census taken in the year 1865 it was ascertained that the Christians of the Orthodox rite in Antioch and the neighbourhood numbered 17,000 souls, of which the number in the city itself were variously computed by three several informants, at 1800 souls, all told; 1000 males—men and boys; and 800 families. They are ministered to by three priests and a deacon.

Such then are the past glories, and such the present state of decay, of the capital and central district of that vast diocese of Antioch which once embraced within its ample limits—according to its ambitious title—"all the East;" conterminous with the second Patriarchate of Christendom, that of the New Rome, towards the west; with the third Patriarchate, that of the Evangelical Alexandria, on the south; and of illimitable extent towards the east; out of which were carved the Patriarchate of Jerusalem, and the autocephalous Churches of the Armenias, Georgia, Seleucia, and others. This volume, it is true, travels over a very small part of this wide field, whether in its geographical extent or its chronological limits: but it is hoped that the *cunabula* of the Catholic Church, and the chequered fortunes of its earliest champions, sketched by the graphic pen of one who so thoroughly appreciated the historical, theological, and ecclesiastical importance of Eastern Christianity, may not be without value as a contribution to a revived branch of sacred literature, to which the enlarged and ever-widening sympathies of the Anglican Church, reanimated from her long and death-like lethargy, have given a fresh impulse—the evidence of a new and vigorous life, the quickening spirit of which is Love of the Brotherhood.

The Feast of the Transfiguration,
1873.

THE

PATRIARCHATE OF ANTIOCH.

BOOK I.

1. IN commencing the History of the Great Patriarchate of the East, I cannot conceal from myself how far more formidable is the task than was the compilation of the Annals of Alexandria. We shall no longer be confined to one land, to a Church, if patriarchal in power, yet metropolitical only in extent. The throne to which we are now to direct our attention, claimed, in itself or by its offshoots, the spiritual dominion of well-nigh the whole of Asia. We shall trace the rise of a smaller Patriarchate in the centre of its elder sister: we shall see a Catholicos thrown off into the far east: in Antioch we shall find, almost always a double, frequently a triple, succession of bishops: we shall see the Catholic Faith engaged in conflict at once with Nestorians, Jacobites, and Monothelites; we shall follow heretical missions into the territories of the Lama, into the strongholds of Buddhism, into the foul abominations of Schamanism: we shall finally see both the Catholic and heretical communions well-nigh overwhelmed by the scimetars of Mahomet, and the tremendous hordes of Tatar invasion. We must at once embrace the half of Asia Minor, Persia, Arabia, India and China, if we would have a clear idea of the history of the Patriarchates of the East.

Difficulty of the task.

S. James, first Bishop of Jerusalem.

2. With respect to the Church of Jerusalem, ecclesiastical tradition unhesitatingly[1] asserts that its first bishop was James, the LORD's brother, surnamed the *Just*. Abundant traces of this may be found in the Acts of the Apostles. When S. Peter had been miraculously set free from prison, and had visited the saints assembled in the house of Mary the mother of Mark: "Go," said he, "shew[2] these things unto *James*, and to the brethren." When S. Paul first visited Jerusalem[3], S. Peter and S. James only were seen by him; the one probably as the chief of the Apostles: the other as diocesan bishop. In the Apostolic Council[4] it is James who sums up the arguments, and pronounces the definition of faith. As diocesan bishop it probably is that S. Paul, writing of those that "seemed to be pillars[5]," names him before S. Peter: lastly, when the same Apostle came up for the last time to Jerusalem, it was to James[6] that he made his report, and to James that he looked for advice. May we not connect this prerogative of S. James with the appearance of our LORD to him when apart from the other Apostles[7]?

---

[1] Eusebius, H. E. II. 1, where he is quoting the Hypotyposeis of S. Clement. Πέτρον καὶ Ἰάκωβον καὶ Ἰωάννην......μὴ ἐπιδικάζεσθαι δόξης, ἀλλ' Ἰάκωβον τὸν δίκαιον ἐπίσκοπον Ἱεροσολύμων ἕλεσθαι.—So again, H. E. VII. 19. So S. Epiphanius, Hæres. 78, and the Apostolic Constitutions, VIII. 35. It is beyond my plan to enter into the much-disputed question, whether James was the son of Joseph by a former wife, as Eusebius, S. Epiphanius, S. Gregory Nyssen, and Hippolytus assert;—or of Mary, the sister of the Blessed Virgin, as S. Jerome, S. Chrysostom, and Theodoret hold. Dositheus (p. 2) inclines to the latter opinion, but in such a manner as to shew that his Church had no tradition on the subject: modern scholars seem generally to prefer the former. Nor shall I enter into the question whether he were the son of Alphæus, or not;—and if so, how far this parentage is reconcilable with either of the foregoing statements. The Bollandists, Henschenius on May 1, and Papebroch in the Historia Chronologica Pattr. Hierosolym. (which will be a household word in this history) follow S. Epiphanius, and stoutly deny that he was an Apostle, till made so by our Lord's appearance to him after His Resurrection (and as they will have it, after His Ascension). I confess that to this the election of S. Matthias appears an insurmountable opposition. Baronius dwells at length on this point, Tom. I.

[2] Acts xii. 17.
[3] Galat. i. 18, 19.
[4] Acts xv. 13.
[5] Galat. ii. 9.
[6] Acts xxi. 18.
[7] 1 Cor. xv. 7.

FOUNDATION OF THE CHURCH OF ANTIOCH.

Thus much of the First Bishop of Jerusalem. We now turn to Antioch.

3. It is thus that S. Luke introduces us to that great city[1]: "Now they which were scattered abroad upon the persecution that arose about Stephen travelled as far as Phœnice, and Cyprus, and Antioch, preaching the word to none but unto the Jews only. And some of them were men of Cyprus and Cyrene, which when they were come to Antioch spake unto the Grecians, preaching the LORD JESUS. And the hand of the LORD was with them: and a great number believed, and turned unto the LORD. Then tidings of these things came unto the ears of the Church which was in Jerusalem: and they sent forth Barnabas, that he should go as far as Antioch." After describing his joy at the success of the Faith, S. Luke proceeds: "Then departed Barnabas to Tarsus for to seek Saul: and when he had found him, he brought him unto Antioch. And it came to pass that a whole year they assembled themselves with the Church, and taught much people. And the disciples were called Christians first in Antioch."

Antioch, notwithstanding the account given by S. Luke of its illumination,

4. Notwithstanding this account of the Evangelist, Ecclesiastical History asserts nothing more positively than that S. Peter[2] was the Founder of the Church of Antioch. Dismissing the chronological enquiry to an Appendix, I will here merely give the most probable[3] opinion as to the date

acknowledged S. Peter as its founder,

---

[1] Acts xi. 19.

[2] So S. Jerome, in his Commentary on the second chapter of the Epistle to the Galatians, mentions, as one of the things not alluded to by S. Luke in the Acts; "Primum Episcopum Antiochenæ Ecclesiæ Petrum fuisse, eumque Romæ translatum." So the Eusebian Chronicle: Πέτρος ὁ κορυφαῖος τὴν ἐν Ἀντιοχείᾳ πρῶτον θεμελιώσας ἐκκλησίαν. So again, Eusebius, H. E. III. 36.

[3] Here I follow the same system as in the History of Alexandria; namely, that propounded by Henschenius and Papebrochius, and defended at length in the 29th of the Bollandist June. Le Quien, on the contrary, O. C. II. 675, defers the commencement of S. Peter's pontificate at Antioch till A.D. 44. I will only observe that the early tradition, preserved by Apollonius, who wrote against the Montanists in the second century, and which represents our LORD as commanding the Apostles to remain twelve years in Jerusalem, is scarcely opposed to the Cathedra of S. Peter at Antioch at a much earlier period, since his tem-

of this event. Assuming that our LORD suffered four years before the period which the Vulgar Era would fix, that is in A.D. 29, and that S. Paul was converted in the following year, we know from the testimony of that Apostle that three years elapsed before he "came to Jerusalem to see Peter:" and, alone of the remaining Apostles, saw James, the LORD'S brother. Immediately after this, and while Peter passed through all quarters, we may imagine that he visited Antioch, and formed there a Church of Jewish converts. Over this Church he presided, according to ecclesiastical tradition, seven years: that is, till A.D. 40. In his frequent absences from Antioch he is said to have constituted S. Euodius his vicar; it is more certain that he ordained him his successor[1].

and first Bishop, A.D. 33—A.D. 40;

he consecrates EUODIUS 2nd Bishop of Antioch, A.D. 40.

porary absences there are scarcely more than his "passing through all parts" in Palestine. At all events, the chronology I have adopted has the authority of the Paschal Chronicle, and of Joannes Malalas, himself an Antiochene:—τετάρτῳ ἔτει, says the Chronicle, τῆς εἰς οὐρανοὺς ἀναλήψεως τοῦ Κυρίου, Πέτρος ὁ Ἀπόστολος ἀπὸ Ἱεροσολύμων ἐν Ἀντιοχείᾳ τῇ μεγάλῃ τὸν λόγον τοῦ Θεοῦ ἐδίδασκεν· καὶ τὴν χειροτονίαν τῆς ἐπισκοπῆς δεξάμενος, ἐκεῖσε ἑαυτὸν ἐνεθρόνισεν πεισθεὶς τοῖς ἀπὸ Ἰουδαίων γενομένοις Χριστιανοῖς· καὶ τοὺς ἐξ ἐθνῶν πιστοὺς οὐκ ἐδέξατο, οὔτε ἠγάπα, ἀλλ' οὕτως ἐάσας αὐτοὺς, ἐξῆλθεν ἐκεῖθεν.
The Festival of the Cathedra of S. Peter at Antioch is of considerable antiquity. It had its rise, as was natural, in that city: and has never been adopted by any other Church in the East. S. Jerome first inserted it in his Martyrology under the title of the Birthday of Antioch;— S. Ambrose received it at Milan, and composed those prayers for it which are now also in the Roman Missal;— S. Augustine thence introduced it into Africa, and we have a Homily of his on the Festival. The S. Maur editors believe this sermon not to be Augustine's, in which supposition they were preceded by Verlinus and Vindingus. But their case does not seem made out. Delpezzo, La difesa de' libri Liturgici, Cap. 2. It was also inserted in the Gotho-Hispanic Calendar: and at least as early as the eighth century. The second Council of Tours, A.D. 567, forbids a heathen custom of offering bread and wine on the tombs of the departed on this day, whence, according to Beleth and Durandus, it was sometimes known as the Festum S. Petri Epularum. In the sermons of S. Augustine before alluded to mention is made of the same practice: and we find S. Monica rebuked by S. Ambrose for so far condescending to it as to distribute bread to the poor in memory of the departed. The Cathedra of S. Peter at Rome was unknown to the Roman Breviary, till inserted by Paul IV. in 1557.

[1] Euseb. H. E. III. 22. Nicephorus Callistus, H. E. III. 11, and S. Ignatius himself, writing to the Antiochenes, μνημονεύσατε Εὐοδίου τοῦ

EUODIUS SECOND BISHOP. 5

He it was, if we may believe Joannes Malalas, himself an Antiochene, who first invented that name of Christians which was adopted during the visit of S. Paul and S. Barnabas to Antioch. It is probable that he ended his course by martyrdom.

5. It is impossible to trace the progress of the Gospel in Palestine, Syria, or Cilicia, further than the scanty notices in the Acts of the Apostles may open a path to conjecture. Tyre[1] and Sidon claimed S. Peter as their founder. The Apostolic Constitutions[2] make him to have consecrated Zacchæus first bishop of Cæsarea. The fertile invention of pseudo-Dorotheus of Tyre supplies a long list, from the Seventy disciples, and from[3] names mentioned in the Epistles, of the earliest prelates of the Churches round Jerusalem and Antioch. But we shall be content to hold nothing as certain beyond the fact that Euodius was already second bishop of Antioch before the miraculous liberation of S. Peter from the prison of Herod. *Founders of the Church-es round Antioch and Jerusalem.*

6. While the Gospel, by the preaching of Apostles and Apostolic men is thus spreading in Western Asia, while S. James at Jerusalem, S. Euodius at Antioch, S. Barnabas in Cyprus, are feeding the Church of GOD, while S. Paul is labouring more abundantly than they all, in journeyings often, in perils of waters, in perils of robbers, in perils by the heathen, in perils in the wilderness, we must glance Eastward to watch the further triumphs of the Faith.

7. It appears, from the universal consent of Eastern writers, that to the Apostle Thomas, also named Judas[4], fell the *S. Thomas evangelises Persia,*

ἀξιομακαρίστου ποιμένος ὑμῶν, ὃς πρῶτος ἐνεχειρίσθη παρὰ τῶν Ἀποστόλων τὴν ὑμετέραν προστασίαν.

[1] So the Liber de Gestis Petri, which though apocryphal is ancient, and contains apparently a good deal of truth.

[2] Constit. Apostol. VII. 47.

[3] An irrefragable proof of the falsehood of these lists of the Seventy is the express assertion of Eusebius that no such list was extant in his time, H. E. I. 12: τῶν δὲ ἑβδομήκοντα κατάλογος μὲν οὐδεὶς οὐδαμῇ φέρεται.

[4] Eusebius expressly, I. 13: Ἰούδας ὁ καὶ Θωμᾶς. Valesius says, "Judam esse cognominatum, alibi quod sciam non reperitur. Itaque et hoc nomine narratio ista in suspicionem venit." Heinichen (I. 82) does not correct him. But S. Ephraim expressly says the same thing:—Assem.

preaching of the Gospel in Parthia[1], and the further East. He extended his labours through Syria, Mesopotamia and Persia, till he reached the borders of India. Here he first evangelised the coast of Malabar, where multitudes received the Faith. He then crossed over to that of Coromandel, and there pursued his labours with equal success. In Malabar, the churches[2] of Angamala, afterwards metropolitical Cranganor, and Coulan, were more especially flourishing;—in Coromandel, that of Meliapore, where the king and all his people believed. Hence it seems matter of certainty that the blessed Apostle passed eastward; but whether to China[3], or merely to Siam and Cochin China, is a question of more difficulty. At Cambala[4], however, wherever the exact posi-

---

B. O. I. 101: "Weigh both in the balance,—the Centurion, who believed, and Judas Thomas, who desired to touch and investigate." See also B. O. I. 318.

[1] Euseb. H. E. III. 1: Θωμᾶς μὲν, ὡς ἡ παρδδοσις περιέχει, τὴν Παρθίαν εἴληχεν. Fortunatus:
Bellica Persidis Thomæ subjecta vigori;
Fortior efficitur victa tiara Deo.
The Menolog. for Oct. 6: οὗτος Μήδοις καὶ Πέρσαις, Πάρθοις καὶ Ἰνδοῖς τὸν λόγον τοῦ Θεοῦ κηρύξας.

[2] The traditions of the country at the arrival of the Portuguese are best given by Ant. Gouvea, Hist. Orient.

[3] It is very certain that S. Thomas preached to some nation called Chinese. In the Malabar office for his day we have, "By the blessed S. Thomas the illumination of the life-giving doctrine arose upon all the Hindoos. By the Blessed S. Thomas the Kingdom of Heaven was opened to the Chinese." It appears, from the records of the church of Angamala, on the Malabar coast, as quoted in Gouvea, that it formerly used to send a suffragan to the Island of Socotra, the other to S.

China. The official title of the Archbishops of Malabar is *Metropolitan of India and China.*—There are innumerable other proofs that some *China* was early evangelised:—but as Cochin China and Pegu were called by the same name, this does not absolutely settle the question. The probability, however, is, that S. Thomas did visit the actual China.—1. It is not likely that the Apostle's zeal should have led him to Pegu or Siam and there have stopped short, when he must have heard of the vast empire that stretched, at comparatively so short a distance, to the N. E. 2. Du Halde has shewn that Quan-yem-Chang, who lived in the beginning of the second century, certainly had a knowledge of our Lord. This throws the introduction of the Gospel very nearly to the time of S. Thomas. 3. Though this China certainly *may* mean the Indian peninsula, no argument has been adduced to shew that it *has* that signification.

[4] Cambala, as Hyde has shewn, simply means in Mogul Tatar, the imperial city. It seems probable that Pekin is intended. To imagine that Cambala is the same with Cam-

tion of that city may have been, he founded a church, and thence returned to Meliapore. Here the innumerable conversions which he effected excited the indignation of the Brahmins;—a popular commotion was easily raised;—the Apostle was stoned, two[1] Brahmins being the principal ringleaders in the attack: a third, observing some signs of life in the battered form, thrust it through with a lance, and thus dismissed the Apostle to his crown. This occurred, according to Indian tradition, in the year 68, and in the reign of Saliochan, king of Meliapore. The remains of the martyr were carried to a hill near the city, then called Calamina, but afterwards S. Thomas's Mount; ever since that period a place of frequent pilgrimage. But in the year 380[2] the relics,—or as the Indian Church will have it—the coffin only, were translated to the cathedral of S. Thomas, in Edessa: thenceforward regarded with the highest degree of veneration. His translation is not only commemorated as a festival by the Indian Church at the present day, but even by their Pagan neighbours. *his Martyrdom at Meliapore, A.D. 68,. and translation.*

8. The Eastern Church, however, regards Mar-Addai, or S. Thaddæus[3], one of the Seventy, as its especial Apostle. He is by some regarded as the same with Nathanael, and is said to have been the son of Tolmai: hence may have arisen the tradition which makes S. Bartholomew the Apostle the same person with "the Israelite indeed in whom was no guile." It was this Thaddæus who is represented by tradition as sent, after our LORD's Ascension, to Abgarus *His disciple, S. Thaddæus, of the Seventy,*

boja, as Yeates does, because there is some little similarity in the name, is quite arbitrary.

[1] The Greek account is different, and evidently less authentic. The Stichos of the Synaxarion, however, agrees with the account of the lance: ὁ χεῖρα πλευρᾷ σῇ βαλεῖν ζητῶν πάλαι πλευρὰν ὑπέρ σου νύττεται Θωμᾶς, Λόγε.

[2] Chronic. Edessen. ap. Asseman. B. O. I. 395.

[3] Eusebius, H. E. I. 13: Θαδ-

δαῖον τὸν ἀπόστολον, ἕνα τῶν ἑβδομήκοντα. S. Jerome read the first three words hastily, and made the messenger the same with Lebbæus the Apostle—as is noticed by V. Bede. See Asseman. B. O. I. 10. So Bar Hebræus in his Catalogue of Jacobite Patr. B. O. II. 391:—and the four Nestorian Catalogues, those of Solomon of Bostra, Annus Bar Matthew, Elias of Damascus, and an anonymous one.

King of Edessa. The genuineness of this history will probably remain a disputed point for ever: to my own mind the evidence[1] slightly preponderates in its favour. Nestorian addition asserts that Thaddæus, after healing Abgarus, refused the money offered by that prince, with the words, "Freely we have received, freely we give." He thence, accompanied by his two disciples, Mar Mari and Mar Achi, went to Nisibis, and there dismissed his associates to their separate labours.

He himself, after discipling the country round Mozul, returned to Edessa, where, twenty-two years after the commencement of his mission, he received the crown of martyrdom from Maan, the son of Abgarus[2], who was attached to the old superstition. He is reckoned the first Patriarch of the East.

9. His disciple, Achi[3], preached Christ, on leaving Nisibis, in Bezabde; on learning the death of his master, he went to Edessa to console the faithful, and to settle the

---

[1] Heinichen says, "Nunc quidem nemo vindicare conabitur." Nevertheless Cave, Pearson, and, to a certain degree, Asseman, believed in it:—the latter holding that the letter of Abgarus is absolutely genuine, while that of our Lord, though not of His own writing, was the substance of the message He sent. The three arguments principally which are against the authenticity of the Epistles are: 1. That S. Gelasius in the Council of Rome, 594, denied it; 2. That Abgarus calls himself τοπάρχης, instead of by the title which every petty Eastern prince used, βασιλεύς; 3. That to keep Abgarus waiting so long would have been contrary to our Lord's goodness (!). The folly of this last kind of argument is evident, and reflects nearly as much on the history of the Syro-Phœnician woman as on the present story. It is presumptuous to say whether any composition like this is, or is not, worthy of our Lord: but the quotation seems just in the style of those in the N. T. "For it is written concerning Me, that they which have not seen should believe on Me, to the intent that they who have not seen, they may believe and live." This is precisely the way in which the N. T. quotes the sense rather than the words, and mixes up two passages in one: as here, Isaiah vi. 9 and lii. 15. Surely a forger would have made a more literal reference.

[2] This is the account of Gregory Bar Hebræus, B. O. II. 391; and it agrees best with the chronology. But Maris Bar Salomon makes him to have died in peace, while Abgarus was yet reigning.

[3] B. O. Chronic. Edessen. I. 421, and II. 394.

LABOURS AND DEATH OF MAR MARIS. 9

affairs of the Church. Here he also suffered martyrdom about the year 51[1].

10. Mar Maris, after leaving Nisibis, betook himself to Ctesiphon[2], a city which will play no small part in these annals of the East. Situated on the eastern bank of the Tigris, it was the winter-quarters of the kings of Parthia. On the opposite bank stood the city of Seleucia, which owed its origin to Seleucus Nicator. By degrees these towns stretched their suburbs along the banks of the river, till they formed one large city: and hence, the aggregation was in after-times called by the Arabs Almodani, the double city. Here Mar Maris fixed that see which afterwards became the head of the vast Patriarchate of the East: he is reckoned its second, though, in point of fact, its first Catholicos. At this time it was the seat of the Parthian monarchy, and inhabited chiefly by Magi. He then discipled Doorkan, Cashgar, the two Irâks, El Ahwaz, Yemen, and the island Socotra, and returned to Ctesiphon. Two of his miracles are recorded. In Doorkan a woman named Kani, grievously afflicted with the leprosy, received in baptism bodily as well as spiritual health. In Ctesiphon itself the master of a feast, where Maris was invited, was seized with sudden illness, and healed by him with the sign of the Cross. At Cascar he consecrated a bishop; and that see became, in after ages, protothronus of Seleucia, and its prelate guardian of the vacant patriarchate. At length, full of years and good works, Mar Maris departed to his reward after an episcopate of thirty-three years. To his disciples, who anxiously enquired as to his successor, the dying prelate is reported to have said, "Seek him at Jerusalem."

Mar Maris founds the see of Ctesiphon, called the second Catholicos; evangelises the Irâks and El Ahraz; his miracles, and death, July 19, A.D. 82.

11. The Apostolic Council of Jerusalem, the visits of S. Paul both to that city and to Antioch, and other matters narrated in the Acts of the Apostles, it does not fall within my purpose to relate. S. James presided with increasing

---

[1] The length of the episcopate of S. Thaddæus requires us to place the martyrdom of S. Achius as late as we can in the reign of Maan. But he, according to the Chron. Edess. died *cir.* 52. He was succeeded however by a brother of the same name, under whom it is possible that S. Achius suffered.

[2] Le Quien, Or. Christ. II. 1094.

reputation for sanctity;—he was venerated by the Jews as well as by the Romans, and received from both the name of *the Just.* Oblias is also recorded to have been one of his surnames, in what sense the learned are not agreed[1]. The year in which his Epistle was written cannot be determined; we may, however, safely consider it as but little anterior to the close of his life. Ananus (the son of that Annas who has an immortality of infamy from the New Testament, but whom the Jews regard as the happiest of men, because his five sons attained to the pontifical dignity which he had himself enjoyed) was raised to the High Priesthood by Agrippa in the interval which elapsed between the death of Festus and the arrival of Albinus, his successor. Ananus, whose influence was more considerable on account of the absence of the governor, desired to signalise the commencement of his pontificate by some act of vengeance on the Church. S. Paul was beyond his power; but S. James would be a victim hardly less illustrious. Josephus assures us that, having been accused to, and sentenced by the Sanhedrim, he was stoned to death; but Hegesippus, a better-informed historian, gives a more circumstantial account of his martyrdom. Brought before the Sanhedrim, at the time of the Passover, he was commanded to ascend the terrace of the temple, and thence to disabuse the people of the worship of CHRIST. He mounted that august erection, and from the summit, glittering with snow-white marble, looked down on the vast multitude below. "Tell us, O just one," demanded the Scribes and Pharisees, "what we are to believe touching that JESUS, whom this people ignorantly worship." "Why ask ye me," replied the Apostle with a loud voice, "concerning JESUS the Son of Man? He sitteth in heaven at the right hand of God, and will come again in the clouds of heaven." The multitude cried, "Hosanna to the Son of David!" The Scribes and Pharisees, after regretting the error which had thus produced another testimony to the CHRIST, and crying out, "The Just one too hath gone

---

[1] Sherva ebn Johanna, MS. (See the Preface) Maris Bar Salomon.

astray," mounted the terrace, cast S. James down from the summit, and bade stone him. Falling on his knees, while a shower of stones was rained in upon him, he cried, "I beseech Thee, LORD GOD and Father, forgive them; for they know not what they do." A man of the house of Rechab, who stood by, exclaimed, "What do ye? the Just one prays for you." A fuller, fearing, it should seem, that, after all, the Apostle should escape, struck him on the head with a club, and thus dismissed him from his sufferings to his crown. So great was the horror which this deed caused among the more moderate part of the Jews, that Josephus unhesitatingly ascribes the destruction of the city to the just vengeance of GOD on so barbarous a murder. <small>and is cast from the top of the temple.</small>

12. Such of the Apostles as were able to be present, and other surviving disciples of our LORD, elected Symeon the son of Cleophas to the vacant throne. He is mentioned in the New Testament, where the Jews asked concerning CHRIST, "Is not this the brother of James and Joses and Judas and Simon?" His relationship to our LORD according to the flesh, no less than his eminent holiness, pointed him out as a fit successor to the Apostle: and he administered the affairs of the infant Church during the tremendous storm that burst over the land. The history of the siege of Jerusalem, the recognition by the Christians of the Roman standards as the abomination of desolation, the retreat of Cestius Gallus, the flight of S. Symeon and his Church to Pella, and their preservation there during the war, fall beyond the limits that I have proposed to myself in this work. <small>S. Symeon, Patr. II. of Jerusalem.</small>

13. The period during which S. Euodius held the see of Antioch is uncertain: there is a tradition that he suffered martyrdom[1] under Nero. Nor can we positively assert whether his successor, the glorious martyr Ignatius, was consecrated by S. Peter[2], S. Paul[3], or merely by some Apos- <small>S. IGNATIUS, Patr. III. of Antioch.</small>

---

[1] Bollandus, Feb. 1. 18 D, unhesitatingly adopts this account. It seems strange, however, on this supposition, that S. Ignatius when eulogising him (see p. 4, n. 1) does not speak of him as a martyr.

[2] Theodoret. Dialog. "Immutabilis," Op. IV. ad finem, ἀκήκοας δὲ πάντως

tolic prelate. It has been asserted, on doubtful authority, that he sat at the same time with Euodius, the one as bishop of the Jews, the other of the Gentiles. A better supported belief makes him to have been the child whom our LORD set before his disciples as a pattern of himself. That he was the disciple of S. John the Evangelist is certain, and these are all the particulars recorded of his earlier life. During his episcopate he suffered much both by exile and imprisonment; and it has been supposed that it was the persecution under Domitian which gave him the opportunity of thus playing the man for CHRIST. Of his other acts, *Prosperous condition of the Church.* during the long period that he governed the see of Antioch, we know little; learning only, in general terms, that the faith grew and prospered, and that multitudes were added to the LORD.

14. In compliance with the injunctions of the dying Maris, a prelate for the East was demanded at Jerusalem[1]. *Successors in the Catholicate of Chaldæa.* Abres, who is said to have been a kinsman of S. Joseph, was selected for that purpose by Symeon the son of Cleophas. During his episcopate of sixteen years he is said to have consecrated a large number of bishops, and to have been greatly beloved for his charity. His successor Abraham[2], of the same family, was consecrated at Antioch; and had to contend against the inveterate enmity which the Parthian king evinced towards the true Faith. The persecution is said to have ceased in consequence of the deliverance of that monarch's daughter from an evil spirit. But all these accounts must be received as extremely doubtful: though it would seem that the succession of names is tolerably certain. Abraham[3] was succeeded by James, also of the same family, and also consecrated in the same city. To what extent the Faith, during these successive episcopates, had penetrated

'Ιγνάτιον ἐκεῖνον, ὃς διὰ τῆς τοῦ μεγάλου Πέτρου δεξιᾶς τῆς ἀρχιερωσύνης τὴν χάριν ἐδέξατο. And Felix III. writing to the Emperor Zeno against Peter the Fuller: sanctamque sedem pontificatus Ignatii Martyris, qui Petri dextra ordinatus est, polluisse.

[3] So the Apostolic Constitutions: VII. 45.
[1] So says Amrou. But Bar Hebræus (B. O. II. 395) will have him to have been consecrated at Antioch.
[2] Bar. Hebr. B. O. II. 395.
[3] Bar. Hebr. Ibid.

the East, it is hopeless to enquire. There is a strong tradition, however, that Jundishapoor, in the modern province of Khuzistan, was one of the earliest of Chaldæan sees[1]: and its proximity to Bosrah, which we know to have been a bishoprick of Apostolic foundation, renders the account sufficiently probable.

15. The degeneracy of the Parthian empire opened an easy passage to the Eastern expedition of Trajan. On his march through Antioch it does not appear that he offered any molestation to S. Ignatius or to his flock: and his conquest of Bosporus, Colchos, Iberia, and Albania, afforded him no opportunity for persecution. In Osrhoene, however, the case was different. Barsumas, bishop of Edessa[2], had converted a large number of heathen to the faith of Christ; and had baptized, among others, Sarbel, a priest, and his sister Bebæa. They received the crown of martyrdom, and are—so far as records go—the protomartyrs of the Patriarchate of Antioch. Sarbel, probably as an apostate priest, suffered fearful tortures, and was finally beheaded in company with his sister. Barsumas himself confessed CHRIST under Lysias the præfect (of what place is not told), but survived the blows to which he was exposed, and at a subsequent period departed this life in peace.

The expedition of Trajan against Parthia.

Martyrdom of SS. Sarbel, Bebæa, and Barsumas.

16. Trajan, prosecuting his Eastern conquests, became master of Seleucia, Ctesiphon and Babylon. On a general review of his troops, eleven thousand[3] soldiers, who professed themselves Christians, were banished into Armenia. Romulus, præfect of the Horse, having expostulated, and owned himself a worshipper of the Crucified, was scourged and beheaded. The soldiers are probably the same who are

The 11,000 martyrs of Armenia.

---

[1] But at that time, under the title of Laphat, or Beth Laphat. The metropolitan of Jundishapoor is protothronus of the Catholic of Seleucia, sits at his right hand in synods, and consecrates him.

[2] Le Quien (O. C. III. 955), following the Roman Martyrology, expressly calls him a martyr; but the Menæa, which are here likely to be a better authority, say (Jan. 30)—ἐν τῇ ἰδίᾳ γενόμενος ἐκκλησίᾳ, καὶ τῷ Θεῷ εὐαρεστήσας (leg. εὐχαριστήσας) ἐν εἰρήνῃ πρὸς αὐτὸν ἐξεδήμησε, which is a rifacimento of the account given on Jan. 29.

[3] Baron. and Bollandist in d. 2 Jan.

commemorated in the Martyrologies as the Eleven Thousand crucified in Mount Ararat. Their passion is indeed fixed under Hadrian; and it may possibly have been procrastinated to that period. Notwithstanding the fables with which it has been adorned, and the difficulties which some details present, there seems no reason to doubt of the main historical fact.

17. The Eastern expedition of Trajan added two illustrious martyrs, and, as it would seem, in the same year, to the catalogue of the Church. Symeon, bishop of Jerusalem, now one hundred and twenty years old, was accused to Atticus, proconsul of Syria, of being descended from the royal house of David[1]. His accusers were certain Judaising teachers, who probably counted on the nervous apprehension with which the Romans regarded any descendant of the kingly line, as having suffered so much from pretended chiefs and Messiahs. His relation to the family of David could not be denied: as the son of Cleopas, the brother of Joseph, his descent from that monarch was perfectly clear. Whatever might have been his fate, could nothing else have been laid to his charge, the boldness with which he testified to the Son of David was not to be forgiven. After enduring the most cruel tortures for several days, with a firmness that, joined to his great age, elicited the admiration of his judge and of the bystanders, he was crucified, and thus ended his course. S. Symeon was probably the last survivor of those who had seen our LORD in the flesh[2]; and it is the mournful complaint of the earliest church historian, that the hearers of His doctrine, and the eye-witnesses of His acts being now removed, heresies began to shew themselves more boldly, and to draw away greater numbers from the faith. In his place Judas, surnamed the Just, was elected bishop. Of a princely Jewish family, he is said to have been con-

Martyrdom of S. Symeon, the kinsman of CHRIST.

S. Judas, third Bishop of Jerusalem.

[1] Euseb. H. E. III. 32, who does little more than quote Hegesippus.

[2] Judas, another of our LORD's "brethren," lived, according to Eusebius into the reign of Trajan, and if S. Ignatius were the little child who was set before the disciples, he was a still later survivor than S. Symeon. But had he remembered our LORD as man, he could hardly have failed to say so in his epistles.

verted by S. James, and baptized by S. Symeon. He held the see three years. Thebuthis, a competitor for the see, revenged himself for, and justified his rejection, by embracing heresy: his followers were not numerous.

18. But the glory of the bishop of Jerusalem is eclipsed by that of his brother of Antioch. Of the persecutions which in the year 115 and the following spring vexed that city we have no particulars. The number of Christians was so large that danger was apprehended; and it was thought that to remove Ignatius would effectually crush the strength and spirit of the Nazarene sect. He was accordingly presented before Trajan, then in Antioch, and on being interrogated as to his name, replied by that of Theophorus. The ancient Acts thus continue[1]. "Trajan said: And who is he that carries GOD? Ignatius said: He that hath CHRIST in his breast. Trajan said: And think you not that we have the gods in our breast, finding them, as we do, our helpers against the enemy? Ignatius said: And do you call the divinities of the heathen, gods? You err. For there is One God, who made heaven and earth, the sea and all that therein is: and JESUS CHRIST, His Only-Begotten SON, whose friendship I have gained. Trajan said: Do you mean Him that was crucified under Pontius Pilate? Ignatius said: I mean Him that hath crucified sin and its author, and who justifieth not the slaves of idols[2], but them only who bear Him in their heart. Trajan said: Do you, then, carry CHRIST within you? Ignatius said: Yea: for it is written: I will dwell in them, and walk in them. Trajan said: We ordain that Ignatius, who affirms that he carries CHRIST within him, shall be bound in chains, and conducted to Rome by soldiers, there to be devoured by beasts for the diversion of the people. Ignatius cried out: I render hearty thanks to Thee, O LORD, for that Thou hast honoured me with perfect love to Thee, so that I am bound with chains of iron, as Thine Apostle Paul." He was given in charge to ten

Examination of S. Ignatius, A.D. 116.

[1] Act. ap. Bolland. Feb. 1, p. 29.
[2] The very ancient Latin Acts have "illum qui non justificat idolorum servitutem, sed qui in corde suo hunc sapit;" but Trajan's reply shews the clause to be corrupt.

soldiers, "ten leopards," as he terms them in the Epistle to the Romans: and thus left Antioch about the middle of the summer.

19. His journey to Smyrna, whatever his sufferings from the cruelty of the guard, of which he more than once complains, was nevertheless a kind of triumphal progress. Gavias[1] and Agathopus accompanied him from Syria: in Cilicia he was joined by the Deacon Philo, whom he mentions with great affection; and as he passed on his way the principal cities vied with each other in welcoming this athlete of CHRIST, if honoured by receiving him, or saluting him by embassies of their bishop and priests, if he passed at a little distance. He reached Smyrna partly by water, partly by land, in August; and there had the satisfaction of being welcomed by Polycarp, his fellow-disciple under S. John.

S. Polycarp and the Church of Smyrna. Polycarp, primitive as the times still were, was fifth bishop of that see[2]. Strataeas, the second, was nephew of Eunice, the daughter of Lois, and thus cousin to Timothy. Bucolus, the fourth, retains no small reputation in the Eastern Church as a holy prelate; and at his dying wish Polycarp was named his successor. To Smyrna also came Onesimus, bishop of Ephesus, without doubt the same in whose behalf the Epistle to Philemon was written, and the successor of Timothy, when his course had been ended by martyrdom. He was accompanied by his priests, Burrhus, Euplus, Fronto, *Deputies to S. Ignatius.* and Crocus. Tralles and Magnesia sent their bishops Polybius and Damas; and how much the spirit of the aged champion was refreshed by their exhortations and prayers, his epistles amply testify. For, while his escort was waiting for a convenient passage, he employed his leisure time in the beginning of September, in addressing the churches which had thus consoled him: and these most precious

---

[1] Ad Philadelph. Sect. 11.

[2] The Apostolic Constitutions give the first three, Aristo, Strataeas, Aristo II. (VII. 47). The relation of Strataeas to Timothy is mentioned in the Acts of S. Polycarp. S. Bucolus is named by Suidas, though mistakenly, as the *first* Bishop. S. Bucolus is named on the 6 of February: his stichos is:

Σμύρνης ὁ ποιμὴν, Βουκόλος θνηπόλος,
Ἄγρυπνός ἐστι καὶ θανὼν ποίμνης φύλαξ.

monuments of Christian antiquity, so often attacked as supposititious, so often proved genuine, rendered his enforced sojourn at Smyrna, however tedious to his desire of martyrdom, a happy event to the whole Church. "I do not pretend," writes he to the Ephesians, "to give you instructions as if I were something; for, though a prisoner for the sake of JESUS CHRIST, I am not yet perfect. I am only beginning to be a disciple, and I speak as to those who are as much masters as I am: for need were that you should prepare me to the conflict, and inspire me with faith, patience and courage." "I am bound," he says to the Trallians, "for the name of CHRIST, but not even so am I worthy of CHRIST; but when I shall be offered up, then perchance I shall be worthy." Against heresy he again and again exhorts: "Be deaf," he tells the Trallians, "when any man speaks to you without JESUS CHRIST, who is of the seed of David, who was truly born of Mary, who ate and drank, who was truly persecuted under Pontius Pilate; who was truly crucified and died in sight of all that are in heaven and in earth; who was truly raised again by the power of the Father, and who will raise us up in like manner, if we trust in Him. If He only suffered in appearance, as some wicked men say, I mean them that believe not, why am I bound? Why do I desire to fight with the wild beasts? I should die in vain. No, most surely: I lie not against the Lord." "I write to all the churches," he says to the Romans, to whom he sent an Epistle by an accidental opportunity, "that I shall die of my own free will, if ye prohibit me not. I beseech you welcome me not with unseasonable kindness. Suffer me to become the food of wild beasts, by means of whom I may obtain the fruition of GOD. I am the corn of GOD: I must be ground by the teeth of beasts, that I may be found the pure bread of GOD."

His epistles.

20. It is, however, the abundant testimony which the Martyr-Bishop bears to the honour and divine institution of the episcopate, which has made his works the objects of such bitter attacks in former times from the sworn defenders

18   PATRIARCHATE OF ANTIOCH.

<small>and testi-
mony to
episcopacy.</small>
of the Presbyterian theory, who held them as false, and, in our own days, from ingenious *littérateurs*, who regard them as bigoted. "Ye must be Christians," he says to the Magnesians, not in name only, as they are who recognise the name of bishop, and do everything without him." "All," writes he to the Trallians, "must respect the deacons, as established by the order of JESUS CHRIST: the bishop, as him who is the image of the FATHER: the priests, as the Senate of GOD, as the company of the Apostles. Without them there can be no such a thing as a Church." "Let us take care not to resist the bishop," is his exhortation to the Ephesians, "to the end we may be obedient to GOD. It is plain that we should honour the bishop as the LORD Himself." "As JESUS CHRIST," he tells the Magnesians again, "did nothing either by Himself or His Apostles without the Father, with whom He was one, so do nothing without the bishop and the priests."

21. At length the aged bishop was apprised that his journey must be continued; and his next resting-place was in Troas. Here the bishop of Philadelphia came to do him honour: it is useless to enquire why this duty of love was postponed till the martyr had reached so much greater a distance from the place whence it was paid. Hence, too, he wrote to the Ephesians, to the Trallians, to the Smyrnæans, and a second time, it would appear from these, to the Magnesians. It cannot but be regarded as by the special providence of GOD that these letters were in the first place writ-
<small>His clear
testimonies
to the
teaching of
the Church</small>
ten, and in the next, have come down to us: so marvellous a testimony do they afford to the faith and doctrine of those primitive ages, at a time only twenty years subsequent to the conclusion of the Canon of Scripture: and had S. Polycarp rendered no other service to the Church than the care with which he collected and preserved these most precious monuments of antiquity, his name would deserve to be had
<small>on the
Blessed
Eucharist,</small>
in everlasting remembrance. So, of the Blessed Eucharist: "Obedient to the bishop and the presbytery, with undivided heart, breaking the one Bread, which is the medicine of im-

mortality, the antidote of death, obtaining life in GOD through JESUS CHRIST, the remedy which purges vices, and chases away all ill." And again: "I rejoice not in corruptible nourishment, nor the pleasures of this life: I desire the Bread of GOD, the Heavenly Bread, which is the Flesh of JESUS CHRIST the SON of GOD; Who in these last days was made of the seed of David and Abraham: and I desire the drink of His Blood, which is incorruptible love and eternal life." So *the Ecclesiastical* of the Ecclesiastical Hierarchy: "Do nothing without the *Hierarchy,* bishops: for they are priests, and thou"—he is writing to the deacon Heron—"the minister of priests." "They baptize, they minister, they elect, they lay on their hands: and thou art their servant, as blessed Stephen was to James." So again of those who, even in these primitive ages, had *the merit of Virginity.* learnt the excellence of the place and the name better than of sons and daughters: where he most distinctly asserts the superiority of chastity to marriage, yet guards himself against all heretical suspicion on the subject of the latter. "Let the wives be subject to their husbands in the fear of GOD: the virgins to CHRIST in all purity: not abominating marriage, but embracing that which is more excellent: not as casting reproach on matrimony, but that they may be at leisure, with hearts more free for meditation on the Divine Word."

22. No sooner had this illustrious Martyr left Antioch, than the Church was left in peace. Heron, a deacon who had distinguished himself by his courage and zeal, seems to have exercised the principal authority in ecclesiastical matters. Meanwhile, Ignatius was again on his journey to Rome. Before leaving Troas he besought Polycarp to take charge of his widowed Church, and then, accompanied by most of the bishops who had visited him on his journey, he sailed to Neapolis, and thence proceeded to Philippi, whence he again addressed his beloved church of Antioch. Hence he passed through Epirus, and so, taking ship, landed, after a circuitous voyage, at Puteoli. Here he had desired, after the example of S. Paul, to disembark. But the wind was unfavourable, and then having veered round, speedily

brought them to the port of Rome. Here a vast multitude of Christians of all ranks and ages met him: sorrowing that their first acquaintance with him in the flesh was but the prelude to their eternal separation from him in this world. He, it is said, knew all their names by inspiration: consoled them, exhorted them, besought them, as he had done in his letter, not by their prayers to impede his passage to his LORD; and so, amid mingled tears and rejoicings, he went towards Rome.

23. It was the twentieth of December, the Feast of the *Sigillaria*. The amphitheatre, tier behind tier, row beyond row, full, crowded, overflowing: the consuls, with the lictors, in their places, the centre of the podium; crowds pressing up from the Suburra and the Via Sacra, from the Forum of Augustus and the Mount Palatine: the designators showing spectators to their places: the alytes describing the victories of Trajan, and the progress of the execrable superstition; patricians complaining of the press and heat; a soft December breeze chasing some few white clouds over the intense blue of the sky; sometimes a roar or snarl from some of the wild beasts in the dens under the caveæ. Ignatius comes forth: eighty-seven thousand heads are turned towards him: he stretches forth his hands with a holy joy towards the den: the gate flies open: a long roar, a spring, and then there is nothing but the crunching and crashing of the martyr's bones, and the savage exultation of the lion as he stands above him. Only some of the larger bones remained. It had been the desire of the martyr that his relics should not be collected: they were wrapped in linen, and sent as a precious treasure to Antioch. But that night, as the brethren after long watching slept through sorrow, the martyr appeared to them in various ways—as standing by them, as embracing them, as praying for them, as entering into the joy of his LORD. "And these things," they say in their encyclic Epistle, "filled us with gladness: therefore, glorifying GOD and praising His saints, we declare to you the day and year of his martyrdom, to the end that we may

have part with the noble athlete, glorifying in his holy memory our LORD JESUS CHRIST[1]." They are noble words in which S. Chrysostom speaks of the martyr's triumph, and the return of his relics. "Short was the time for which GOD took him from you, and with greater grace hath He restored him to you again. And as they who borrow money return that which they have borrowed with usury, so GOD, taking from you this precious treasure for a little while that He might display it at Rome, returned it to you with the greater glory. Ye sent him forth a bishop, ye received him back a martyr; ye sent him forth with prayers, ye welcomed him home with crowns; and not ye only, but all the cities in the intervening lands."

24. Heron, the friend and deacon of Ignatius, was his successor[2]. His episcopate of twenty years has left no materials for ecclesiastical history[3]. The successors of S. Justus in the see of Jerusalem have, in like manner, left their names, but no record of their actions[4]. Zacchæus, or Zacharias, followed Justus: next came Tobias: then Benjamin, after him John, and then Matthias. The last-named

<small>HERON, IV. Patriarch of Antioch. Of Jerusalem: S. ZACCHÆUS, IV. TOBIAS, V. BENJAMIN, VI. JOHN, VII. S. MATTHIAS, VIII.</small>

---

[1] Baronius had fixed 110 as the date of the martyrdom of S. Ignatius; but Pagi, understanding that fuller information was given on the subject in the then unpublished Chronicon of John Malelas,—the same Chronicle which was afterwards to lay the foundation-stone of Bailly's reputation—wrote to Bishop Lloyd for particulars. Lloyd, in his answer, which Pagi has inserted in his *Critica*, under the year 109, so irrefragably demonstrates the true date to be 116, that the matter has not since been questioned. The Eastern Church celebrates this great Martyr on the day of his passion. The Canon, however, is of the Proeortia of the Nativity. In the Roman Church, the Festival is transferred to Feb. 1.

[2] Euseb. H. E. III. 36, *ad finem*,

also in his Chronicon.

[3] The address of Heron to S. Ignatius, given from a Vatican MS. by Baronius (A. 110, VII.), though not without beauty, is so manifestly of a later age that it is wonderful how the great annalist could have believed it genuine.

[4] This dry list is from the Chronicon of Eusebius. S. Matthias is the subject of eulogium by Usuard, in his Martyrology, under Jan. 30, who says that he had read "mira et fide digna" about this prelate.—Papebroch suspects these wonderful things to have been adopted from the apocryphal acts of S. Matthias the apostle. The bishop of Jerusalem is however named in the Roman Martyrology: in the Eastern he finds no place.

PHILIP, IX.
SENECA, X.
JUSTUS 2,
XI.
LEVI, XII.
EPHRES,
XIII.
JOSEPH,
XIV.
JUDAS, XV.

prelate is said, by an uncertain tradition, to have confessed under Hadrian, but to have ended his life in peace. Then came in order: Philip, Seneca; Justus II.; Levi; Ephres; Joseph; Judas: with him, as we shall hereafter see, ended the bishops of the Circumcision in A.D. 135.

25. We must bear in mind how different was the condition, at this early period, of the later patriarchates of Antioch and Jerusalem from that which we found to be the case at Alexandria. The Pope of Alexandria had, from the very beginning, a definite and acknowledged headship over his patriarchate; which was, in fact, merely his province. The position of Antioch was far different. The prelate undoubtedly took the lead among the churches that were afterwards his suffragans; but the larger cities, Damascus, Apamea, Tyre, Edessa, and others, as yet owned no decided inferiority. The prelates of Seleucia did indeed come to Antioch for consecration, but in their missionary enterprises eastward they were already autocephalus. It would be interesting, in these primitive times, to know how far the heralds of the Cross had won their way eastward; how far that church of Malabar, triumphant for five or six centuries, was then bearing plenteous fruit; how far the light of the Gospel had dawned on China. This only is evident, that even in the second century vigorous efforts were made for the propagation of the faith eastward, from Seleucia and Edessa: and that, at that epoch, central Asia afforded a far brighter promise of an evangelical harvest than central Europe. Jerusalem, of which we must next speak, was a mere provincial church of comparatively small importance: willingly acquiescing in the primacy of Cæsarea, and asserting no other pre-eminence than that which attached itself to the place where the salvation of the world had been wrought, and where the Holy Ghost had descended on the birthday of the Catholic Church. Whether the rapid succession of bishops in this see argues—as some have imagined—a savage persecution, seems doubtful. If the dates we have assigned be correct, thirteen prelates sat in nineteen years; let the widest limits be assigned, and their united episcopates

only occupied forty[1]. Still, it seems hardly credible that the church of Jerusalem should have been honoured by the successive, or nearly successive martyrdoms of so many of her bishops, while ecclesiastical history remains silent on the fact: especially when the glorious passion of S. Symeon and the names of his successors are equally known.

26. Hadrian, in the eleventh year of his reign, passed some time at Antioch. The fatal and final vengeance denounced on the Jews was now come to the full. The emperor had refounded Jerusalem by the title of Ælia Capitolina, had forbidden circumcision, and had raised a temple to Jupiter on Mount Moriah. The famous revolt of Barchochebas, 'the Sun of the Star,' was the consequence. In Judæa first, and then, but almost simultaneously, through the whole Roman Empire, that miserable people arose in their last and bloodiest rebellion: perpetrating in every country of their dispersion the most horrible atrocities, massacring their Gentile fellow-subjects by tens and hundreds of thousands, sawing their victims asunder, drinking the warm blood, and girding themselves with the entrails of the murdered men. Turnus Rufus, the general first charged with

Revolt of Barchochebas.

---

[1] The earliest date assigned to the martyrdom of S. Symeon is A.D. 107, but Dodwell, and Bishop Lloyd, followed by Pagi, seem to have made it clear that 116 is the correct epoch. The year of the death of Judas, the last bishop of the Circumcision, is more uncertain. Eusebius (H. E. IV. 5) seems to assert that the line of the first fifteen Bishops came to an end in the time of Adrian, that is before A.D. 138. But Epiphanius (Hær. 66. 20) says that it lasted till the eleventh year of Antoninus Pius, A.D. 148. And it is very conceivable that, after the edict which forbade the Jews to enter Jerusalem, there might have been for some few years two successions; the one, specially Hebrew for the exiled Hebrews, the other, Gentile, from its founder Mark. If we are to take 116 as the date of the martyrdom of S. Symeon, and 138 as that of the death of Judas, it does seem incredible that in twenty years thirteen bishops should have succeeded. At the time when the position of Roman Pontiff was the most dangerous in the Church, thirteen prelates were never compressed into a century, If we procrastinate the death of Judas till A.D. 148, we lessen the difficulty,—and if, notwithstanding the great authority of Lloyd and Dodwell, we might take the old date of A.D. 107 for the martyrdom of S. Symeon, we should still further obviate it. S. Judas is celebrated in some Martyrologies on May 4, under the additional name of Quiriacus.

the war, was unequal to the emergency: Severus, called from Britain, brought it to a final and terrible termination. Five hundred and eighty thousand Jews perished: nine hundred and eighty-five cities were levelled with the ground: it was forbidden to a Jew to reside in, or even to look from a distance at, Jerusalem, and the image of a swine was erected over the gate that led to Bethlehem. This annihilation of the Jews as the natives of Palestine, spoke to the Church in terms which could not be misunderstood; that now the last relic of the law was to be done away; now the rite of circumcision was no longer to be practised on any Christian; now evangelical liberty was to be fully and finally proclaimed. Accordingly, on the death—it would seem by martyrdom—of the last bishop of the Circumcision, Judas, Mark, a gentile, was elected in his place; and after fulfilling every duty of a good shepherd, gloriously accomplished his course as a martyr[1].

27. S. Heron, having sat twenty years, finished his course[2] by a glorious martyrdom. Cornelius[3] was elected in his place: and to him succeeded Eros[4]. His successor, Theophilus[5], who flourished under Aurelius Verus has left a somewhat more illustrious memory in the Church. The

[1] S. Mark is celebrated in the Roman Martyrology on October 22.

[2] Boschius of course fixes the martyrdom of S. Heron to A.D. 128. Ado and Usuardus give Oct. 17 as the day of his triumph. He does not appear to be mentioned in the Martyrology.

[3] Eusebius, H. E. IV. 20. Terzi in the *Syria Sacra* affirms that this prelate governed his church admirably by word and deed: on which I can only say with Boschius, "non dubito equidem, sed tamen id alibi nusquam reperi."

[4] Eusebius, u. s. I suppose that this is the same Eros who is mentioned in the Menæa (Cod. Clifford) on the 24th of June:—it is strange that Boschius does not allude to the commemoration.

Ἐρῶν ὑπῆρχεν οὐρανῶν κάλλους Ἔρως,
Πρὸς οὓς μεταστὰς, ὥσπερ ἦρα χαιρέτω.

[5] Eusebius, H. E. u. s. He is mistaken in the date, as given in his Chronicon, assigning the death of S. Theophilus to A.D. 177, which was, in fact, the year of his accession. Le Quien vindicates the date given in the text, which, on the whole, though not without difficulties, seems the most satisfactory. Those difficulties may be seen in Boschius, pp. 11, 12, who fixes the date 181. It is also disputed by Halloix and Tillemont, and perfect certainty is unattainable in the matter. William of Tyre absurdly makes this Theophilus the same with him to whom S. Luke wrote.

doctrine of Marcion was at this time troubling the East. The son of a bishop of Sinope in Pontus, he had sullied a youth of purity and religion by the violation of a consecrated virgin. To all his prayers and tears his father, with a sternness which resembled that of a Brutus rather than that of a Christian prelate, was inexorable; and the Roman priests, when the offender had betaken himself to that city, refused him their communion, unless he could produce the dimissory letters of his father. "I will rend your church in pieces," was the reply of the enraged man;—and he founded a heresy which extended far and wide, and lasted for centuries. Embracing the doctrine of a good and evil principle, he rejected the Old Testament, and the GOD of the Jews: he held the innate evil of matter, condemned marriage, encouraged voluntary death, fasted on Saturday in hatred of the Creator of the world, refused the use of meat and wine, and celebrated in water only. A little condescension and tact might, at the outset, have stifled this heresy: but it soon assumed formidable proportions, and ravaged the diocese of Antioch. Theophilus composed[1] a treatise, in three books, against the new doctrine, which is much praised by S. Jerome. He also confuted the errors of Hermogenes, an African heretic, who joined the teaching of the Porch to that of the Church: he affirmed the eternity of matter, and taught that the Body of JESUS CHRIST was in the sun. These treatises of Theophilus were distinguished by their elegance; a quality which did not attach to his commentaries on Proverbs and on the Gospels.

28. His principal work, however, and that which has alone come down to us, is his Treatise to Autolycus, a book of singular elegance[2], and which, considering its extreme

His Treatise to Autolycus, Book I.

---

[1] A list of the works of S. Theophilus is given by Eusebius, H. E. iv. 24, and Nicephorus, iv. 9: see Grabe, Spicileg. ii. 220, 221. The four books of Allegorical Commentaries on the Gospels, extant under the name of S. Theophilus, seem to be considered by Grabe as probably genuine.

[2] The editions of Bishop Fell (Oxford, 1684), Wolf (Hamburg, 1724), and the Benedictine (1722, Paris), are all good; but the best and most convenient is that of Mr Humphry (Cambridge, 1852). There is an English translation by Joseph Betty (Oxford, 1722).

antiquity and its intrinsic merits, has scarcely obtained the attention which it deserves. The three books of which it is composed were not written at the same time: the third is clearly, from its very commencement, of a later date, and is referred to as a separate treatise by Lactantius. Autolycus, it seems, had been amusing himself with some of the usual jokes against the name and the tenets of Christians: and, more particularly had made the usual heathen demand, "Shew me your God."—Hence the bishop takes occasion to commence his treatise. He demonstrates that GOD cannot be seen with the bodily eye, nor yet by the mental vision, unless it be purged and purified from sin: that to image Him under any form would be to be guilty of a representation which must necessarily do Him dishonour: that although GOD cannot be discerned by the eye, even in this world He can be perceived by His Providence and by His works: and that He will then be seen perfectly and eye to eye when this mortal shall have put on immortality. Hence arises the question of the Resurrection of the Dead. Faith, argues the bishop, is necessary in the pursuance of human art and science: how much more is it due to GOD by whom we are created?—"Are you not aware that faith precedes as leader in all things? What husbandman would ever reap, unless he first committed the seed to the earth? who could pass the sea, unless he first trust himself to the bark and to the pilot? What sick man can be healed, unless he first confide himself to the physician? Who can learn any art or science, unless he first give himself over to, and trust, the master? If then the husbandman trusts the earth, the voyager the ship, the patient the physician, will not *thou* trust in GOD, from whom thou hast so many pledges?" Hence he takes the opportunity of relating the characters and enormities of the gods,—and more especially the superstitions of Egypt: and contrasts them with the character, as allowed by all, of Christianity. Autolycus had said that, could he see any one who had risen from the dead, then, and not till then, would he believe. Theophilus expresses his doubt whether, even in that case, belief would be the result:

reminds him of the legends of Hercules and Æsculapius, and argues from the analogy of the changes of night and day, the reflorescence of trees, the renewal of flowers, the waning and waxing of the moon, the restoration of the sick to pristine health and vigour. "Be not thou," he says, "faithless, but believe. I once disbelieved that this would ever take place: but now, after having diligently considered it, I believe, at the same time having happened upon the holy writings of the Divine Prophets, who through the HOLY GHOST related in what way things past took place, in what way things present are being done, in what way things future shall be completed. When therefore I have received a demonstration from the occurrence of those things which were predicted, I disbelieve not: but I believe in obedience to GOD; to whom do thou also, if thou wilt, obey, lest if thou shouldest be unbelieving now, thou shouldest believe hereafter in eternal punishment." A clear proof that the eloquent bishop of Antioch had himself been a convert from heathenism.

29. In the second book our author returns to the follies of Gentile superstition: and remarks that, as statuaries attach no especial reverence to their work while in hand, but, when once it is placed in a temple, they fall down and worship it; so mythologists confess that the beings whom they have set forth as gods were originally mortals like ourselves. Why,—he argues,—has the generation of Divine beings ceased? Why are the ravines and peaks of Ida silent and solitary, when they ought to be alive and peopled with divinities? Thence he turns to the self-contradictions of poets and philosophers: some denying the very existence of a God, some affirming that every man's only god was his own conscience. This discrepancy he compares with the one and uniform tenor of the sacred narrative; which, commencing with Adam, he follows to the curse of Cain and the inventions of his posterity. He dwells on the historical and geographical knowledge which we obtain from Holy Scripture, and that at a time when the narratives of profane writers are a chaos of contradictory accounts. He dwells on

Book II.

the maxims of the prophets as indicative of Divine wisdom, and quotes the Sibylline Oracles in further illustration of his subject.

30. In the third, which, as I said, appears a later production, and of which one MS. only is extant, Theophilus proceeds to the defence of Christian doctrine. Autolycus fluctuated between a truer belief and the assertions of those who charged it with promiscuous concubinage and banquets of human flesh. Both charges he retorts on heathen philosophers: Zeno, Diogenes, Cleanthes, had taught the latter eminently: Plato, a community of wives: Epicurus had defended and even applauded incest. After dwelling on the various abusive theories, he next comes to Christian doctrine: the Unity of the Godhead: the Providence by which He supports, and the laws by which He rules the world: the Ten Commandments: the injunction of hospitality: the commendation of penitence, justice and charity: and, in the New Testament, the avoidance of vainglory, and the duty of obedience being exhorted. Could men, living in obedience to such laws, be guilty of the horrible crimes vulgarly laid to their charge? Next follows a long chronological dissertation, —not always perfectly accurate—that the superior antiquity of the Christian Scriptures may be demonstrated;—and the work is concluded with an attempt to assign the reasons why the Hebrew writings have found so little mention in Grecian literature. The date of the work is sufficiently settled by a passage in this last book: where the chronology ends with the death of Verus. It was therefore published, in all probability, at the commencement of the reign of Commodus—or in A.D. 181.

31. The mystical meanings in which, even in addressing a heathen, our bishop delights, are still more prominently brought forward in the fragments which we possess of his commentary[1] on the Gospels, and of the Song of Solomon. He seems to have survived the publication of his treatise to Autolycus about five years. From his own writings we

---

[1] Grabe, Spicileg. II. 228.

learn that he was[1] a native of Chaldæa; he nowhere mentions his bishoprick: but accidentally mentions another work of his, a "First Book on Histories[2]." Baronius speaks of his books as altogether divine. Natalis Alexander calls them a treasure-house of profane and divine learning[3]. His acquaintance is profound with the heathen poets and philosophers: and his love of mystical interpretations gives a peculiar charm to his style[4]. It must be confessed, however[5], that some passages regarding the eternal generation of the SON OF GOD have what would now be called an unorthodox sound, although he no doubt taught the same doctrine, though in a more loose and less theological language, which the Arian heresy obliged the Church to express in more definite and formal terms. Yet he is clearly one of the authors who stood in need of the greatest amount of charitable explanation from our own Bull[6]. So far as the remains of antiquity enable us to discover, S. Theophilus is the first writer who employed the term of the Trinity. The Church celebrates him[7] on the 18th of October. He was succeeded in the see of Antioch by Maximinus[8], of whom nothing is recorded but that his episcopate lasted thirteen years. *MAXIMINUS, Patr. IX. of Antioch, A.D. 186.*

32. The deepest uncertainty rests over the early bishops of Seleucia, so far as the dates of their accession and the period of their episcopates are concerned. James was succeeded by Achadabues[9], who is said to have been his son. This, if we may believe Amŕu,—and I confess that his explanation appears to me as probable as any—was in A.D. 190. Achadabues was sent, along with an ecclesiastic by name Kam-Jesus, after the ancient rite, to Antioch, with a request that the bishop of that see, who must, according to our

---

[1] Lib. II. 24. οὗτοι (the Tigris and Euphrates) γειτνιῶσιν ἕως τῶν ἡμετέρων κλιμάτων.
[2] Lib. II. 30.
[3] Vol. v. p. 46.
[4] Tillemont, Vol. III. p. 51.
[5] Petavius, Theolog. Dog. Vol. II. Cap. 3.
[6] Lib. III. Cap. 7.
[7] So the Martyrologies of Ado and Usuard; by the Eastern Church he does not seem to be commemorated.
[8] Euseb. H. E. IV. 24.
[9] Assem. B. O. II. 396. J. A. Assem. Cath. Chald. 5.

chronology, have been none other than Maximin, would ordain whichever of the two he thought most worthy of the dignity for which they were selected. They were arrested, by the vigilance of the Roman prefect, as Persian spies. Kam-Jesus, with his host, was crucified: Achadabues made his escape to Jerusalem, and was there ordained—as we should now speak—on letters dimissory from the bishop of Antioch. But the imminent dangers by which this journey was beset induced the bishop of Antioch to abdicate his right of ordination; and thus the see of Seleucia became autocephalus. How far this step opened the door to the heresies by which the Catholicate of Chaldæa was afterwards infected; how far it was one of those necessary concessions which, if not granted to entreaty, will be taken violently, are questions which we need a better history of these early times to determine. Achadabues appears to have held his dignity for fifteen years: he was succeeded by Shachlupha: whose pontificate of twenty years was equally glorious to himself, and beneficial to the Church.

Succession of Bishops at Jerusalem.

33. The succession at Jerusalem again presents a mere catalogue of names[1]. To write of Cassiau, Publius, Maximus, Julian, Caius, Symmachus, Caius II., Julian II., Capito, Maximus II., Antoninus, Valens, Dolichianus, must be to write of many a glorious athlete of JESUS CHRIST, of great things done and suffered for His sake, of the increase of the faith, and the edification of the Church: but the fifty years occupied by their episcopates are unmarked by any recorded event in the annals of the Church. The

---

[1] These Bishops are known from the Chronicon of Eusebius, and his H. E. v. 12. Of the separate dates of each, we find from this writer that Capito's episcopate lasted till the consulate of Maternus and Bradua, A.D. 185; while Epiphanius (Hæres. 66. 20) tells us that the episcopate of Caius II. ended in the 8th year of Verus (A.D. 168); Maximus II. to A.D. 176; Dolichianus to A.D. 180. So uncertain are these dates, it is fortunate that they are equally unimportant. The first Caius is also called Gaianus, and Capito is sometimes named Apion. Boschius doubts whether Maximus II. be not the same who is commemorated in the Roman Martyrology on the 8th of May, with the title of Confessor. He does not seem mentioned in the Menæa.

successor of Dolichianus, Narcissus, has left a more distinguished memory.

34. In the year 198, the question of Easter, never yet settled, again vexed the Church. The greater part of the churches in Asia observed it on the 14th day of the moon, whatever day that might be: the West kept it by the same rule as that which now appropriates to it the Sunday. The question had lately assumed a practical importance at Rome, where the schism of Blastus. had principally based itself on this question, and S. Victor, who then held the chair of S. Peter, requested the celebration of councils through the whole Church, in order that, if possible, the question might be settled at once and for ever. Among the prelates to whom he wrote was Theophilus of Cæsarea[1]—and under his presidency, and that of S. Narcissus of Jerusalem, a synod was held in the former city. It is singular that the only detailed account we have of the acts of this assembly has been preserved to us by our own Bede in his treatise on the Vernal Equinox; and there have not been wanting learned men who have denied its genuineness. But it was likely that in a country where the Paschal controversy raged so long and furiously as in our own, a document of this kind should have been preserved with more than usual care: while the ecclesiastical intercourse between Britain and the East adds a still greater probability to the authenticity of the document. To me, however, its acts seem to have the very appearance of genuineness, apart from every other consideration; and I shall therefore insert them. In the first place, I would observe that the church of Jerusalem had, in all probability, symbolized with the Jews in observing the fourteenth day of the moon, during the line of bishops of the Circumcision. But nothing is more likely than that, in disconnecting itself as far as possible from the Jews, that church should have adopted the Western and more distinctively Christian Easter:—whether Cæsarea had preceded or anticipated Jerusalem in the change, we have no data to determine. Ven. Bede speaks

Quartodeciman Controversy.

S. Theophilus of Cæsarea.

---

[1] V. Bede gives the acts of the Council in his *Commentarius de Æqui-noctio Vernali*. Baronius transcribes it at length, Vol. II. p. 371.

of the letter of S. Victor, as if that pontiff had appointed Theophilus his legate for the convocation of the Church: with how little accuracy, the celebrated reply of Polycrates, who had received a similar letter, may sufficiently show. Of the other prelates present we only know the names of two,—Cassius of Tyre, and Clarus of Ptolemais. The Acts, as given by Bede, run thus:

<small>Acts of the Council of Cæsarea.</small> 35. "When all that multitude of priests had assembled, the bishop Theophilus produced the authority sent to himself by Pope Victor, and explained the task which had been enjoined them. The bishops said unanimously: Unless we first investigate in what way the world was created in the beginning, we cannot satisfactorily ordain anything respecting the observance of Easter. The bishops therefore said: What day should we believe to have been the first, except the Lord's Day? Theophilus said: Prove what you declare. The bishops replied according to the authority of Scripture: The evening and the morning were the first day; then the second, third, fourth, fifth, sixth, seventh; in which seventh day GOD rested from all his works; and which day He called the Sabbath. Since, therefore, the Sabbath is the last day of the week, what except the Sunday can be the first?

36. "Theophilus the bishop said: You have proved that the Lord's Day is the first;—what say you with respect to the time of year? We usually reckon four seasons, spring, summer, autumn and winter. Which of these was first made? The bishops answered, Spring. Theophilus the bishop said, Prove what you say. And they answered, It is written: Let the earth bring forth grass, the herb yielding seed, and the fruit-trees yielding fruit after his kind; but this takes place in spring. Theophilus said: When do you believe the world to have been created? In the beginning, middle, or end of the year? The bishops replied; In the equinox on the 25th of March. Theophilus the bishop said: Prove what you say. And they answered: It is written that GOD made the light and called it Day; and made the darkness and called it Night: and divided equally between the light and the darkness. Theophilus said: You have proved

with regard to the day and the year; what do you believe about the moon? Was it created by GOD a crescent, or full, or waning? The bishops answered: Full. And he: Prove what you say. They answered: And GOD made two great lights, and set them in the firmament of heaven: the greater light for the beginning of the day: the lesser light for the beginning of the night: this could not have been unless the moon were full. We have therefore investigated the manner in which the world was created: that is, on Sunday, in the vernal equinox, on the 25th day of March, and at the full moon.

37. "Theophilus said: We must now discuss the manner in which we ought to celebrate Easter. The bishops said: Is it possible to pass by the Lord's Day, so as not to celebrate Easter on it, when it has been sanctified by so many and such benedictions? The bishop Theophilus said: Tell me what benedictions it has received, that I may write them. The bishops said: Its first benediction was that on this day the darkness was removed and the light was made. Its second, that the people were liberated from the land of Egypt, as from the darkness of sin, by means of the Red Sea, as by the fountain of baptism. Its third benediction, that on the same day celestial food, namely manna, was given to men. Its fourth, that Moses commanded the people, Let this day be observed by you. Its fifth, that which is written in the 117th Psalm, They came about me like bees, and are extinct, even as the fire among the thorns. For he speaks of the Resurrection of the Lord, when he says, This is the day which the Lord hath made, we will rejoice and be glad in it, even to the horns of the altar. Its sixth benediction is that the Lord on that day arose. You see then that the day of the Lord's Resurrection ought most emphatically to coincide with Easter.

38. "Theophilus said: God commanded Moses respecting the time on this wise: This month shall be unto you the beginning of months: keep the Passover therein. Therefore all its thirty days were consecrated to the Lord. The bishops said: We have already replied that the world began at the equinox on the 25th of March: and we read that

the days from the 25th of March to the 24th of April were consecrated. Theophilus said: Would it not be impious that the Passion of the Lord, the mystery of such a sacrament, should be excluded from these limits? For the LORD suffered on the 22nd of March, on the night of which He was betrayed by the Jews, and rose again on the 26th. How then should these three days be excluded from the limit? All the bishops said: The time of this Sacrament should in no wise be excluded: but those three days should be included within the limit above mentioned."

Importance of their acts. 39. The care with which the records of this Council were preserved in Britain, where the Quartodeciman controversy raged more fiercely and for a longer period than in any other portion of the Church, sufficiently shows its importance, and the esteem in which the prelates who composed it were held. The violence of Victor, his threatened excommunication of the bishops of Asia Minor, and the final settlement of the question at Nicæa, are not matters on which it is necessary for me at present to enlarge. How long Theophilus survived the synod, we have no means of ascertaining:—he is reckoned by the Western Church among the saints[1]. His coadjutor in the Council of Cæsarea, S. Narcissus, stands forth as one of the more prominent heroes of those early times.

S. Narcissus, Patr. of Jerusalem XXX. 40. We find him presiding over the Church of Jerusalem[2] with great reputation towards the close of the second century[3]. On an Easter Eve it happened that the oil for the lamps in the church failed, and the people were distressed by the occurrence. "Draw water," said Narcissus to one of the acolytes, "from yonder well,"—pointing at the same time to one within the precincts of the building, "and bring it to me." He prayed over it, and then commanded the bystanders to pour it, with earnest faith, into the lamps: it was at once converted into oil. A portion of this oil was not unnaturally preserved among the treasures of the Church; and was seen, as we are informed by Eusebius, by several of

---

[1] S. Hieronym. *de Script. Ecclesiast.* 43; Niceph. Callistus, IV. 19, 36. He is celebrated in the Roman Martyrology on the 5th of May.
[2] Euseb. H. E. VI. 9.
[3] Tillemont, Vol. III. p. 178.

the brethren in his time,—a hundred and twenty years subsequently to the miracle. The sanctity of this eminent prelate raised up against him a band of calumniators. He was accused of a sin of impurity; and three witnesses stood forth to lay it to his charge. "If I speak not the truth," said the first, finding the people incredulous, "may I be burnt alive!" "And I," cried the second, "may I perish of the leprosy[1]!" "And may loss of sight," exclaimed the third, "be my fate, if my words are not the very truth!" The accusation remained unbelieved; but such was its effect on Narcissus that he left the city, and betook himself into the wildest part of the desert. He was long sought in vain: till at length the neighbouring bishops, unwilling to leave the Church of Jerusalem in longer widowhood, raised Dius to that see. Ere long, divine vengeance fell on the persecutors of Narcissus. The first, with all his family, was burnt at night,—the origin of the fire never being explained. The second died miserably of the leprosy which he had invoked. The third repented, publicly confessed his crime, and lost his sight with continual and bitter weeping. S. Dius[2] is praised for the excellent management of his Church: his episcopate, however, must have been of the very shortest duration. To him succeeded Germanus, or Germanion, and to him Gordius. During the prelature of the last, S. Narcissus, his innocence being now made clear, reappeared from the desert: and, at the instance of all, resumed the government of his Church.

S. Dius, Patr. Jerusal. XXXI.
Germanus, Patr. Jerusal. XXXII.
Gordius, Patr. Jerusal. XXXIII.
S. Narcissus again.

41. On the death of Maximin, S. Serapion succeeded to the see of Antioch, and claims no mean place among those early theologians. He distinguished[3] himself by a treatise against Montanus, addressed to Pontius and Caricus; by a letter to one Domninus, who in the time of persecution had embraced Judaism; and by a treatise on the so-called Gospel of Peter, in which he pointed out its mistakes. This was addressed to a diocese within his own jurisdiction,

S. Serapion, Patr. of Ant. IX. A.D. 199.

---

[1] See Valerius's notes on the σκαιᾷ νόσῳ of Eusebius. It is odd to see the literal translation, *scævo* morbo, given in Baronius as *sævo* morbo.

[2] Euseb. H. E. u. s. See his eulogy in the Horarium, which fixes Jan. 11 as his festival.

[3] Euseb. H. E. vi. 12.

Rhossus[1], on the gulf of Cilicia. "We, my brethren," thus he wrote, "receive Peter and the rest of the apostles as we receive CHRIST: but writings which falsely bear their name, we, as having skill in the matter, repudiate: knowing that we never received such things by tradition. When I came among you, I imagined that you were all conversant with the orthodox faith. And not having as yet perused the Gospel offered me under the name of Peter, I said,—'If this is the only matter which excites ill feelings among you, let it be read.' But now, when from what was then read there, I plainly perceive that their minds contained a hidden heresy, I will hasten to you. Therefore, brethren, you may expect me shortly." The extract is remarkable, as shewing the power yet possessed by individual bishops in the settlement of the Canon of Scripture[2]. The letter of Serapion against the Montanists or Cataphrygians would appear to have been a circular, and was signed by other prelates as well as the writer. Thus: "Aurelius Cyrenius, martyr: I bid you GOD speed. Ælius Publius Julius, bishop of the colony of Debeltus in Thrace: I do you to wit that blessed Sotas of Anchialus desired to cast out the dæmon of Priscilla, but the hypocrites suffered him not." The personal influence of Serapion must have been widely extended, when the bishops of the far distant province of Thrace were found following his lead.—In the time of S. Jerome[3] many letters of Serapion were extant, answerable to his reputation and the holiness of his life[4].

S. Alexander, Patr. of Jerusalem XXXIV. A.D. 212.

42. The growing infirmities of Narcissus at Jerusalem rendered it necessary that he should be provided with a coadjutor. Alexander[5], a Cappadocian bishop[6], who had

---

[1] Introduction to Eastern Church, I. 134.
[2] Euseb. H. E. v. 19.
[3] Catalog. Script. Eccles.
[4] Tillemont. Vol. III. p. 168. I do not understand what this author means when speaking of S. Serapion's letter to the inhabitants of Rhossus; he says that it would appear from hence that at that time the Church of Antioch had ecclesiastical rights over Cilicia. There can be no doubt that from the very beginning the case always was so.
[5] Euseb. H. E. vi. 8.
[6] None of the ancient writers mention the city of which Alexander had been bishop. Some of the modern

gloriously confessed in the persecution of Severus, happened to visit Jerusalem for the sake of a pilgrimage to the holy places;—and its aged prelate was miraculously warned to adopt the stranger as his present assistant and future successor[1]: the same revelation is also said to have been made to others of the brethren. A letter of Alexander to the inhabitants of Antinous was extant in the time of Eusebius, in which he said: "Narcissus salutes you, who held this episcopate before me, and now, having passed his hundred and sixteenth year, is joined with me in prayer, beseeching you with me to be of one mind." It would seem that at the very commencement of his episcopate the valiant confessor was again thrown into prison. For on the death of S. Serapion of Antioch, S. Asclepiades[2], himself a confessor in the persecution of Severus, having succeeded, Alexander wrote to express his congratulations: "Alexander a servant and prisoner of JESUS CHRIST, to the most blessed church of the Antiochenes, greeting in the LORD. The LORD hath made my bonds during the time of my imprisonment light and easy, since I have heard that Asclepiades, a man most fitting on account of his faith, has been, by the divine providence, charged with the episcopate of your holy Church." The letter was sent by a priest named Clement,—no other than the celebrated S. Clement of Alexandria, who, it would seem, had governed the Church of Jerusalem during the imprisonment of its prelate; to whose zeal and piety the writer bears ample testimony. It was S. Alexander who—injudiciously, to say the least—elevated Origen to the priesthood, and who was thus involved in a dispute with S. Demetrius of Alexandria, as I have related in the Annals of that Church[3].

S. Asclepiades, Patr. of Ant. X. A.D. 211.

[1] Valesius observes, there were two infringements of the Canons: the fact of a translation, and the appointment of a coadjutor with right of future succession during the life-time of a prelate. Dr Routh, however, very justly remarks that the intimation of S. Alexander's succession is expressly said to have been miraculous: and therefore cannot be brought within the strictness of Canon law.

Greeks will have it to have been Flaviopolis, in Cilicia Secunda; and he is thus mentioned in the Jus Græco-Romanum, Lib. IV. p. 295, as an early example of translation of one church to another. This subject is discussed by Dr Routh, Reliq. Vol. II. p. 178.

[2] Euseb. H. E. VI. 11.
[3] Hist. Alex. I. p. 27.

43. We must now, despite the exceeding difficulty of their chronology[1], turn to the affairs of the far East. Jacob,

---

[1] The extreme difficulty of arranging anything like an accurate chronology of these early patriarchs may be seen by a comparison of the dates as given by Gregory Bar-Hebræus and by Amrou. (Compare J. A. Assemann, *de Catholicis Commentarius*; J. S. Assemann, *Bibl. Orient.* (II. 390), and Le Quien, II. 1103, sq.)

		Bar-Hebræus.	Amrou.
Mares	died	82	82
Abres	...	98	99
Abraham	...	110	152
Jacob	...	128	170
Achadabues	...	133	220
Shachlupha	...	156	244

The dates, sufficiently perplexed in themselves, are still further confused by J. A. Assemann, who follows neither one computation nor the other, but yet, it seems to me, a very consistent one of his own.

Papas, who is given as the successor of Shachlupha, died in A.D. 326, having sat 70 years, and therefore succeeded in 256. According to the account of Amrou, 12 years remain unaccounted for; according to that of Bar-Hebræus, 74. But the periods assigned by Amrou seem far too great for a reasonable episcopate, and it is more than probable that several names have been lost, just as Elias of Damascus inserts a certain *Tomarsa* between Achadabues and Shachlupha, whom the other Catalogues omit. It will be worth while to give here three other lists discovered by Assemann. The first is by Salomon, bishop of Bostra; the second, by an anonymous writer (Cod. Anod. VII.) in hepta-syllabic verse; the third, by Elias, Bishop of Damascus. They here follow down to the period at which we have arrived.

Salomon.

1. *Adæus* and *Mares*. Adæus was buried at Edessa; Mares in Dair-Kuni.

2. *Abres*, who is called in Greek *Abrosius*. The place of his sepulture is uncertain. He was ordained at Antioch.

3. *Abraham* received imposition of hands at Antioch. He came of the race of Jacob the son of Joseph. His sepulchre is in the city of Ctesiphon.

4. *Jacob* received imposition of hands at Antioch. He also was of the race of Joseph the husband of Mary, and his sepulchre at Ctesiphon.

Anonymous.

1. The first in order the most blessed *Thaddæus* and *Mares* of the 70.

2. *Abres*, full of all sanctity and kinsman of the blessed Virgin.

3. *Mar Abraham* of Cascara, who appeased the king of the Persians, and delivered his daughter from the possession of the devil.

4. *Mar Jacob* the athlete, the kinsman of Joseph the carpenter.

Elias.

1. *Adæus.*
2. *Mares.*
3. *Abres.*

4. *Abraham.*

5. *Jacob.*

fifth Catholic, was succeeded by Achadabues[1]: he was sent, Achadabues, Cath. VI. A.D.? with one Jabjesus, or Kamjesus, to Antioch; the bishop of that city being requested to elect him whom he considered the fitter candidate of the two for the episcopate of Seleucia. Jabjesus took up his abode in the house of a friend, in company with whom he was arrested on a charge of Christianity, and crucified. Achadabues fled to Jerusalem; was there consecrated, and filled the episcopal throne for twenty years. On his death, one of the catalogues represents him Tomarsa, Cath. VII. as succeeded by a certain Tomarsa:—the rest name, as his A.D.? immediate successor, Shachlupha. At the time of his accession war was raging between the Roman emperor Aurelius Shachlupha, Cath. VIII. A.D.? and Vologeses II.[2] of Parthia; and access to Antioch was thus rendered impossible. Hence, but not till after a delay of three years, a synod of oriental bishops was assembled at Seleucia, and the prelate-elect there received the imposition of their hands. Thus the link between the ancient metropolis and her eastern daughter was finally severed; the various

Salomon.	Anonymous.	Elias.
5. *Achadabues* received imposition of hands at Antioch. His sepulchre is at Ctesiphon.	5. *Achadabues* verily introduced salvation to the East.	6. *Achadabues.*
6. *Shachlupha* received imposition of hands at Ctesiphon, and was there buried.	6. *Shachlupha*, of Cascar, instructed with doctrine, enlightened the countries of the East, and was illustrious with spiritual merchandise.	7. *Tomarsa.*
		8. *Shachlupha.*

[1] J. A. Assem. *De Cath.* p. 6. B. O. 396.

[2] This was commenced in A.D. 161. The chronology therefore of Amrou, who makes Shachlupha to have succeeded in 244, is manifestly absurd, nor can that of Bar-Hebræus be entirely reconciled with history. Bar-Hebræus makes the liberation of the see of Seleucia to have been occasioned by the murder of Kam Jesus, and affirms that the Western bishops, i.e. the other three Patriarchs, gave a *Systaticon* by which that liberation was confirmed,—and the names of 'Catholic' or 'Patriarch' conferred on the Bishop of Seleucia, 'which,' says he, 'was displeasing to the Patriarch of Antioch.'—A manifest fable, yet offering a certain confirmation to the fact that Seleucia was independent of Antioch as early as the second century.

inconveniences and risks of so anomalous a separation came to an end; and the delay between the vacancy of the see and the appointment of a new prelate ceased to be a necessity. With the death of Shachlupha a gloom of eighty years settles down on the history of the see of Seleucia. The political circumstances of that city may in great part account for this silence. The capital of the Macedonian conquests, it had a population of six hundred thousand citizens, and formed an independent government, under a senate of three hundred nobles, in the very heart of the Parthian empire. In the wars of Aurelius[1] it opened its gates to the Roman generals: in base violation of treaties it was sacked and burnt; and three hundred thousand of the citizens fell victims in a general massacre. From this blow it never recovered: and Ctesiphon, previously a dangerous rival, now succeeded to its wealth and importance. In the same war, Edessa, of which we shall have more to say in the sequel, was wrested from the feeble grasp of its native princes, and became a constituent portion of the Roman empire.

Pantænus: his mission to India.

44. But in these obscure times the first light breaks in on the vast peninsula of India. Pantænus, who had taught Christian philosophy with no small reputation at Alexandria[2] under S. Julian, bishop of that see, conceived the idea of preaching the Gospel to the Indians. It is said that a deputation of Brahmins requested from S. Demetrius, successor of S. Julian, a missionary, and that the philosopher was nominated by that prelate to the arduous task. He undertook the task; and found, it is said, that S. Matthew's Gospel, in Hebrew, was not unknown to the Indians, and that it had been introduced to them by the preaching of S. Bartholomew. It gives us but small reason to admire the zeal of Pantænus, when we find that, after having laboured some years in that evangelical field, he returned to the literary ease and philosophic indulgence of Alexandria. Not by such apostles has the Catholic Faith been livingly and substantially propagated.

[1] Eutropius, VIII. 10; Dion. 71. xxxii. 4. S. Hieronym. Epist. ad
[2] Euseb. H. E. v. 10. Niceph. Magn. (84).

MARTYRDOM OF S. ALEXANDER. 41

45. The episcopate of Alexander was eminently beneficial to the Church of Jerusalem. We read of a library[1] founded by his care, and possessing, in the days of Eusebius, a rich treasure of ecclesiastical writings. In remarkable contrast with the shortlived rule of his predecessors, he occupied the episcopal throne thirty-eight years. A few fragments of his epistles[2] remain, as if to make us sensible of the injury which we have sustained from the loss of his works. In that dreadful persecution of Decius, when it seemed as if the elect, were it possible, must fall away, he confessed with great constancy at Cæsarea[3]. Neither the weakness of his old age, nor the tortures of the persecutor, had any other effect than to cover the venerable prelate with honour, and to magnify, through him, the name of his LORD. The Menæa tell us that he was exposed, in the theatre of Cæsarea, to the wild beasts: that his prayer was, "LORD, if it be Thy pleasure that my life is to end now, Thy will be done:" and that the animals let loose against him licked his feet, and crouched down before him. Cast into prison, he thence departed to his reward, and though not actually undergoing a violent death is most rightly reckoned[4] among the martyrs. His successor was Mazabanes[5]. *Martyrdom of S. Alexander, A.D. 249.*

Mazabanes, Patr.
46. S. Asclepiades presided over the church of Antioch only eight years[6]; and was succeeded by Philetus. After an episcopate of eleven years, he was followed by Zebennus;—and he, after ruling the Church eight years, by the more famous S. Babylas. These catalogues of dates and names, *XXXV. of Jerusalem A.D. 250.*

S. Babylas, Patr. XIII. of Antioch.

---

[1] Euseb. H E. vi. 20.
[2] They have been published by Gallandius, Biblioth. Tom. ii. 301: and by Routh, Reliquiæ, ii. 159.
[3] Euseb. H. E. vi. 46, where the historian is quoting a letter of S. Dionysius of Alexandria to S. Cornelius of Rome.
[4] By the Latins he is celebrated on March 18: by the Greeks on Dec. 12 (Papebroch, by a misprint, I suppose, and Le Quien copying him, say the 22d). His *stichos* is:

ὁ Ἀλέξανδρος εἶς ἦν τῶν θυηπόλων,
ἄνευ αἵματος εἶς ὢν καὶ τῶν Μαρτύρων.

[5] The fragments of S. Alexander's writings are given by Dr Routh in his Reliquiæ Sacræ, Vol. ii. p. 165—179. They consist of a few sentences of his Epistles to the Antiochenes, to the Antinoïtes, to Origen, and to S. Demetrius of Alexandria.

[6] Baronius has reckoned S. Asclepiades among the martyrs; but it would seem without sufficient reason. Tillemont, Vol. iii. p. 648.

wearisome to the writer to enumerate, more wearisome to the reader to peruse, what deeds of honour do they not, in all likelihood, contain! what noble confessions! what acts of faith and patience! written, indeed, in the Book of Life, but unrecorded by the Church militant! It may easily be that the first two centuries and a half was the period in which Antioch brought forth a more abundant harvest than in all the other ages of her existence together: and yet how brief the mention of the former, compared with the detailed extent of baneful prosperity or beneficial reverses, of heresies, schisms, and divisions in the latter.

<small>Martyrdom of S. Babylas, Jan. 24, A.D. 251.</small>

47. In his pontificate of fourteen years S. Babylas saw Antioch taken by the Persians. If we are to believe the account of S. Chrysostom, that the emperor Philip was put by him to public penance, we should have an action of heroism which might vie with the courage which S. Ambrose displayed in his treatment of Theodosius after the massacre of Thessalonica. It is not to be wondered at that the eloqence of S. Chrysostom should have been excited by the acts of this noble-minded prelate: but even in his time the actual facts of his history were so much corrupted that already a considerable degree of obscurity hung over them. After fourteen years pontificate, S. Babylas was honoured with confessing the name of CHRIST; whether by death in prison, or by actual martyrdom, it is impossible to affirm with certainty. Eusebius clearly asserts the former: S. Chrysostom is no less positive that the saint was dragged from the prison into which he had been thrown and beheaded. It would seem more probable—however much we might wish to believe the other account—that Eusebius is right: and that S. Chrysostom, misled as he certainly is in part by falsified memoirs, mistook the term martyr,—applied in those early ages more vaguely,—as if our prelate had actually suffered death for CHRIST'S sake. With him, either in the prison, or in the amphitheatre, suffered three children, whom the Latin martyrologies name Urbanus, Prilidianus, and Epulonius. Meletius, who was bishop of Mopsuestia about 430, wishes for the courage of that child, seven years old, who suffered

with S. Babylas[1]. The dying request of the bishop, to have the chains of his imprisonment interred with him, seems well authenticated. We shall have occasion, at a later period, to speak of the removal of his relics from the grove of Daphne, and the world-famous miracle which accompanied that event. And the Menæa thus celebrate him:

> Himself the Lord's anointed, who of old
> To God's Anointed Son his mortal frame
> Had sacrificed, through torments manifold
> The Prelate Babylas to glory came[2].

48. S. Babylas having thus accomplished his course, Fabius[3] was chosen his successor in the widowed Church. It was to him that S. Dionysius of Alexandria addressed the celebrated letter on the effects of the Decian persecution, which I have given at length in my history of that Church. He was however involved in a longer and more important correspondence. The schism of Novatus and Novatian had broken out at Rome; and it was of the greatest importance

---

[1] S. Babylas is celebrated by the Eastern Church on the 4th of September with the three children who are mentioned in Western Martyrologies. The Menology says of him, but with manifest incorrectness, "Who when the Emperor Numerianus entered into his own church, drove him therefrom, on account of his having put to death the son of the Persian king whom he held as a hostage. Wherefore, he was bound in iron fetters, was publicly mocked, and had his head struck off with the three children." But on the same day they keep the Festival of another S. Babylas, a teacher at Antioch, who is said to have suffered with eighty-four of his scholars under Galerius, who was present at the martyrdom. The account, which is very long, seems of later date, and altogether uncertain. The story of the three children is confirmed by S. Chrysostom, who, in an Antiochean story, has more than usual authority; by Suidas, and by the Arian historian Philostorgius. The testimony of Meletius is to be seen in the Epistolæ of Christianus Lupus, page 355.

[2] Bollandus, under the 24 of January, gives three lives of S. Babylas; of which Tillemont very truly says, that "the first, which is the most simple, is the best, or rather the least bad." This depreciatory criticism highly offends the Bollandist Boschius, who in his Chronological History of the Antiochene patriarchs, endeavours, but not very successfully, to defend their authenticity.

[3] He is called by Ruffinus, Fabian; by Eutychius and S. Jerome, Flavian: by Georgius Syncellus, sometimes by one name, sometimes by the other; by S. Nicephorus of C. P. and the Chronicon Alexandrinon, Flavius.

to S. Cornelius, the canonically-elected bishop of that see, to obtain the support of the most influential prelates in his struggle. Fabius, from whatever cause, had imbibed[1] a prejudice in favour of Novatus, and Cornelius in a series[2] of four letters, fragments of which are preserved by Eusebius, set forth at length the history of the schism. S. Dionysius of Alexandria also addressed the bishop of Antioch; and though the latter does not seem to have acted decidedly against the party of Novatus, he, at all events, convoked a synod at Antioch for the discussion and settlement of the question. Deprecating, as I always would do, the introduction of controversy into pure history, I cannot but observe that the *ipse dixit* of the Roman pontiff did not satisfy the Church of Antioch; and that, as many a council assembled in Rome to discuss the affairs of other bishoprics, here an Eastern synod was convened to take into consideration the internal dissensions of Italy. The letter which invited Dionysius[3] of Alexandria to attend this council was subscribed by Helenus bishop of Tarsus, as one of the chief suffragans of Antioch, by Theoctistus of Cæsarea, whom we have already seen engaged in the Quartodeciman controversy, and by S. Firmilian of Cæsarea in Cappadocia, whom we shall hereafter find one of the most distinguished supporters of the Eastern dogma on the subject of re-baptism. By the same letter, however, he received intelligence of the death of Fabius, who had held the episcopate for less than two years. He is described as a man of spirit and courage, as indeed his acceptance of the throne yet reeking as it were with the blood of Babylas, proves him to have been: but neither by the East nor by the West is he reckoned among the saints.

S. Demetrian, Patr. XV. of Ant. A.D. 252.

49. The convocation of the Council was probably felt to be a cause why the vacant see should be filled up without loss of time. Demetrian[4], a priest of Antioch, succeeded:

---

[1] Eusebius expressly says so: ὑποκατακλινομένῳ πῶς τῷ σχίσματι. H. E. VI. 44: words which I cannot conceive why Valesius should omit in his translation.

[2] They are given in H. E. VI. 43. See also S. Nicephorus, VI. 3.

[3] Euseb. H. E. VI. 46.

[4] Euseb. H. E. VI. 46.

FIRST COUNCIL OF ANTIOCH. 45

and his first care was the celebration of the synod. A vigorous effort was made by the partizans of Novatus to procure his recognition; but the synod unanimously determined against his claims, and intimated in a similar synodal letter to S. Cornelius their rejection of the schismatic. The acts of this council have perished; but it has been spoken of in the highest terms of commendation, and evidently exercised no small influence on the final settlement of the question. The episcopate of Demetrian was distinguished by no other event of importance. An obscure tradition reckons him among the martyrs, but the general silence of contemporaries, the fact that when a subsequent synod of Antioch[2] are speaking in his praise, they say nothing of his martyrdom[3], and the time of his death, which took place in a period of peace, render it more probable that he has no real claim to that highest of honours. His successor, Paul of Samosata, the celebrated heresiarch, will unfortunately afford us larger materials for history.

Council of Antioch, March, A.D. 252.[1]

Paul of Samosata, Patr. XVI. of Ant. A.D. 260.[4]

50. Of all the great sees, Antioch was the first which fell into heresy. The elevation of Paul to that throne had

---

[1] Pagi seems to me to have settled this date beyond the possibility of doubt. His whole chronology of the schism of Novatus exhibits more even than his usual ingenuity.

[2] In the second synod convoked againt Paul of Samosata, the fathers speak of "Demetrian the bishop of blessed memory, who governed this Church with great praise."

[3] His name is in the Martyrology of Usuard; whence it found its way into the Roman. Blasius Terzi, in his Syria Sacra, positively affirms Demetrian to have been a martyr, (I. 33); Baronius (II. 62. 70) is content to leave it uncertain. Usuard, who calls him Demetrius, gives him as his companion Anianus a deacon, Eustachius a layman, and twenty others. There is no reason to think that the Demetrius who is commemorated in the Menæa is our bishop. He, at all events, is honoured as a martyr. But it is worth notice that a Demetrius who suffered under Maximian, is commemorated on November 15; and on the same day a martyr named Eustochius. Is it possible that Usuard should have derived a mistaken account from these Menæa, and thence taken the name of Eustosius, a name which I do not remember to have met with elsewhere?

[4] In this date, I follow Pagi, though it is not absolutely certain. George Syncellus and S. Nicephorus give only four years to the episcopate of Demetrian; Scaliger, six; the Chronical of Eusebius, in the edition Pontao, seven.

His luxury and pomp. not been brought about without simony. Originally[1] of low birth, and miserably poor, he had employed his powers, which were considerable, in the acquisition of wealth; and in the possession of the see at Antioch he appears to have beheld nothing more than a profitable speculation. His riches and luxury were thought remarkable, even in the wealthy and luxurious city of Antioch. The clergy were kept waiting in his outer chambers; he affected a retinue and an attendance which might almost vie with those of the prefect of the East; his harangues to the people were rather the glittering declamations of a sophist than the addresses of a Christian bishop; and it is particularly recorded of him that he abolished the ancient hymns of his Church, and in their stead introduced new and florid compo-
His innovations in the rites of his Church. sitions of himself and his followers. On a certain Easter-day he filled his church with a choir of women, who desecrated the festival by odes in praise of the many virtues of their bishop—an angel, they said, descended from heaven for the protection and sanctification of happy Antioch. His private life was notoriously immoral: and yet in his discourses he made a point of speaking in a slighting manner of his predecessors, even of those whose names were as household words in the universal Church,—S. Euodius, the great Ignatius, and S. Babylas. His arrogance and effeminacy were no less offensive to the pagans than to his own flock. It was intolerable, they said, that such a man should be a preacher of the law of humility, of temperance, and of purity. But the political circumstances of the East were destined to elevate the bishop of Antioch to yet higher power, and to prepare the way for his ruin.

Empire of Palmyra. 51. For now the empire of Palmyra had blazed out in all its short-lived splendour. Odenathus, remarkable for his own vigour and talents, still more remarkable in his wife, the celebrated Zenobia, had raised himself from a humble situation to the virtual empire of the East. Twice he had

---

[1] This account of the misdeeds of Paul is given by the Fathers of the Second Council of Antioch summoned against him: Euseb. H. E. VII. 80.

driven the Persian monarch to the gates of Ctesiphon; and was not less successful in his encounters with the Roman legions. His murder by a nephew only gave a greater opportunity for the display of the talents of Zenobia. From that city of palaces, Tadmor in the wilderness, she ruled not Syria only, but obtained influence nearly supreme in Armenia and Arabia. She ruled the empire of the East as far as the borders of Bithynia: Antioch opened its gates to her:—and she added Egypt to her other conquests. A Jewess by education, though deriving her descent from Cleopatra, she expressed a wish to be instructed in the principles of the Christian religion: and Paul of Samosata, not only as the highest ecclesiastical dignitary in the East, but as the most fashionable preacher in Asia, was selected for her teacher. The scheme of religion which he presented to her was certainly one which she could adopt without surrendering any essential portion of her former belief[1]. He taught that Christ had no existence before He took flesh of S. Mary: that from the instant of His Incarnation, the Word and the Eternal Wisdom dwelt in Him, but only at that instant began to have a hypostatical existence, distinct from the everlasting Father: that yet, though a new divinity, CHRIST, having been eternally predestined to that dignity, might in some sort be Himself called Eternal. Consequently that there were two distinct persons united in CHRIST: the one by nature the Son of GOD, who existed before the worlds; the other the Son of David, born in the world, and no otherwise the Son of GOD than as Jerusalem might be called the city of GOD. With this, Paul united many of the opinions of Sabellius; denying the separate existence of the Persons in the ever-blessed Trinity, and making the LORD and the HOLY GHOST the mere prolations or efficiencies of the FATHER.

Zenobia requests instruction from Paul of Samosata.

Character of his heresy.

---

[1] The heresy of Paul of Samosata may be best learnt from the aforesaid letter of the Fathers of Antioch, S. Epiphan. Hæres. 65; S. Augustin, de Hæres. 44: and the Epistle of S. Dionysius of Alexandria to the hæresiarch himself. See what I have said in my Hist. of Alexandria, I. p. 81, note 4. Natalis Alexander sums up the teaching of Paul as briefly and lucidly as his custom is.

Leontius in his work on the sects states clearly and accurately the difference between the doctrine of the followers of Paul, who assumed the name of Paulianists, and those of Sabellius and Nestorius. "There existed," says he, "in these times another sect, that of Paul of Samosata, who erred both concerning the Divinity and concerning the Incarnation. Concerning the Divinity, in acknowledging the FATHER alone; concerning the Incarnation, because he affirmed that CHRIST was pure and simple man, in whom the Word of GOD did not exist" (that is, did not exist as a distinct hypostatical essence), "herein differing from Nestorius: because Nestorius, although affirming CHRIST to be pure man, affirmed also that the self-existent Word and Son of GOD abode in that man. For the doctrine of Nestorius, with regard to the Trinity, was not erroneous. But Paul of Samosata taught that the self-existent Word of GOD was not in CHRIST; but that the expression Word signified a certain order or command; that is, as he expressed his own meaning, that GOD commanded that which He willed to be done, that GOD made that which He willed to be made by that man. Nor was the teaching of Paul with regard to the Trinity the same with that of Sabellius. For Sabellius taught that the same person was FATHER, SON, and HOLY GHOST: calling GOD an existence with three names, and utterly abolishing the Trinity. Paul, on the contrary, did not teach this, but asserted that the FATHER was the GOD that had created all things; the SON, that pure man of whom we have already spoken; the HOLY GHOST, that grace which descended upon the apostles." To this we must add, that, according to this heresiarch, the Word, though it wrought in the man CHRIST, did not suffer in Him—another variation from the schism of Sabellius: and that the Paulianists, at least, though perhaps not their leader, made some alteration in the form of baptism which compelled the Council of Nicæa to decree that, on their reception into the Church, such heretics should be re-baptized.

52. It was not to be expected that such heretical teaching would pass unnoticed by the Church. A council, prin-

FIRST COUNCIL OF ANTIOCH.

cipally convoked by the assiduous efforts of Dionysius of Alexandria—though he himself was prevented by declining health from attending it, met at Antioch. Among those who were present, were S. Firmilian of Cæsarea[1], one of the most illustrious prelates of the East, S. Gregory the Wonderworker, and his brother Athenodorus, also reckoned among[2] the saints, and bishop of Amasea in Helenopontus, and Nicomas of Iconium: these, though not in the diocese of Antioch, were probably invited on account of their great reputation: for the same reason, Hymenæus, bishop of Jerusalem, and Theotecnus of Cæsarea, were also summoned. Among the most illustrious suffragans of Antioch, were Helenus, bishop of Tarsus, who had been present in the former synod against Novatus, and Maximus of Bostra, whose administration of that Church is mentioned in terms of the highest praise. Besides these, there were a vast number of other bishops, priests and deacons, and the followers of Paul mustered in some force. That prelate used every art of sophistry and eloquence for the good of his cause: he was pursued from one hiding-place to another by the theological skill of Fermilian, who seems to have presided in the council[3]. This synod is remarkable, in the history of controversy, by its rejection of that word "Consubstantial," which was afterwards made an article of faith at Nicæa. "Our Lord," said Paul, "had no existence before Mary: from her He derived His being, and from being man, He became GOD; were it not so, He would not be consubstantial with the FATHER, but it would follow that there were three substances; the one superior, the other two inferior." In order to expose this sophism[4], and taking the word in its grosser sense, the fathers of Antioch denied the consubstantiality of

First council of Antioch against Paul, A.D. 264.

Its rejection of the word Homoousion.

---

[1] Euseb. H. E. VII. 28. He is commemorated in the Menæa under Nov. 7th, with this Stichos:
ἐκ γῆς καλοῦσιν Ἀθηνόδωρον νόες
πρὸς τὰς νοητὰς δωρεὰς τοῦ Κυρίου.
[2] Euseb. H. E. VI. 39. S. Epiphan. Hær. LXVI. 20.
[3] The proceedings of this council are related both by Euseb. H. E. VII. 22; and by Theodoret, Hæret. Fab. 2. 8: also by S. Athanasius, De Synod.
[4] The rejection of the term *consubstantial* by the fathers of Antioch is admirably explained by our own Bishop Bull, *Def. Fid. Nic.* 2. 13.

the SON with the FATHER. It was not to be expected that the Arians would allow the verbal discrepancy between the two synods to pass unnoticed; and S. Athanasius exerts himself to shew that the difference was simply one of words, and that the dogmatic teaching of the synod of Antioch, touching the divinity of the SON of GOD, was the same with that of the three hundred and eighteen who inflicted the deathblow on Arianism. Paul had no mind to be a martyr to his own tenets; and after defending them as long as the patience of the council lasted, avowed himself convinced by the arguments of its president and gave in his nominal adherence to the Catholic faith. How far the temporal power of his protectress Zenobia induced the council to leave him undisturbed in the possession of his see, is a point which we have not data to determine.

Feigned recantation of Paul.

53. No sooner, however, had the council dispersed, than the bishop of Antioch returned to his former teaching. Depending on the protection of the Queen of the East, from whom he obtained the title of Ducenarius[1], or Imperial Procurator,—a title which he is said to have prized beyond his episcopal dignity,—he added to his perversion of the faith, more scandalous immorality than before. Constantly entertaining two of the most beautiful women of Antioch as the companions of his leisure, he connived at any amount of irregularity or vice in his priests, so they only would profess themselves supporters of his doctrine. It is not clear whether any synods of inferior note[2] had been previously assembled: but the heterodoxy and crimes of Paul becoming more notorious, another council assembled at Antioch in the autumn of 269. The numbers are variously reckoned; S. Athanasius assumes that there were but seventy: S. Hilary counts them at eighty; while Basil, the deacon in the council of Ephesus, makes the number to have amounted to 180[3]: a reckoning which appears manifestly exaggerated.

His renewed heresy and immorality.

Second council of Antioch, autumn of A.D. 269.

---

[1] The office of Ducenarius was worth 200 sestertia. See Suetonius, Aug. cap. 34.

[2] Tillemont expressly asserts that there were three councils in all, Mem. Ecc. IV. 297; but does not allege any absolute proof.

[3] So Tillemont very justly ob-

SECOND COUNCIL OF ANTIOCH.

The fathers postponed the opening of the synod for some time, in hopes of the arrival of S. Firmilian, who had been the presiding spirit of the former assembly. At the beginning of November, however[1], a despatch arrived at Antioch[2], with the news of the death of that illustrious prelate. Notwithstanding his great age and infirmities, he had commenced his journey and had advanced as far as Tarsus. There, worn out with years and labours, he departed to his reward on the 28th of October, A.D. 269.

54. S. Firmilian having thus been taken to his rest, Helenus[3] of Tarsus, whom I have mentioned as having been present at the first council, presided in his place. Among the other principal prelates were Hymenæus of Jerusalem, to whom I shall presently have occasion again to refer, Theotecnus of Cæsarea, and Theophilus, whose see is unknown; Maximus of Bostra, and Nicomas of Iconium were also there; and a certain Theodorus, whom I should like to believe none other than S. Gregory the Wonderworker. The opening of the council presents a remarkable contrast to the vehemence with which some of the synods had proceeded against a suspected heretic. Six of the principal bishops—it would appear, during the interval while the fathers were expecting the arrival of S. Firmilian—addressed a letter[4] to Paul, in which they gently but clearly laid down the Catholic faith; such, they say, as they had received it by tradition, such as it had been handed down from apostolic times; and they invite the bishop of Antioch, by affixing his signature to it, to render further proceedings unnecessary. They laid down the union of the divine and human natures in the One Per-

Letter addressed to Paul.

---

serves; though he charges a blunder on the document itself, which is only a printer's error in the edition of Labbe, as Boschius points out in his Hist. Chron.

[1] All these particulars are given in the synodical letter of the council, Euseb. H. E. vii. 30.

[2] So Pagi very clearly demonstrates, 272. ii.

[3] Euseb. H. E. vii. 30.

[4] The authenticity of this letter, (printed in the third Vol. of the Bib. Max.) has been contested by no one with the single exception of Dupin, who however gives no reasons for his opinion; it is received unhesitatingly by Tillemont, by Valesius and by Pagi, 272. iv.

son of the Incarnate Word, while they as clearly establish the personal distinction of the FATHER and the SON, in one and the same Essence. This epistle, however, remained without effect; the synod was duly opened and its acts were preserved at least till as late as the eighth century, though they have now perished. Malchion[1], a priest of Antioch, distinguished himself above the rest in exposing the subterfuges of the heretic, pursuing him to his last shifts, and reducing his dogmas to their naked deformity. The crimes of Paul were also objected against him, and the council unanimously pronounced his deposition, and substituted in his place[2] Domnus, the son of his predecessor, S. Demetrion. By this action they manifestly violated the rights of the clergy and people, by depriving them of the power of election; and the fact that they thus infringed on a custom, never before violated at Antioch, seems to prove that Paul had very numerous partizans, and that the assembled fathers feared the re-election of the deposed bishop.

His deposition, and election of S. Domnus.

S. Domnus I., Patr. of Ant. XVII.

55. They announced their proceedings in a synodal letter, addressed to S. Dionysius[3] of Rome, and Maximus of Alexandria. A large portion has been preserved by Eusebius; other fragments by Leontius. It is signed by sixteen

---

[1] Malchion is by the Eastern Church reckoned among the saints, and celebrated with S. Firmilian on the 28th of October. Their Stichos is:

In peace those sons of peace to GOD are gone,
Firmilian and the sophist Malchion.

[2] Euseb. H. E. VII. 30. Zonaras XII. 25. Gibbon of course makes the most of the irregularity by which S. Domnus was substituted for Paul, Vol. II. p. 456. (Edition 1807, which I always quote.)

[3] This is the letter preserved by Eusebius, H. E. VII. 30. See also S. Nicephorus, VI. 29. 30. The names of the bishops who sign it are, Helenus of Tarsus, Hymenæus of Jerusalem, Theophilus, whose see is unknown, and about whom Tillemont offers no conjecture; he may have been bishop of Apamea, and the same who is mentioned by S. Epiphanius as having so entirely confuted the sect of heretics called Angelici, as to put an end to their existence. Blondel (*Primauté en l'Eglise*, p. 544) makes him bishop of Tyre;—a pure guess. Next come Theotecnus of Cæsarea, Maximus of Bostra, Proculus, whose see is unknown, Nicomas of Iconium, Ælianus, Bolanus, Paulus, Protogenes, Hierax, Eutychius, Theodorus, the same who is alluded to in the text, Malchion, and Lucius. Of these Malchion was only a priest; the case was therefore probably the same with Lucius.

prelates, and is said to have been composed by Malchion. Although the term consubstantial had been condemned by the first council, the greater favour of this synod has caused it more usually to be cited as having authorized that condemnation. S. Athanasius and S. Hilary[1] have well shewn that there was no real difference of doctrine between the fathers of Antioch and those of Nicæa. The former intended to condemn a gross and corporeal sense attached to the word "substance," which the latter rejected in that phrase of the Creed, *Light of Light;* and in a similar manner, the Arians afterwards accused the Catholics of Sabellianism, from their adoption of the term in question. The synodal letter was, as I said, addressed to S. Dionysius of Rome; but that pontiff had already been taken from the world (Dec. 26, 269). His successor, S. Felix, replied to Maximus, and acquiesced in the deposition of Paul. That deposition, however, was easier to pronounce than to execute. The favour of Zenobia supported her Ducenarius in his see; and the irregular consecration of Domnus indisposed many of the catholic party to render him assistance. For two years Paul retained possession of the episcopal house; at the expiration of that period the victories of Antioch and Emesa made Aurelian master of the crown and person of Zenobia. Antioch readily opened her gates to the victor; and a representation was made by the catholic bishops to Aurelian, in order that the secular[2] arm might be called in for the expulsion of the deposed prelate:—a fatal precedent, and one not forgotten when subsequent emperors were endeavouring to Erastianize the Church! The spectacle of rival bishops pleading their cause before a heathen Augustus, afforded a fair subject of raillery to the sophists and rhetoricians of Antioch. Aurelian, with the good sense and love of justice which distinguished him, professing his entire ignorance of the point in

The term consubstantial.

Appeal to Aurelian.

---

[1] See this point discussed with his usual ability by Tillemont, Mem. Ecc. IV. 301; also by Bishop Bull, Book II. Cap. 1.

[2] Theodoret, II. 8. Godeau, anxious to spare the reputation of the fathers, makes, without a shadow of authority, Paul to have been the first to complain to the emperor.

dispute, resolved on referring it to a party unconcerned in the quarrel; and accordingly decreed that the bishop's house at Antioch should belong to him of the two rivals with whom the prelates of Italy would communicate. This decision sealed the fate of Paul, who was ignominiously chased from his see, and Domnus, in a method which all must pronounce unsatisfactory, substituted in his stead.

Decline of the Paulianists.

56. The followers of Paul did not return to the communion of the Church[1]. S. Lucian, afterwards a martyr—the same who is commemorated in the English Calendar on the 8th of January—was for awhile one of Paul's favourite disciples, and remained in heresy during the episcopate of the three succeeding prelates. The Paulians or Paulianists existed in considerable strength at the Council of Nicæa, by which, as I have said, their baptism was declared invalid; could exhibit some poor remains in the later years of S. Athanasius; were not absolutely extinct at the beginning of the fifth century; but when Theodoret[2] wrote, about 450, their very name had almost been forgotten.

S. Eusebius and S. Anatolius, bishops of Laodicea.

57. Among those who had been present was S. Eusebius, bishop of Laodicea next-the-sea. His history is somewhat remarkable; and though I have already related it in part when writing of the Church[3] of Alexandria, it must be repeated here. During the civil war which devastated that city, in the local rebellion of Æmilian, this devoted Christian followed the party of the emperor Gallienus, while his friend Anatolius ranked himself in the faction of Æmilian. By their mutual charity, they greatly mitigated the horrors of that war, as they had already by their mutual co-operation assisted the sufferers in the fierce persecution of Decius. When the first council was summoned at Antioch against Paul of Samosata, the great Dionysius of Alexandria, unable, as we have seen, to be present himself, dispatched Eusebius as his deacon to the synod. On its conclusion, the see of Laodicea happened to be vacant. This

---

[1] See on this, Tillemont, IV. 303, and Natalis Alexander, VI. 35.

[2] Theodoret, Hæret. Fab. 2. 11.

[3] See my History of Alexandria, Vol. I. p. 77.

SS. EUSEBIUS AND ANATOLIUS. 55

city, situated on a bluff promontory that overlooks the Mediterranean, extended its diocese to the very suburbs[1] of Antioch. The Alexandrian deacon on his return to Egypt had reached this point, when he was seized almost by force and ordained bishop. In this character he was present at the council by which Paul was deposed, when he had the pleasure of again meeting his friend Anatolius, sent from Egypt to attend the synod. The two[2] returned together to Laodicea, where, very shortly after, Eusebius was taken to his rest. Anatolius who had already been consecrated bishop by Theotecnus of Cæsarea, and had acted as his coadjutor for some time with him, was now elected by the people. He governed this church with considerable reputation; and here it was that he composed his celebrated work on Easter[3]. In that work he mentions that in Laodicea and the adjacent country, the festival was still observed on the fourteenth day of the month; though that custom did not as yet prevail in Syria. His own opinion would appear to have been in favour of it, and his eminent authority as a mathematician, joined to the prestige which he enjoyed as coming from the great school of Alexandria, probably assisted in maintaining the quarto-deciman observance throughout Asia till it was finally abolished by the Council of Nicæa. S. Anatolius was living as late as the reign of Carus, 282 or 283, after which he disappears[4] from the page of ecclesiastical history.

[1] S. Epiphanius, Heresy 73, where he speaks of a bishop of Laodicea and Daphne.
[2] For the lives of S. Eusebius, and S. Anatolius, see more especially Tillemont, Mem. Ecc. IV. 304.
[3] S. Hieronym. Descript. Ecc. Cap. 73.
[4] S. Anatolius is celebrated in the Roman martyrology on the 3rd of July. The Menæa celebrates indeed an Anatolius, but not this. The saint of that day is Anatolius, patriarch of Constantinople. S. Eusebius is celebrated in the Menæa on the 4th of October; the title is, "Faustus, Gaius, Eusebius and Chæremon, deacons and martyrs," and they are said to have been disciples of the great Dionysius. Tillemont unhesitatingly makes this Eusebius the same with our bishop; but surely the double mistake of reckoning him among the martyrs, and not reckoning him among the bishops, must make the point very doubtful; and Eusebius is far too common a name to render it impossible that Dionysius should have had two pupils so called.

58. We must now return to Jerusalem. The persecutions of Decius and Valerian have left no traces in the history of that Church[1]. Mazabanes would appear to have held his see in peace for sixteen years. He was succeeded by Hymenæus[2], the same whose presence at the council of Antioch I have already mentioned. He held the see for thirty-two years, during the last fourteen of which Diocletian was emperor. Jerusalem, however, either enjoyed singular tranquillity during that persecution, or ecclesiastical annalists have remarkably neglected its martyrs. It would appear that to this prelate is due the conversion of S. Maurice, and the ever-memorable Theban legion[3]. They had been sent for by Maximian from Asia into Europe to put down the revolt of the Bagandæ: and it is expressly related in the acts of their martyrdom that they had received the faith from the bishop of Jerusalem. His successor, was Zabdas[4], called by some, Bazas, who would appear to have held the see for four years only. His successor, elected just before the outbreak of the tenth persecution, was S. Hermon[5]. This prelate distinguished himself by his missionary

Hymenæus, Patr. of Jerusal. XXXVI. A.D. 266.

S. Zabdas, Patr. of Jerusal. XXXVII. A.D. 298.

---

[1] Hieronym. Chronic. He is called Flavius in the MS. of Rulæus; which induced Papebroch at one time to imagine that a prelate of this name must have held the see of Jerusalem as successor of Mazabanes whose name had been accidentally omitted by other historians. He is also mentioned by S. Epiphanius: Hæres. 66. cap. 20; and in the letter from S. Dionysius of Alexandria to S. Stephen of Rome, a fragment of which is preserved by Eusebius, H. E. VII. 5, he is spoken of as successor to S. Alexander.

[2] Euseb. H. E. VII. 14. With this prelate the catalogue of S. Epiphanius ends, Hæres. 66. 20; though he afterwards accidentally mentions some of the succeeding bishops.

[3] Theodoricus Pauli, and the author of the Florarium Sanctorum, speak of Zabdas as the patriarch to whom the Theban legion were indebted for the faith. A comparison of dates, however, as Lequien and Papebroch shew, makes this impossible. The revolt of the Bagandæ, a rebellion very strongly partaking of the character of the rising of our own Jack Straw and Wat Tyler, and the peasant war which desolated France in the fourteenth century, gave Maximian a triumph on April 1, 286: the martyrdom of the Theban legion must therefore have taken place in the preceding September.

[4] Hieron. Chron. Euseb. H. E. VII. 32. S. Zabdas is commemorated under the name of Zambdas by the Roman Martyrology, on the 19th of February.

[5] Euseb. H. E. VII. 32; S. Nicephorus, VI. 34; S. Hieron. Chron.

zeal; he consecrated several bishops for the wild region of Tauric Scythia, and sent them forth to preach the faith to its barbarians.

59. The pontificate of Domnus was of no long duration; it is variously reckoned as having occupied five, or three years[1], manifestly as the historians fixed its commencement at the *de jure* deposition of Paul, or else his *de facto* expulsion from the episcopal mansion. His successor was Timæus[2], whose actions were equally destitute of materials for history. To him succeeded S. Cyril; his pontificate appears to have been rendered comparatively obscure[3] by the superior lustre of his namesakes of Jerusalem and Alexandria.

Timæus, Patr. of Antioch. XVIII.
A.D. 274. S. Cyril, Patr. of Antioch, XIX. A.D. 283.

60. It is a most melancholy picture that Eusebius draws of the state of the Church in the years which immediately preceded the breaking out[4] of the great tenth persecution. He is writing of the East, and his words no doubt apply more especially to the dioceses of Antioch and Jerusalem. Mutual dissensions and follies of bishops; illegal and simoniacal ordinations; ambitious endeavours of rival churches for the pre-eminence; schisms originated or fomented by the confessors themselves; innovations on the ancient canons by relaxations of ancient discipline; luxury and effeminacy prevailing to an extent till then unknown; these were the characteristics of the Church at the time she was called to meet the greatest storm that ever imperilled her existence.

Worldliness of the Church.

61. S. Cyril had almost concluded his pontificate of twenty years, and S. Hermon had but just commenced his episcopate at Jerusalem, when on the Feast of the Terminalia, Tuesday, Feb. 23, A.D. 303, went forth at Nicomedia

Commencement of the Great Tenth Persecution, Feb. 23, A.D. 303.

Lequien, 354, says that S. Hermon is commemorated in the Menæa on the 7th of March; I can find no reference to him on that day.

[1] Eusebius gives him five years; S. Nicephorus, two. There is a tradition that he died a martyr, to which Tillemont seems to attach some credit.

[2] Euseb. H. E. VII. 32; Zonaras. 12. 30; S. Nicephorus, VI. 34. For the time of his accession I follow Lequien rather than Boschius. Eutychius calls him Timotheus.

[3] Euseb. H. E. VII. 32. Boschius fixes the accession of S. Cyril in 280, and his death, therefore, in 300. This would make his martyrdom less likely. He is celebrated in the Roman martyrology on the 22nd of July.

[4] Euseb. H. E. VIII. 2; and De Martyribus Palestinæ, Cap. VIII.

PATRIARCHATE OF ANTIOCH.

the ever-memorable edict of Diocletian and Galerius for the destruction of the Christian religion. From the emperor's palace the persecution gradually spread with greater or less severity in every direction; churches were thrown down; the sacred books ordered to be delivered up, and committed to the flames; priests and bishops either obtained the crown of martyrdom by refusal, or became libellatics by acquiescence; and thus, about Easter-tide—Easter-day in that year fell on the 18th of April—the wave of persecution approached Antioch and Palestine. The first martyrdom in the former city was attended with some remarkable circumstances. A deacon and exorcist, by name Romanus[1], attached to the church of Cæsarea, happened to be on a visit at Antioch. Indignant at seeing the churches everywhere demolished, and the edict of persecution carried out by the prefect Asclepiades with the more energy because the emperor Galerius was himself in the city, he endeavoured, without any regard to his own safety, to animate the dismayed spirits of his brethren, to keep up the congregations which the fury of the persecutors threatened entirely to disperse, and to supply, as far as in him lay, the lack of the priests—there were many in this great and luxurious city who had apostatized. Eusebius enters into a long detail of the agonies which the saint endured on the rack, by the leaded scourges; how the flesh was not only torn from his sides and back, but from his forehead and cheeks; and how all that art could

Passion of S. Romanus, April, A.D. 303,

---

[1] Tillemont relates the history of S. Romanus with his usual fulness and accuracy. The original authorities for it are Eusebius in his account of the Martyrs of Palestine, and at greater length in his work on the Resurrection; a sermon of S. Chrysostom delivered on the festival of the saint; and another printed among his works, but apparently supposititious; it is probably of the end of the fourteenth century. Besides which, Prudentius has celebrated him in a long and tedious hymn, the tenth of the Peristephanon: it runs to the length of 1140 lines, and is the weakest of all the compositions of that poet. Eusebius and S. Chrysostom say nothing of S. Barulas. They are celebrated in the Menæa on the 18th of November: the name of S. Barulas is not mentioned, and S. Romanus is commemorated twice; a similar account being given of his martyrdom in both cases. The Mozarabic office commemorates him on the same day.

invent was put in practice to shake the constancy of so courageous a confessor. In the midst of his tortures the martyr, upbraiding his judge with the folly of worshipping those idols which "have mouths and speak not, eyes have they and see not," offered to take the decision of a child on the question between the one GOD of the Christians and the gods many and lords many of their persecutors. A child who happened to be in the court, and whose name was Barulas, was by order of the judge brought forward; and being interrogated as to his faith, answered boldly, There is but one true and living GOD, and He is JESUS CHRIST. Furious at being thus baffled, the prefect summoned the mother of the child, and gave orders that in her presence he should be scourged almost to death. While many of the spectators wept, the Christian mother exhorted her child to remember the crowns bestowed on the infants at Bethlehem, and was with him committed to prison; whither also Romanus, after having been subjected to fresh torments, was sent as their companion. A few days later, the prefect gave orders that Barulas should be beheaded, and Romanus burnt at the stake. The martyr child, unable through weakness to walk, was carried by his mother to the place of execution: the deacon, on his arrival there, expressed his joy at suffering in such a cause. "And yet," said he, "not for my own sake, but for the weakness of the faith of many among my brethren, I appeal to our LORD to give us such a sign of His presence and support as our enemies shall not be able to gainsay." Barulas was first beheaded, after his mother had recommended herself to his prayers, and requested him to become her patron instead of her son. But just as the faggots were about to be lit, there arose so fearful a tempest of wind and rain that the execution was necessarily postponed; and the wood was then so thoroughly drenched, that while fresh faggots were being procured, it was thought proper to request the further instructions of Galerius. "Since GOD has so manifestly interfered," said the emperor, "to set the prisoner free, let us not be found fighting against His will: let him be set at liberty." Asclepiades, however, though not daring so far to disobey as to take the life of the martyr, attributed his deliverance to magic, and gave orders that his tongue should be cut out by the roots. Unhappily for himself, one Ariston, a Christian who had fallen away through fear, happened to be present: he was a surgeon and had the instruments of his profession about him; and now he was induced, under a threat of immediate execution, to obey the command of the prefect. As in the more celebrated instance of the confessors in the Arian persecution of the savage Huneric, Romanus retained the use of his voice. He was remanded to prison, and lay there for several months, his feet being stretched to the fifth hole of the stocks. In this torture he remained till, on the 18th of November, every other prisoner in Antioch was set at liberty in honour of the completion of the 20th year of Diocletian. On that day S. Romanus was strangled as he lay in the stocks; and thus entered into the possession of a more glorious liberty than that which was bestowed on his fellow-prisoners.

S. Romanus is strangled in prison, Nov. 18, A.D. 303.

62. It would appear that S. Cyril's[1] death took place somewhere in the course of this year; and the obscure tradition, that he received the crown of martyrdom, seems likely enough. In his place Tyrannus[2] was elected bishop; his acceptance of the office in the midst of so fiery a trial is enough, did we know nothing further of him, to stamp him at once as a Christian hero. That he suffered, however, or that Antioch was *severely* visited by the persecution, is perfectly uncertain. We only know that he survived till peace was restored to the Church. Some of those, however, who confessed at Antioch have left a name in the annals of their Church. Some were broiled on gridirons: some, of their own accord, stretched forth their right hand to the

Martyrdom of S. Cyril.

Tyrannus, Patr. of Ant. XX. A.D. 303.

His death, A.D. 314.

---

[1] I do not exactly see why the acts given by the Bollandists (July 16) of a S. Cyril, called "a bishop from Antioch," in Pannonia, should not apply to the present prelate: but Boschius unhesitatingly ascribes them to some one else. The Chronicon of Eusebius attributes to him a twenty years' episcopate, from the 4th of Probus (A.D. 283). S. Nicephorus gives him fifteen only.

[2] Euseb. H. E. IV. 32. Eutychius calls him Euris.

THE CRIMEA EVANGELIZED. 61

flames: some, resolved to avoid temptation, in order to escape from their persecutors, precipitated themselves from a high cliff. S. Augustine[1] would excuse them by supposing, in their case, a special inspiration of the SPIRIT of GOD. Of Antioch's most famous martyr, S. Lucian, we shall hereafter have to tell.

63. The mission despatched by Hermon, bishop of Jerusalem, into the Chersonnesus, was not without its fruit. Ephraim was sent into Scythia—by which we are probably to understand Russia—Basil into the Crimea. The latter preached CHRIST in "the city"—no other name is given to it—without any immediate effect; and being expelled thence, as a setter forth of strange doctrines, betook himself to some of the caves with which that region abounds, probably those of Inkermann, which we know to have been famous a few years later. In the meantime, the son of the prince or chief of the Crimea, fell sick and died. As his relations were keeping watch at his tomb, the spirit of the deceased appeared to them, and besought them, if they would have him restored to them, to call the stranger preacher, and to believe his doctrine. They did so; and being instructed by him, professed that JESUS CHRIST was the SON of GOD. On this, he called for water, and poured it on the grave, and the child arose[2].

64. But, if we are taught but little regarding the immediate martyrs of Jerusalem and Antioch, we may expatiate with greater fulness on those glorious athletes whom Syria, Cilicia and Palestine offered to GOD. Of these[3], the twenty

---

[1] De Civitat. Dei, I. 26. Sed quædam, inquiunt, sanctæ feminæ tempore persecutionis, ut insectatores suæ pudicitiæ devitarent, in rapturum atque enecaturum se fluvium projecerunt; eoque modo defunctæ sunt: earumque martyria in Catholicâ Ecclesiâ veneratione celeberrimâ frequentantur. De his nihil temere audeo judicare. Utrum enim ecclesiæ aliquibus fide dignis testificantibus, ut earum memoriam sic honoret divina persuaserit auctoritas, nescio; et fieri potest ut ita sit. Quid si enim hoc fecerunt, non humanitus deceptæ, sed divinitus jussæ; nec errantes, sed obedientes?

[2] The history of the mission in the Crimea is given in the Menæa, under March 7: the narrative is simply written, and seems trustworthy, —and is so judged by Papebroch in his Hist. Patr. Hierosl.

[3] Act. Bolland. May 14. See also the notes of Baronius to the Roman martyrology on the same day. He is

Martyrs of Tarsus claim the first place. Even now, the passion for relics was attaining a considerable height; so much so, that more worldly feelings were brought into play by the search directed over them, and they were beginning to become the regular subjects of merchandize. No marvel, when the healing powers bestowed on them were as yet such objects of every day experience; and that GOD, always wonderful in His saints, was still marvellous in the cures and miracles wrought by their ashes. The cruelty and ferocity of Simplicius, Proconsul of Cilicia, had made Tarsus a very slaughterhouse of martyrs; and its convenient maritime situation rendered it a commodious emporium for the traffickers in relics.

65. There dwelt at Rome a lady by name Aglais, a Christian by profession, but disgracing that name of purity by gross and open immorality. The partner of her sin was named Boniface, her slave, but supported in luxury by her as the minister of her infamous enjoyments. Whether by the increase of the severity of the persecution, or by the unassisted grace of GOD, her heart was touched, and she resolved that her repentance, so far as might be possible, should equal her crime. And nothing doubting but that her prayers would speed the better for the intercession of the martyrs, she employed Boniface to procure, at whatever cost, the relics of those who had suffered for the faith of CHRIST. Hearing of the multitudes that were confessing at Tarsus, he sailed thither; and arrived there in time to be a spectator of the tortures and of the triumphs of twenty valiant athletes of their LORD, in whom Simplicius had exhausted the science and the perseverance of cruelty. Changed by the sight into another man, he embraced the corpses, and expressed his envy of their happiness, who by hours of misery obtained eternal years of glory. Apprehended himself, he was exposed to the severest tortures: his nails were torn from the flesh, he was tormented with boiling pitch and with molten lead; and, constantly persevering in his profes-

celebrated in the Menæa with this epigraph, on Dec. 19:

Ζητῶν Βονιφάτιος ὀστᾶ Μαρτύρων
'Εαυτὸν εὗρε Μάρτυρα τμηθεὶς ξίφει.

sion, he was beheaded. His companions, after long searching for him in vain, were amazed on learning the truth. They satisfied themselves by redeeming his body, and conveyed it to Rome. Here it was received with rapture by Aglais; and by her honourably interred in the Latin Way.

66. Tarsus was also illustrious for other martyrs. The virgin S. Pelagia[1] was shut up in a brazen bath, which was heated red hot. S. Cyriacus and S. Julitta require a more especial notice. Julitta, a young widow, in order to escape the persecution then raging in Cilicia, made her way to Tarsus, thence intending to escape by sea. She took with her her young son Cyriacus[2], a child of three years old. Arrested, and carried before the Proconsul, they were asked if they were Christians; and both replying in the affirmative, Julitta was ordered to the torture of the leaden whips, while Cyriacus was fondled by the persecutor, as too young to be aware of the meaning of his words. But the child, with courage beyond his years, upbraided the cruelty of the persecutor, and Simplicius, yielding to his rage, dashed the martyr infant against the steps of the tribunal. The blow sent him to glory; and his mother, giving thanks to GOD, endured her own torments valiantly, and so entered into rest. In the same presence, Chemas and his companions triumphed gloriously, and at Pompeiopolis, Sozon[3] in like manner obtained the martyr's crown.

Martyrdom of S. Cyriacus and Julitta.

67. But the martyrs of Palestine, as the most illustrious, so they have been also the most fortunate in finding a chronicler. Eusebius of Cæsarea, however much we may revolt from his time-serving and worldly character, is at all events an unexceptionable witness of that which he had seen himself; and the very coldness and scepticism of his natural disposition gives additional value to his accounts. S. Procopius was the first among these martyrs. A native of Ælia

Martyrs of Palestine.

---

[1] She is celebrated in the Menæa on May 4:
ἄθλου πέλαγος ἐμπλέει Πελαγία,
νεωρίῳ νῦν σάρκα δοῦσα καμίνου.

[2] Martyrolog. Roman., June 16.

[3] Menæa: Sep. 7:
ἀντεῖχε Σώζων σώματος πρὸς αἰκίας,
πρὸς τὸν μόνον σώζοντα τὴν ψυχὴν
βλέπων.

Capitolina, he was at this time attached to the church of Scythopolis, otherwise known as Bethshan. He united in himself the offices of reader, of Syriac interpreter—turning the Greek of the New Testament into the vernacular language of his countrymen—and exorcist. He had grown up in the practice of virginal purity; he tasted nothing but bread, and that only every second or third day; and applied himself entirely to the study of Holy Scripture. Sent to Cæsarea, he was commanded to sacrifice to the gods, and to offer an oblation to the four Emperors; he amused himself by quoting the verse of Homer:

οὐκ ἀγαθὸν πολυκοιρανίη· εἷς κοίρανος ἔστω·

July 7, A.D. 303. and was beheaded on Wednesday, July 7th. At the same time several bishops of Palestine were exposed to the torture. Some yielded; some were dragged to the altar, obliged by main force to throw on incense, and then treated as if they had done so willingly. None received the crown of martyrdom, which was however attained by S. Alphæus and *Nov. 17.* S. Zacchæus: the latter a deacon of the church of Gadda. This was on the same day that S. Romanus triumphed at Antioch.

Martyrdom of S. Timotheus, Thecla, and eight others, March 24. 68. I have related, in the History of Alexandria, the passion of the Egyptian martyrs at Tyre. The martyrdoms of Palestine we will relate by themselves, following the invaluable work of Eusebius as our guide. In the second year of the persecution at Gaza, Timothy, whether a layman or in orders is not certain, after suffering lengthened and excruciating tortures, was at last roasted at a slow fire. Agapius and Thecla, the latter no unworthy follower of the virgin martyr, confessed with him, and were condemned to the wild beasts. As the show in which they were to be exposed was one of unusual solemnity and grandeur, six Christian youths generously resolved to dare the rage of the persecutor; and, though with a zeal not according to knowledge, confessed themselves worshippers of the Crucified. They were: Timolaus, a native of Pontus; Dionysius, from Tripolis in Phœnicia; Romulus, a subdeacon of the church of Diospolis or

Lydda; two Egyptians, Pausis and Alexander; and another Alexander, a native of Gaza. They were committed to prison, where they were confined for some days; during which period a second Agapius, who had already suffered cruel torments, was added to their little band, and another Dionysius gladly ministered to their wants. Finally they were beheaded together at Cæsarea on the 24th of March[1]; the first Agapius being reserved for another fate.

69. Apphian, a native of the small but flourishing town of Pagae in Lycia, and the son of rich parents, was sent to Berytus in order to complete his education. Here he set an edifying example of Christian life and conversation. Disgusted, on his return home, with the paganism of his father's house, he came to the resolution of leaving it and of returning to Cæsarea. Here he was instructed by the friends with whom he lodged in the deeper mysteries of his religion; and was stimulated with the desire of martyrdom. Leaving the house without their knowledge, he went boldly to the proconsul Urbanus, who happened to be engaged in a sacrifice; laid hold on his arm, and conjured him to desist from the folly of those rites, and worship the true GOD, who had made heaven and earth. The soldiers of the guard threw themselves furiously on the youthful confessor, and almost tore him to pieces on the spot. Rescued from them, he was committed to gaol, and there remained a day and a night with his legs stretched in the stocks. On the following morning, dragged before the tribunal, and refusing to sacrifice, his back and sides were lacerated with the iron hook, until the flesh hung down in slips! linen was then dipped in oil, applied to the wounds, and set on fire. Remanded to prison, and brought up half dead for judgment on the third day, he was condemned to be thrown into the sea. The miracle which accompanied the execution of this sentence is evidently related by Eusebius with hesitation. He speaks of a loud sound and roar which appeared to arise from the sea

of S. Apphian,

---

[1] They are thus noticed in the Menæa: Σωτῆρος ὀκτάριθμος ἐτμήθη φάλαγξ,
Τοῦ πρὶν περιτμηθέντος ὀκταημέρου.

and to be echoed by the sky; and that at the same moment the body of the blessed Martyr was ejected close to the city gate. He suffered in the twentieth year of his age, on Friday the 2nd of April[1]. A brother of Apphian, by name Ædesius, suffered some little time after at Alexandria, and by the same kind of death. At Tyre, Ulpian, after suffering dreadful agonies, was sewn up in a leathern sack with a dog and an asp, and also thrown into the sea.

S. Ædesius, and S. Ulpian;

70. In the fourth year of the persecution, towards the middle of November, Maximin was himself at Cæsarea, and on the twentieth of that month gratified the people, in honour of his birth-day, with a spectacle of more than ordinary splendour. Beasts from Ethiopia were exhibited, and received with great applause: after which two malefactors were introduced;—a slave who had murdered his master, and that Agapius whom I have recently mentioned. The slave was pardoned by the emperor; the amphitheatre rang with the applauses of his generosity:—a spectacle, remarks Eusebius, resembling that of Barabbas. Life and liberty were offered to Agapius, if he would renounce his faith; on his quietly refusing, he went forward to meet the she-bear that straddled towards him, and presently hugged him in her terrible embrace. He was dragged half dead from the arena, and surviving, the next day was thrown, stones having been attached to his feet, into the sea.

of S. Agapius;

71. On Easter-day—it was the second of April, in the fifth year of the persecutions—Theodosia, a girl of eighteen years of age, a native of Tyre, paid a visit to some of the confessors then in prison at Cæsarea, for the sake of enquiring after their welfare, and, the historian adds, probably also for the purpose of imploring their remembrance when they should be before the throne of GOD. The soldiers on guard reported her to the pro-consul, by whom she was arrested,

S. Theodosia, April 2, A.D. 307.

---

[1] The Menæa:

Τὸν 'Αμφιανὸν ὁρῶν λαβόντα στέφος,
Ἔσπευδεν Αἰδέσιος θανεῖν προθύμως.

I cannot reconcile the dates of Eusebius. He implies that the martyrdom took place in the second or third years of the persecution. But the date, Friday April 2, gives the Dominical letter C, and the year 303.

and her sides and breasts having[1] been lacerated to the very bone with iron hooks, she was thrown, as the others, into the waves. The confessor whom she had visited was immediately condemned to the mines at Phænon in Palestine.

72. The cruelties exercised by the pro-consul Urbanus were such as to give him a peculiar notoriety among his fellow-ministers of Satan. He sentenced three Christians to gladiatorial combat; how the compulsion was carried out is not related: a venerable old man, by name Auxentius, was given to the beasts; and Pamphilus, of whom more presently, was exposed to the most cruel tortures. But GOD's righteous vengeance overtook this man; the very city, Cæsarea, which had beheld so many of his iniquitous sentences, saw himself stripped of rank and power, a miserable suppliant to the Emperor for life, and even that boon denied him. He was succeeded by Firmilian, before the sixth year of the persecution. Under this judge, a meeting of the Christians at Gaza was discovered, and many of those present arrested. The women among them suffered with more than manly courage. While one was undergoing the torture of the Little Horse, a woman in the crowd, by name Valentina, of insignificant outward appearance, but who had dedicated her virginity to GOD, exclaimed with a loud voice, "How dare you torture my sister in so barbarous a manner?" Dragged to the altar, she spurned it with her foot, and was tortured in a more barbarous manner than any other, the flesh being torn from her in slips. After this, manacled to her whom she had called 'sister,' both were thrown into the fire. Paul suffered on the 25th of July. Condemned to be beheaded, he requested a short time for prayer. That granted, he interceded for the restoration of peace and security to the Church; for the conversion of the Jews and Samaritans; for the illumination of the Gentiles; for the judge under whom he was suffering, and lastly, for the Emperors: his prayer ended, his head was struck off.

S. Auxentius.

S. Paul, July 25, A.D. 308.

73. Injunctions for greater severity having been issued

---

[1] She is called Theodora in the Menæa:

Σεμνοπαρθένος καὶ Μάρτυς Θεοδώρα,
Προσήχθη τερπνὸν ὡς δῶρον τῷ Κυρίῳ.

Martyrdom of S. Pamphilus, and twelve others. by Maximin, and willingly obeyed by the prefects, Firmilian was engaged in some sacrificial rites, when three Christians presented themselves to him, and exhorted him to desist: Antoninus, a priest, Zebinas of Eleutheropolis, and Germanus. They were simply beheaded, without being exposed to any previous tortures. But on the same day, Nov. 5, a virgin, by name Ennathas, was arrested and scourged; and then, given over to one Maxys, a subordinate official, was by him stripped naked, and led about through the city, scourged by him as she went. Returned to the judge, she was sentenced to be burnt alive. Those who suffered were no longer allowed to be burned, so that the streets of Cæsarea were a pitiable spectacle from the putrefying and lacerated bones dragged hither and thither at random by jackals and birds of prey. Multitudes were deprived of their eyes and feet, or of one eye and one foot. At Ascalon, Ares perished at the stake; Probus and Elias at the block. Peter, a hermit, otherwise called Apselamus, a native of Anea, near Eleutheropolis, though exhorted by the judge to pity his own youth, suffered at the stake; after him Asclepius, a bishop of the Marcionites: it may be hoped that his martyrdom was accepted in atonement of his heresy.

74. A more celebrated martyr was Pamphilus, the friend and tutor of Eusebius, who from him assumed his second name. A priest, and possessed of a considerable fortune, he devoted himself most energetically to the study of sacred literature, and founded a school at Cæsarea for its promotion. With him was Valens, a deacon of the Church of Jerusalem; a venerable old man, he had the whole of Holy Scripture by heart, and could as easily recite it from memory as read it from the book in the divine office. The third was Paul, of the city of Jamnia; already a confessor; for he had previously endured the torture of red hot iron. These three had been in prison two years, when certain brethren from Egypt, on their way to visit the confessors condemned to the mines in Cilicia, entered Cæsarea. Interrogated as to who they were, and what was their errand, and frankly confessing the truth, they, to the number of five, were thrown into

prison. On the following day, which was the 16th of March, they, together with Pamphilus and his original companions, were set before the judge. It seemed the Egyptian comers had at their baptism received the names of Jewish prophets; and their interrogatory not a little enraged and vexed the judge; as did the reply that they were citizens of Jerusalem. It would appear that the original name of Ælia Capitolina was so entirely forgotten, that Firmilian could obtain no satisfactory reply to his questions. The Egyptians were the first to receive the crown of martyrdom, and the like sentence had been passed on Pamphilus and his companions, when a young man, by name Porphyrius, upbraided the wickedness and cruelty of the judge. Cruelly tortured, he was burnt alive; and Seleucus, Theodulus, and Julianus, arrested on different pretexts, completed the apostolic number of twelve; all crowned on the same day as Pamphilus. Left unburied for four days, their corpses were not touched by birds or beasts, and at length received Christian sepulture from the hands of their friends[1].

75. And here the historian takes occasion once more to dwell on the ambition, sloth, and negligence of the bishops, and the quarrels between the confessors themselves. One of the most illustrious prelates who suffered in the 8th year of the persecution, was Silvanus of Gaza; he had been a confessor before he was raised to the episcopate. As many as forty suffered at Cæsarea in that and the last year, before it pleased GOD to give peace to His afflicted Church.

76. The name of Pamphilus is not only glorious for his martyrdom, but illustrious as one of the early writers and leading divines of the primitive Church. His theological library is the first on record: and is mentioned by S. Jerome in terms of the highest praise. Among its contents were the works of Origen, written out by the collector's own hand; a treasure, S. Jerome observes, beyond the riches of Crœsus.

S. Pamphilus:

---

[1] These as well as the following martyr, S. Silvanus, are commemorated in the Menæa on Nov. 5:

Ἐν τοῖς μετάλλοις Σιλβανὸς βεβλημένος,

Λείπει μέταλλα, καὶ μεταλλάττει βίον.
* * * *
Φρουρᾷ δαμασθείς, καὶ πρὸ τῆς φρουρᾶς ξέσει,
Διπλοῦν λάβοι Πάμφιλος εἰκότως στέφος.

For if one letter of a Martyr be of such inestimable value, what *his library.* must be the price of so many thousand lines traced by the hand that afterward sealed its testimony with its blood? An Apology for Origen[1], extant in the time of S. Jerome, went under his name; but whether his or not, or whether composed by Eusebius and attributed to him, is doubtful. S. Pamphilus was probably ordained by S. Agapius of Cæsarea. His name has undoubtedly been injured by its close juncture with that of Eusebius:˙ the ecclesiastical historian, while intending to honour himself, by the distinctive title of *Eusebius Pamphili*, has rather dishonoured his friend.

Martyrs in Isauria: 77. We may now take a glance at the other martyrs of CHRIST, who glorified the provinces of Antioch with their blood. Though no catalogue of those who suffered in Isauria and Cilicia and the adjacent parts have reached us, we know enough to be sure that the persecution there raged fiercely. *S. Tation;* In Isauria we find the martyr Tation[2], and the 'Wonder-*S. Azas, with 150 companions.* worker' Azas. The latter was a soldier, who having embraced the faith, betook himself[3] to the conventual life, and was honoured by an especial gift of miracles. Betrayed to the prefect Aquilinus by certain hunters, he was accompanied in his confession by 150 of his late comrades. They were confined in prison till they could be set before the tribunal; and, on their suffering from thirst, Azas, by his prayers, procured a plentiful supply of water. The legend proceeds to relate his sufferings on the wheel, by the scourge, by the iron hooks, and his being cast into the fire, which was at once extinguished; he was afterwards beheaded, the hundred and

---

[1] Cf. S. Hieron. de Scriptor. Eccles. in Pamphilo et Epist. LXV. See also Baronius, 256, XXXVIII. and 308, XV.

[2] Named in the Menæa on August 24. I do not understand to what his travels, mentioned in the Stichos refer:
"Ἔλξει μετρήσας πολλὰ πολλὰ γῆς πλέθρα
Ἐδὲμ λάβοις ἄμετρα πλέθρα, Τατίων.

[3] His history is in the Menæa for Nov. 19. The Stichos for him and his companions:
Διψητική τις ὡς ἔλαφος εἰς ὕδωρ
Ἄζης ὁ Μάρτυς ἔτρεχε πρὸς τὸ ξίφος.
and
Τετμημένας τρεῖς, Χριστὲ, πεντηκοντάδας
τριττῇ στεφῶν γέραιρε πεντηκοντάδι.
The conversion of the wife and daughter of the præfect appears to me to have somewhat of a fabulous appearance.

S. LUCIAN OF ANTIOCH. 71

fifty soldiers, and the wife and daughter of the prefect, having first received the crown of martyrdom. To these we must add SS. Cleonicus[1], Eutropius, and Basiliscus; who confessed under Asclepiades. All were cruelly tortured with burning pitch; the two former were then crucified; the latter was remanded to prison, and finished his course. Apollos, Isaac[2], and Quadratus, were, the first starved, the two others beheaded.

78. I have related in my History of the Church of Alexandria, and I expect the reader to keep in mind here, the various political events which occurred in this persecution; —the death of Maximian Herculius, the illness of Galerius, the edict, extorted by agony from the tyrant, in favour of the Christians; his death, and the renewal of the persecution, by Maximin. The sufferings of S. Lucian are the most illustrious at this epoch. He was the most learned priest in the city of Antioch; and devoted his talents and erudition to the completion of an edition of Holy Scripture, as celebrated as that of Pamphilus in Palestine, or Hesychius in Egypt. His teaching, however, was unfortunate enough to incur suspicion, as tainted with the heresy of Paul of Samosata; and three successive bishops separated him, justly or unjustly, from their communion: these must have been S. Domnus, Timæus, and S. Cyril. He was, it appears, restored to the church by Tyrannus; and having attracted the notice of the Emperor by his writings, he was set before Maximin at Nicomedia. Having presented to the governor of that city an Apology for Christianity, he was cast into prison; and there, as an early[3] writer says, making good his name, derived from light,—and shining in his life, shining in his faith, shining in his perseverance, he endured many bitter torments. From Nicomedia he wrote a letter to the Church of Antioch, in which he communicates the intelligence that "the Pope An-

Martyrdom of S. Lucian, Oct. 15, A.D. 311.

---

[1] They are commemorated in the Menæa on March 3.
[2] They are in the Menæa for April 21. Baronius gives their names incorrectly, as Apollos, Isacius and Crotates.

[3] Pseudo-Origen in Job. II. As Baronius well observes, this very citation proves that the commentary in question is wrongly attributed to Origen, who had deceased long before.

thimus" had finished his course by martyrdom. Exposed for a long time to the torments of hunger, and then offered meat that had been dedicated to an idol, he still remained firm; thus several days he uttered no other words than his usual phrase, "I am a Christian." And with these, he gave up the ghost[1], when the officials came to see whether he were still living.

Orthodoxy of S. Lucian. 79. There seems no reason to doubt the orthodoxy of S. Lucian. Like S. Dionysius of Alexandria, carried away by his energy in attacking Sabellius, he used here and there an incautious phrase, which seemed to encourage the Arians, and of which they were not slow to take advantage. S. Alexander of Alexandria[2] even called those heretics by the name of Lucianists; and Arius termed his followers[3] "*Collucianists.*" But the positive testimony of S. Athanasius, who had no need to go out of his way in defending a priest of Antioch, is amply sufficient. In his Synopsis that great Father mentions the address of S. Lucian with the highest eulogium on his faith and perseverance to the end. It cannot, however, be denied that Lucian's disciples[4] did somewhat to blemish his fame. Eusebius of Nicomedia, Theognis of Nicæa, Marinus of Chalcedon, Antonius of Tarsus and others, called him their master; and all, more or less, gave in to the teaching of the arch-heretic Arius. In point of fact, the rationalistic character of Antiochene teaching, which I have[5] already had occasion to notice, in contradistinction with the mystical dogmatism of Alexandria, as inclining the one Church rather to Arianism, the other preferably to Sabellianism, may probably have left its impress on the teaching of Lucian; but in no such degree as to render him unworthy of the place which he holds among the martyrs[6] of JESUS CHRIST.

[1] Symeon Metaphrastes gives the acts of this blessed Martyr at great length, and Baronius copies them from him. I wish I were able to believe them, and the story of the Dolphin, genuine.

[2] Epist. ad Alexandr. Pap. And so Marius Victorinus, adv. Arianos, Lib. I.

[3] Ap. S. Epiphan. Hæres. LXIX.

[4] S. Niceph. Hist. Lib. VIII. 31.

[5] Hist. Alexandr. Vol. I. p. 37.

[6] The Latin Church commemorates him in the 7th, or (as our own Calendar) as the 8th, of January: the Menæa on October 15, which is

80. S. Lucian was one of the last among the Martyrs of the East. It is not my duty to repeat the already told tale of the gradual steps by which Constantine rose to the purple; his war with Maxentius; the miraculous Cross; the battle by the Pons Milvius; the defeat and death of Maxentius; the edict of Constantine and Licinius in favour of the Christians; the war between the latter and Maximin, the battle of Heraclea, the victorious entry of Licinius into Nicomedia, and restoration of peace to the Church, and the miserable despair and death of Maximin Daia. Henceforth, Antioch will take a more definite place in the annals of the Church; we shall be able to pursue, with less doubtful hand, the clue of the history; and her patriarchs, instead of being little more than names, will be living and acting realities. As may be gathered from a preceding section, when the edict of pacification went forth from the palace of Nicomedia, Tyrannus held the See of Antioch, and S. Hermon that of Jerusalem. Neither of them, however, very long survived the commencement of happier times. Tyrannus was succeeded by Vitalis; Hermon by the more celebrated S. Macarius.

<small>Restoration of peace to the Church.</small>

<small>VITALIS, Patr. XXI. of Ant. 314[1]. S. MACARIUS, Patr. of Jerusal. XXXIX. A.D. 313.</small>

81. I have already mentioned the mission of certain bishops, by Hermon to Tauro-Scythia. The legend, and I see no reason to doubt it, is in substance as follows[2]. The names of these evangelizers of that savage region were—Ephraim, Basil, Eugenius, Agathodorus, and Elpidius. Ephraim is vaguely said to have gone into "Scythia," Basil into the Crimea. Here, obtaining no success in the principal city of those barbarians, he concealed himself in a cave; probably one of that series of caves now made illustrious by Inker-

---

probably the right date, with this Stichos:

"Ἄρτου στερήσει Λουκιανὸς ἀντέχει
τοῦ ζῶντος "Ἄρτου μὴ στερηθῆναι θέλων.

[1] This date may be ascertained by two circumstances. Theodoret says that Tyrannus saw peace restored to the Church, that is, he survived the death of Maximin, August 31: while the name of Vitalis appears in the Synod of Ancyra, A.D. 314.

[2] It is given in the Menæa under March 7. Papebroch's opinion is that these Acts are "relata stylo simplice et perquam accurato." He has a parergon on the subject, but it only relates to certain Spanish fragments connected with it.

mann, then named Parthenium. The eldest son of the petty king of the Chersonnese happened to die, and was about to be interred with the ordinary funeral ceremonies. The preceding night his spirit appeared to the mourners. "If," said the spectre, "you would recall me to life, go to the Christian emissary now residing in the southern caves, and implicitly follow his advice." Basil sprinkled the corpse with consecrated water, in imitation, says the Menology, of baptism. The young prince was restored to life; and his parents with their dependents believed and were baptized. But—remarkably enough—the *Jews* interfered, stirred up a popular sedition, and induced the barbarians to drag Basil through the streets until he gave up the ghost. His companions are said to have suffered on the same day in a different year. Ætherius was subsequently despatched from Jerusalem, and though at first unsuccessful, obtained assistance, in course of time, from Byzantium, and planted the gospel in the Chersonnese. In his further missionary travels Ætherius was drowned by the Pagans whom he was seeking to convert, in the Danube. Any further account of this mission belongs to the annals of Russia, and consequently, of Constantinople.

82. But a greater harvest was now about to be reaped by the Church. The introduction of the gospel into Armenia will require a longer narrative. During the reign of Valerian, Artaxerxes king of Persia, and his son Sapor, had bent their efforts to the conquest of Armenia. Chosroes, king of that country, of the house of Arsacidæ, made a noble resistance, till assassinated by the emissaries of Sapor, who had now succeeded to the Persian crown[1]. The aristocracy of Armenia implored the assistance of Rome in behalf of Datad, or Tiridates, the infant heir of the murdered monarch. The young prince was by the fidelity of a servant removed to Italy; Valerian perished in the attempt to restore him, and Tiridates was educated under the protection of the emperors. In a luxurious age, he is described as the model of every manly virtue; in a sedition, he had saved the life of Licinius, and the gratitude of Galerius restored him to the

Tiridates, infant Prince of Armenia: driven from his country.

---

[1] Moses Chorenensis, II. 76. See also Gibbon, II. 139.

throne of Armenia. As soon as, after living six years in exile, he appeared on the borders of his native country, the inhabitants, in a fever of patriotism, flew to arms. The nobility vied with each other in offering their services to the exile; Artavasdes, whose father had preserved the infant prince, and whose family had been in consequence massacred, was appointed commander-in-chief. Garrison after garrison yielded; the Persian archers were overthrown; the perpetual fire of Ormuzd, kindled on the summit of Mount Bogaven, was extinguished; and for some time the kingdom of Tiridates appeared secure. But civil broils had distracted Persia; these were at length composed; and then the whole force of that kingdom was turned against Armenia. The odds were too great: Tiridates fled, but returned with Galerius, who resolved to attempt another Persian war. Narses, the monarch of the consolidated Persian empire, gave him battle on the plains of Mesopotamia; two desperate contests were without decisive result; but the third, fought on the very ground that had witnessed the death of Crassus, and the slaughter of ten legions, again saw the defeat of the Roman armies. Tiridates with difficulty escaped; and Galerius was disgraced in the presence of his whole army, by the anger of Diocletian. Persuaded, however, to undertake a second expedition, he was completely successful; Diocletian was enabled to dictate his own terms, one of which provided for the restoration of Tiridates, and enlarged the frontiers of Armenia. The triumph on account of this expedition was the last that Rome ever beheld. *restored:* *again conquered by the Persians:* *defeat.* *Final victory of the Romans, A.D. 297.*

83. A nobler triumph, in the land which was the prize of the victor, awaited the Church. At the time when the infant Tiridates had been snatched from the victorious Persians, a young prince of the royal house, by name Gregory[1], also escaped, and took refuge at Cæsarea in Cappadocia. He was there converted by S. Leontius, one of the most eminent prelates in those parts, and afterwards one of the Fathers of Nicæa. At the first restoration of his kinsman Tiridates, he offered his services to the national party; and *Prince Gregory* *is converted by S. Leontius.*

---

[1] Act. Bolland. Sept. 30. Nicon. Ep. ad Enclyst.

remained high in the monarch's favour, till his refusal to attend a sacrifice of Diana revealed the fact that he was a Christian. On this he was, the legend says, flung into a lake, weights being attached to his hands and feet; but, miraculously delivered from destruction, was confined for thirteen years in a dungeon. The persecution, however, continued. The protomartyr of Armenia was S. Hripsime, a maiden of noble birth and great beauty, who remained firm against all tortures in her refusal to wed Tiridates till he should embrace the true faith. Her commemoration on the 3rd of June is a national festival to the present day; while S. Gayane, her nurse, is commemorated with nearly equal honour. A more uncertain legend assigns thirty-three virgin companions to the triumph of the protomartyr. The church, erected on the scene of her passion, is the oldest in Armenia, and the prototype of that style. After the second restoration of Tiridates, he is said to have been seized with madness; and on its removal by the prayers of Gregory, the king not only embraced the Christian religion himself, but resolved on propagating it through his country. Gregory was therefore despatched to his old friend Leontius, with a letter from the king, requesting from him episcopal consecration. I should be glad to be certain of the genuineness of this letter; but as eminent critics have admitted its authority, I proceed to give it[1].

Martyrdom of S. Hripsime and S. Gayane.

Conversion of Tiridates.

Letter (real or fictitious) of Tiridates to S. Leontius.

84. "The dark shadows both of other sins, but chiefly of open unbelief, long time surrounded us: hence it came to pass, that we were neither able to look to the truth, nor to understand the common Maker of all things. But when He exhibited to us Gregory, another illustrious sun in the earth, and the holy virgins with him, that by these means we might attain to the knowledge of his own goodness and clemency, we, blinded by fury, persecuted them in a most savage manner. The virgins—woe therefore!—were miserably slain by us. Gregory, strengthened by the unconquerable

---

[1] It is to be seen in the Acts, and in Baronius, 311, xxv. Though the historian receives it without the expression of a doubt, I cannot believe it genuine.

might of GOD, survived our cruelty and snares. But not even so did that abyss of mercy, that infinite sea of clemency, despise us when we lay perishing; but by the doctrine and prayers of this divine Gregory, and by the intercession of those glorious virgins and martyrs"—(this phrase makes the letter grievously suspicious)—"removed that black darkness from the eyes of our mind, and brought us to the light of truth, and the recognition of, and belief in Himself. Him therefore who was the author of so much good to us, and the certain leader and dispenser of our salvation, we have not only ourselves chosen to be the teacher and pastor to others of life and virtue, but a vision from heaven has confirmed us in our resolution. And for this cause, having obtained also his own leave, we have sent him to your holiness, that he may be consecrated bishop, and speedily returned to us his flock."

85. S. Leontius gladly complied with the request: and S. Gregory returned with the episcopal dignity, and on his way back destroyed a temple of Hercules. That he consecrated a church on the same spot, with relics of S. John the Baptist, and S. Athenogenes, Bishop of Sebaste in Lesser Armenia, a martyr in the persecution of Diocletian, may be more doubtful. He shortly afterwards erected his episcopal see at Vagarschnebad, in a vast plain about thirty-five miles north of Ararat; and named the church *Etchmiadzine*, or the Descent of the Only Begotten: a Vision of the LORD having there been vouchsafed to him. After the revolutions of dynasties, and the convulsions of empires, the monastery of Etchmiadzine still remains the shrine and sanctuary of the Armenian Nation and of the Armenian Faith[1]. Still the spring of S. Gregory is shewn, the water of which, wherever it is sprinkled, is said to bring the *tettigush*[2], the bird that destroys the locusts which infest those parts. Well did Gregory deserve the title by which he is universally known

Ordination of S. Gregory.

Foundation of Etchmiadzine.

---

[1] Parrott's ascent of Mount Ararat, and Mouravieff's tour in Armenia supply the best accounts of this most venerable monastery with which I am acquainted. Etchmiadzine is derived from two Armenian words, signifying, *descent* and *Only Begotten*.

[2] Parrott, 143.

in Armenia—*Lorisaforich*[1], the Illuminator. The true faith rapidly spread over the country: bishopricks were established everywhere; and the family of Gregory—for he was a married man—were the principal disseminators of the truth.

Consecration of the Church at Tyre.

86. It was natural that the province of Antioch, as the richest and most luxurious of those belonging to the Church, should be the first to feel the influence of revived Christian art, and to vest the daughter of the King with clothing of wrought gold. Paulinus of Tyre had seen his church ruined, and turned into a place for painting during the persecution: he now raised it gloriously from the dust, and its description is the first bright light which is thrown on the subject of Christian Ecclesiology. We find the Bema, the Synthronus, the Iconostasis, the Narthex, and all the other divisions which are so familiar to the student of ecclesiastical buildings. The dedication-sermon, preached by Eusebius of Cæsarea, is a florid, jejune, artificial composition; worthy of the man[2], but not of the occasion. Paulinus himself, whatever were his exertions here, was to acquire an unhappy after-reputation as the favourer of Arius.

Eusebius of Cæsarea:

87. Eusebius was more worthily employed in his Evangelical Preparation, dedicated to Theodotus, probably Bishop of Laodicea in Syria. It is a body of evidence for Christianity both against Jews and Pagans;—and, though abundantly endued with that coldness which seems inseparable from Apologies and Evidences[3], contains a most valuable résumé of the dogmas and artifices of Phœnicians, Greeks, Egyptians, and Romans, of the Jewish religion, its external and internal proof,—and then enters into the promises and obligations of Christianity. And here, at the very first liberation of the Church from her heathen persecutors, we hear it distinctly stated, that the religious is preferable to the secular life;—that evangelical counsels recommend a higher state than that of marriage and implication in worldly cares; in short, we have the whole monastic system in the bud,— and nothing but the new breath of a genial atmosphere

his work.

---

[1] From the Armenian.
[2] Eusebius, H. E. x. 3.
[3] See more especially Demonst. Lib. I. 8.

breathed in all its beauty. It will be convenient here[1], as elsewhere under similar circumstances, to give a brief sketch of the principal works of this author.

88. The Evangelical Preparation consists of fifteen, the Evangelical Demonstration of twenty books, of which the last five have perished. In the first three of the Preparation, he ridicules the vast number of gods in whom popular credulity believed; and not only shews that the accounts of their various actions are mere fables, but enters into a description of the meaning of some of those which are best worthy of study. In the next three books he applies himself, and he evidently considered this the most difficult part of his task, to a consideration of the heathen oracles. I cannot but think that a little more faith, a little more willingness to allow them the supernatural assistance of evil spirits, would have made this part of the work more convincing to the readers, as well as more satisfactory to the author. The seventh, eighth, and ninth books, contain the history of the Jews, not only related from their own writers, but confirmed by the testimonies of Greek authors. The superior antiquity of Hebrew to Grecian theology is demonstrated in the tenth book. The five concluding books shew that all which is best and holiest in the writings of the philosophers is consentaneous with the teaching of the Jews:—and that where, for example, Aristotle departs from Moses, he departs from Plato also. The enormous amount of reading these last books shew, would be wonderful in an age of printing: how is it to be characterized in a period of MSS.—however much we take into consideration that, to the friend of Pamphilus, the library of Cæsarea

The Evangelical Preparation.

---

[1] It may seem almost presumptuous in me, after the admirable abstracts which Lumper at length, and Fleury, briefly, have given of the works of the Fathers, to insert new abstracts in this history. I think, however, that, as the points which are most interesting in the present age may not always be those which would be most salient to historians, I shall be more likely, by a fresh epitome, to consult the taste of my readers, than were I merely to reproduce an old one. In some instances, such an abstract must necessarily be new, as in the Theophania and Eclogæ of our present author, which, in Fleury's time had not been published.

80 PATRIARCHATE OF ANTIOCH.

was open with every advantage? The very names, much more the several dogmas, of many ancient philosophers would be unknown to us were it not for the extracts preserved in, and information given by, this precious work.

The Evangelical Demonstration. 89. The Evangelical Demonstration is a lengthened argument, from the Hebrew Scriptures themselves, that Christ was the Messiah, and that none other is to be expected. The first three books contain the argument which has since become so hackneyed (and which even then was perhaps scarcely novel, although we have no earlier example of it in existence), on the impossibility that the Apostles could have been deceived, or could wish to deceive others. He then enters on the question of the Incarnation; proves that it also was foretold by the prophets; substantiates the pre-existence of the Divine Word, and discusses the prophecy of Daniel concerning the Seventy Weeks. Hence he considers, by the light of prophecy, our LORD'S Nativity, Life, and Passion: and the fifteenth book ends with an interpretation of the 22nd Psalm.

The Holy Places at Jerusalem. 90. The twentieth year of Constantine, a length to which the reigns of few Roman emperors had extended, reminded him that some testimony of gratitude was due to the Power by whom kings rule. It was in the Holy Land[1] that he extended his most remarkable liberalities. Macarius of Jerusalem had distinguished himself at Nicæa, and was one of the most illustrious among the Eastern prelates; and to him the emperor addressed a letter, preserved to us by Eusebius, commanding the erection of a basilica which should excel every similar structure, and should be reared without any regard to expense. "Tell me what you would wish," Constantine says in fact, "and my business shall be to carry out your desires;—what marble you consider preferable for the piers; whether you would have the roof vaulted, and if so, whether you would have gold employed in the work." Dracilian, prefect of the province, was charged to give every possible assistance to the work; which, with such assistance, soon began to rise majestically from

[1] Euseb. Vit. Constantin. Lib. III. cap. 25—40.

the ground. Eustathius, a priest of Constantinople, was the architect, and the work occupied ten years. Of the dedication of the church we shall speak in due time. At the same time two other churches, though on a less enormous scale, were in progress,—the one at Bethlehem, the other at the Mount of Olives. To expedite these erections, as well as to satisfy her earnest desire to visit in person the scenes of our redemption, Helena, the mother of the Emperor, came into Palestine.

91. Helena had, at an advanced[1] period of life, been converted by her son to the true faith. She was at this time in the eightieth year of her age, and had devoted herself for some years to works of piety and mercy alone. Whatever was the guilt of Constantine as regards other branches of his family, to his mother, at least, he ever displayed the most touching filial piety: he conferred on her the title of Augusta, and her effigy was impressed on the public money. She was more especially desirous of visiting the scene of the crucifixion—a task not to be accomplished without great difficulty. The pagans had already, it would seem, under the orders of the Emperor Hadrian, resolved to consign the locality of our redemption to oblivion, and had heaped over it a vast quantity of earth and rubbish, which they paved with stone; and on this a temple to Venus had been erected. One shudders to think that the spot where the *Consummatum est* was heard, should have been so long profaned by the foul abominations of the goddess of impurity.

92. It would seem that no great hopes were entertained of discovering the Holy Sepulchre, which, it was supposed, had been levelled by the impious hand that endeavoured to conceal its locality. Let S. Ambrose relate the feelings of the pious queen. "Helena arrived[2]; she began to visit the holy places; the SPIRIT put it into her heart to seek the Wood of the Cross. She came to Golgotha, and said, There is the place of the battle;—where is the victory? I seek the Banner of Salvation and find it not. I sit on the throne, shall the Cross of the LORD be in the dust? I am in the

---

[1] l. c. cap. 42.   [2] S. Ambros. Orat. de Obitu Theodos. sect. 43. seqq.

royal halls, and shall the temple of CHRIST be in ruins? How shall I believe that I have been redeemed if the instrument of redemption cannot be discovered? I see, O Satan, what has been thy craft, to conceal the sword that destroyed thee. But Isaac removed the rubbish from the wells that had been stopped up by the Philistines; and suffered not the water to remain hidden. Let the heaps of ruins, then, be taken away, that Life may appear. Let the sword be drawn forth, wherewith the head of Goliath was struck off. Let the ground be opened, that salvation may shine out. In hiding the Tree, O Satan, what doest thou, but prepare another defeat for thyself? Mary shall conquer thee; she, the mother of Him that triumphed; who without loss of virginity brought Him forth, that crucified He might conquer thee, and dead He might subdue thee. To-day, too, thou shalt be vanquished, and a woman shall discover thy snares. She, as a saint, bare the LORD:. I will seek for His Cross. She taught that He was born; I will teach that He is risen. She opens the ground; she unpiles the rubbish, she discovers three crosses in a confused heap; overwhelmed with ruins, concealed by the enemy. But the triumph of CHRIST could not be obliterated. She seeks the midmost tree: but it might have happened that ruins should confuse, accident misplace the three."

93. We must honestly confess that, in a matter of such deep interest to the Church, and among writers who flourished so short a time after the events they described, the variations and contradictions of accounts is marvellous. S. Ambrose affirms that the cross was known by its title; Paullinus[1] of Nola relates the usually received story, that by the advice of S. Macarius, the three crosses were applied to a recent corpse; and that the LORD'S vindicated its authenticity by restoring him to life. Ruffinus[2], instead of the corpse of a man, speaks of a lady of rank, in the very agony of death. S. Ambrose wrote sixty-nine years after the event; Ruffinus, at about the same distance of time; but most remarkable of all is the total silence which Eusebius, in his

---

[1] S. Paullin. Epist. XI.   [2] H. E. I. 17.

Life of Constantine, preserves as to the story. He seems, indeed, elsewhere to refer to it, but we might well have expected that so illustrious a miracle, and one, too, which so much redounded to the glory of his hero, could not have been passed over by him without notice. Two things, however, notwithstanding the disagreement of historians, we may assume as certain. The one, that the real spot of the sepulchre was discovered by S. Macarius, and that that spot[1] is the same which is received as such at this day. The other, that by some kind of miracle the "invention of the cross" was decided; and that the real tree whereon the Redemption of the world was wrought thenceforth remained in the treasury of the church of Jerusalem.

94. The Councils of Ancyra and Neocæsarea, though presided over by Vitalis of Antioch, will better fall into my history of Constantinople. The persecution of Licinius had, however, its glorious Martyrs within our province. After embroiling himself with, and having been defeated by, Constantine, a hollow peace was made: Crispus and the younger Constantine, sons of the latter, Licinianus, son of the former, being raised to the dignity of Cæsar. Licinius then commenced a series of irritating laws;—as that no conversions were to be made by the Christian clergy; no communications to be held between neighbouring churches; no councils to be held. Then, that men and women were not, from motives of delicacy, to assemble at the same time for prayer. Then, that no church was to be erected except in the country: the city air might be injurious to the worshippers. These injunctions meeting with no great obedience, the emperor next commenced an open persecution, though he would not permit it to be called so. It was principally directed against bishops who indeed appear in some instances to have indiscreetly given cause of offence by their panegyrics on the superior qualities of Constantine. Blasius[2], bishop of Sebaste in Armenia, was one of

Persecution of Licinius.

---

[*] See this point admirably proved and illustrated in Mr Williams's classical work on Jerusalem.

[2] S. Blasius is commemorated by the Latin Church on the 3rd, by the Eastern on the 11th of February. A S. Blase is indeed celebrated in the Menæa on the 3rd: but this was

the most distinguished Martyrs. He was distinguished for his medical skill, as well as for his ardent piety: and his cures, whether natural or miraculous, or both, made him a conspicuous object of persecution. Arraigned before the præfect Agricola, he was scourged, hung up to a transverse beam, and tortured with a wool-comb (whence he has been, in all ages, the patron of wool-combers). He was then thrown into prison, where seven women and two children, known to be Christians by collecting the blood of the martyrs, were also thrown. And here they were all beheaded together. In the same persecution, Paul, bishop of Neocæsarea, had the honour of confessing: his hands were so injured by red hot iron that he never recovered their use[1].

Second War, and death of Licinius.

95. The unquiet disposition of Licinius soon engaged him in a second war with Constantine. The battles of Hadrianople and Chalcedon, with the sea-fight off Byzantium, declared in favour of Constantine. Besieged in Nicomedia, Licinius came forth as a suppliant; was pardoned and exiled to Thessalonica. Here he again commenced intriguing; and his successful rival, now become master of the world, gave, in the next year, orders for his death.

S. Philogonius, Patr. Ant. XXII. 319.

Dies, Dec. 20, 323.

96. Vitalis held the see of Antioch only for six years: and was succeeded by Philogonius[2]. He had been married[3], and was the parent of daughters. While in the world, he carried on the profession of an advocate: and was especially noted for the zeal and tenderness with which he undertook the cause of the poor. Raised to the episcopate, he completed the church in Old Antioch which had been commenced by his predecessor: and was one of the prelates whom Arius reckoned his most determined opponents. Reckoned among the saints, he has been honoured by a sermon of S. Chrysostom, preached on his "birthday" by him. His successor was Paulinus[4], a very different character; being none other

a shepherd. I have, by mistake (Introduct. H. E. Church, i. 32. note 1), referred the Stichos to the bishop, which indeed belongs to the less distinguished sufferer.

[1] Theodoret, H. E. i. 7.

[2] S. Jerome, Chron. Theodoret H. E. iii. 1.

[3] So we learn from a sermon of S. Chrysostom on his festival, Dec. 20.

[4] S. Jerome's Chron.

than that bishop of Tyre whom I mentioned not far back, and who is mentioned by Arius, in the letter which I have just quoted, as one of his friends. It seems that he was a native of Antioch[1]; and the citizens, says Eusebius, claimed him as their own. However, he could have held the see but a few months, for at the Council of Nicæa it was represented by a far worthier prelate, S. Eustathius. This noble confessor was a native of Side in Pamphylia, and was raised to the bishopric of Berrhœa in Syria. Here he confessed, either under Diocletian or Licinius, and S. Chrysostom has celebrated his suffering and his victory. He had but just ascended the throne of Antioch, when this Council of Nicæa[2] commenced.

Paulinus, Pat. Ant. XXIII. 324.

S. Eustathius, Patr. Ant. XXIV. 325.

97. In commencing my *History of the Eastern Church* on its present plan, I foresaw the difficulty which would beset its earlier portions—owing to my having to relate, or refer to, the same event. Such is the case with Arianism now. I have already narrated its rise in Egypt, its rapid spread both in the East and West: the vain attempts of the imbecile Constantine to regard the controversy between S. Alexander and Arius as a strife about words: the convocation of the ever-memorable Council of Nicæa: the adoption of the Homoousion, the obstinacy of the five prelates, Eusebius of Nicomedia, Theognius of Nicæa, Maris of Chalcedon, and the Egyptians, Secundus and Theonas: the constrained submission of the three former, the banishment of the two latter with the arch-heretic: the sum and substance of the principal canons of discipline.

Council of Nicæa.

98. Of the Canons, those which more immediately concern us, are the sixth, which confirms Antioch in its exarchal authority: and the seventh, which vindicates an especial

---

[1] Euseb. in Marcell. 1. 4.

[2] Sozomen asserts that he was translated to Antioch by the fathers of Nicæa. But S. Theophanes, with greater probability, tells us that he was merely confirmed by that synod (καὶ ἐκύρωσε): indeed it is hardly likely that the Council would have originated a translation, when, in their 15th Canon, the fathers so strenuously opposed the practice: while it might well have confirmed a recent translation like that of S. Eustathius, though in contravention of its own rule.

honour to Ælia, though it is to be without prejudice of the metropolitical rights of Cæsarea.

99. The prelates, who were entrusted with the publication of the decrees of the Council in the dioceses of Antioch and Jerusalem and the dependencies of the former, were S. Macarius of Jerusalem, and Eusebius of Cæsarea, for Palestine, Arabia, Phœnicia; S. Eustathius of Antioch for Cœlosyria, Cilicia and Mesopotamia; John for Persia and the far East.

100. To the affairs of that far East I must now turn. In the former half of the third century, Shachlupha was, as we have seen, Catholicos of Seleucia. In the year 256, Papas, of Arakan, was raised to that dignity. He held it during the unprecedented length of seventy years; but his longevity was the only noteworthy feature of his administration. Some writers affirm that he was himself present at the Council of Nicæa: but it seems more probable that he merely dispatched to it his archdeacon Symeon, afterwards the celebrated Martyr, and Saadost. In the year 314 a synod of Oriental prelates was held at Seleucia, in which, among others, S. Milles of Susa, of whose martyrdom I shall ere long have to tell, was present. The immediate cause was a schism between the Churches of Seleucia and Ctesiphon, originating in the intolerable arrogance of Papas. "Consider, brother," said Milles, "that our LORD Himself, the Bishop and Shep"herd of us all, has left us a command not to domineer over "the Church: *He that will be great among you*, saith He, "*let him be as the least.*" And so saying, he placed the open codex of the Gospel before the Catholicos. Papas, in a frenzy of rage, struck it with his fist. "Speak, book," he said; "speak, book, as my defence: I have no words from "indignation." S. Milles seized the volume, pressed it to his heart, and then denounced the Divine vengeance on Papas[1],

---

[1] The details of the life of Papas are to be learnt, unsatisfactorily enough, from Maruthas, the Nestorian annalist, as quoted by Assemani, B. O. I. 186: from Bar-Hebræus, B. O. II. 397: and from J. A. Assemani, *De Catholicis*, p. 6. But the dates are very uncertain. Thus Amru gives the Council of Seleucia (J. A. Assemani, p. 7) as I have given it in the text: but Bar-Hebræus postpones it till 334, and places the death of Papas in 335. So uncertain is early Syrian history!

in recompence of so ungovernable a rage. At the same moment the right side of the offender was struck with palsy. It would seem, however, that the guilt of the prelate was not universally allowed: and others tell of the insubordination of his suffragans. A letter of S. James of Nisibis is extant in MS. to this synod, exhorting to brotherly love, and to humility. It was moved that Papas should be deposed; but gentler counsels prevailed, and the punishment inflicted by GOD was considered sufficient to obviate the necessity of any ecclesiastical animadversions. S. James of Nisibis and S. Ephraem consoled the aged prelate under his afflictions. Papas died in the year following the Council of Nicæa; and was succeeded by his celebrated archdeacon S. Symeon.

S. Symeon Bar-Saboe, Catholic of Seleucia. X.

101. Eustathius, whether he filled the office of president of the great Œcumenical Synod or not, was at all events a man of too much mark long to escape the persecution of the Arians. That sect was gathering numbers and acquiring influence daily; and Eusebius of Nicomedia, and Theognius of Nicæa resolved on an united effort to remove the great supporters of the Catholic faith in the East[1]. The former prelate, then high in the emperor's favour, was seized with a sudden desire of visiting a magnificent church nearly finished at Antioch, in part through the munificence of Constantine himself, and of the consecration of which we shall have more to say[2]; and having obtained from the imperial liberality the carriage and its expenses, necessary to reach that city, he invited his brother bishop to share his pious expedition. Eustathius, the most simple-hearted of men, received them with open arms; accompanied them to every spot most worthy of note—the "Confession" of Babylas, the church of S. Euodius, and, more especially, that which was the particular object of their journey. In the meanwhile they were not losing time. They enquired into the numbers, resources and influence of the Arians of Antioch; obtained an introduction to the prin-

Eusebius and Theognius

---

[1] Theodoret, H. E. I. 21.

[2] For this, as Baronius observes, is much more likely than, as Theodoret tells us, that it was the new church of Jerusalem, at the dedication of which he had already been present, that Eusebius now desired to see.

intrigue at Antioch,

cipal leaders of that sect; and with their assistance framed the plot that was to deprive Eustathius of his reputation and of his throne.

obtain assistance at Jerusalem,

102. From Antioch Eusebius and Theognius proceeded to Jerusalem, whither they summoned Eusebius of Cæsarea, Patrophilus of Scythopolis or Bethshan, Aetius of Lydda, Theodorus of Laodicea, all Arians of the deepest dye, and having settled with them a plan of operations, the whole party returned to Antioch. Under what colour we are not informed, they proceeded to hold a synod; but some whisper of their intentions had gone abroad, and several of the nearest Catholic prelates came into the city, and insisted on their

A.D. 331;

own right of assembling with the others in synod [1]. The proceedings having been opened, strangers were commanded to withdraw, and a wretched prostitute was introduced to the

and in the Council of Antioch accuse S. Eustathius of fornication.

fathers with an infant at her breast. By her Eustathius was named as the father of the child; and summary punishment was demanded by his adversaries for so great a crime. "What witnesses have you to the fact?" it was next enquired. "I have none," replied the woman, "save GOD, who knoweth all things." "Let her then be sworn," said Eusebius of Nicomedia. But here a great tumult arose. "Against a presbyter," exclaimed the Catholic portion of the assembly, "receive not an accusation, save by two or three witnesses;" how much more against a bishop! how, most of all, against one of the first bishops of the church! and a man against whom calumny had never dared to breathe a whisper. The

---

[1] Few dates are more difficult of satisfactory settlement than this. Baronius places it in 340: Pagi, in 327; Cartagorius in 330; Le Quien and Tillemont in 331; and with them, as out of a choice of difficulties, I am inclined to agree. But S. Athanasius, in his History of the Arians, § 5, expressly says that S. Eustathius was deposed under Constantius, and adds, that one accusation employed to embitter the emperor against him was the charge that the bishop of Antioch had spoken harshly of the licentious life of Fausta his mother. As it is impossible to believe S. Athanasius on such a point mistaken, we must conclude with Tillemont, that S. Eustathius, having been deposed in 331, endeavoured to reascend the throne of Antioch in 340: that then this charge about Fausta was made, and that Constantius confirmed the deposition pronounced first by his father.

woman, however, was sworn; but it would seem that the Catholics commanded a majority in the synod, and the bishop came scatheless from its investigation. The old accusation of Sabellianism was attempted with as little effect; and the Arians saw that they must have recourse to a different method of attack.

103. The Emperor happened to be in that part of Asia; and to him the chiefs of the fathers instantly repaired. The imbecile Constantine forthwith gave orders for the deposition of Eustathius, and he was accordingly exiled to Trajanopolis[1]. It will be well to finish the history of this great confessor here, as he was never restored to the episcopal throne of which he had been so unjustly deprived. He appears to have spent many years in the place of his banishment; but at length, when the Catholic church seemed almost extinct at Constantinople, he was requested by the few remaining believers in the faith of the Consubstantial, to perform episcopal offices for them. He led a concealed life in that city till the year 370[2], when an opportunity seeming open for the consecration of a Catholic bishop, he raised Evagrius—it would appear somewhat irregularly, but the exigencies of the times excused much—to that dignity. The immediate result was the banishment of the good man to Bizua in Thrace, whence he appears to have removed to Philippi[3], and to have ended his long and afflicted life in that city. The exact year of his death is uncertain; but a century afterwards, his remains were translated by Calandion, patriarch of Antioch, to that city. Calandion sat, as we shall see, from A.D. 482 to 486; S. Eustathius therefore must have died, in extreme old age, about 380.

He is deposed by Constantine.

His banishment and death, A.D. 380.

104. The enforced leisure of the latter part of the life of *His works.*

[1] S. Hieronym. Apolog. II. adv. Ruffin.
[2] Socrates, H. E. IV. 14. Sozomen. H. E. VI. 12.
[3] S. Jerome says that he was buried at Trajanopolis: but Theodorus, and after him S. Theophanes, say so clearly that his remains were translated from Philippi, that we must suppose S. Jerome to have concluded too hastily that the aged bishop would return, at the conclusion of his life, to the place where the longer part of his exile had been spent.

Eustathius gave him leisure for the composition of various works, almost the whole of which have perished. His address to Constantine after the Synod of Nicæa, if it be indeed his, has been preserved to us by Gregory of Neocæsarea. In his treatise on the Witch of Endor[1] against Origen, he denies with some vehemence that the phantasm was in very deed the soul of that prophet. Satan, he argues, has no power whatever over the spirits of the just; it was a diabolic apparition which the sorceress invoked. If it were really Samuel, he argues, was he in, or out of, the flesh? and he endeavours to reduce either hypothesis to an absurdity. The prophecy was either a guess of the woman herself—or a permitted vatication of the evil one, undoubtedly sometimes allowed by the Lord of all things to foretell future events. I must confess that, notwithstanding a certain neatness in the language, the arguments of this little work appear to me unsatisfactory, and its perpetual sneer against Origen unpleasing. The *Commentary on the Six Days' Work*, which has been published under the name of S. Eustathius, is, undoubtedly, supposititious. Fragments remain to us of his *Discourse on the Soul*[2], of his sermon on the verse *The Lord possessed thee in the beginning of His ways*[3], clearly composed against the Arians; of another on *Come, eat of My Bread*[4]; several sentences from various treatises against the Arian heresy, and of *Expositions on the 15th*[5] *and 2nd Psalms*[6]. In the time of S. Jerome[7] a very large number of his letters were extant;

---

[1] The κατὰ 'Ὠριγένους διαγνωστικὸς εἰς τὸ τῆς ἐγγαστριμύθου θεώρημα was, with the work on the Creation, first published by Leo Allatus (Lyons, 1629), and the latter treatise was thence reprinted by Bishop Pearson in the *Critic. Sacr.* (1660). S. Jerome refers to the Engastrimythus.

[2] Quoted by Theodoret, by Eustratius of Constantinople (the treatise of this writer, who lived in the 6th century, is printed at the end of the Occident. et Orient. perpetuus de igne Purgatorio consensus, 1655) and S. John Damascene in his *Sacred Parallels*.

[3] Also preserved by Theodoret, H. E. I. 8.

[4] In the 6th Action of the II. Council of Nicæa.

[5] By Facundus Hermianensis, in his defence of the three Chapters: by S. Eulogius of Alexandria, as quoted in the Myriobiblion of Photius, and by S. John Damascene in his *Sacred Parallels*.

[6] By Theodoret in loc.

[7] Extant ejus infinitæ Epistolæ: enumerare longum est.

they would doubtless have thrown much light, had they reached us, on the controversies of his day. Sozomen[1] highly commends the beauty of his language, and the elegance with which the basis of his ideas is carried out[2].

105. How long Macarius of Jerusalem survived the Invention of the Cross is a point which we cannot accurately determine. Sozomen mentions his death between the deposition of Eustathius, which, as we have seen, occurred in A.D. 331, and the Council of Tyre, which was held in A.D. 335. Let the precise year be what it may, the good old man was happily taken away from the evil[3] times to come, in which he could hardly have escaped deposition. A few short treatises of his against the Arians are referred to by S. Athanasius. In his place Maximus[4] succeeded; an arrangement to that effect having been made in the deceased bishop's lifetime. This priest, who had confessed in the persecution of Licinius, had been consecrated by Macarius, bishop of Diospolis (or Lydda); but the laity of Jerusalem, with whom he was a great favourite, were so unwilling to lose him, that another bishop was appointed to the inferior see, and he himself appointed as a kind of associate in the capital city. Macarius, who was fearful lest the Arian faction should seize on Jerusalem after his death, gladly regarded Maximus as his successor; and accordingly, on the decease of the venerable prelate, he was unanimously raised to the vacant dignity. His subsequent conduct unhappily belied the fairer promises of his youth.

Maximus II. Patr. of Jerusal. A.D. 331.

---

[1] H. E. II. 19.

[2] S. Eustathius is celebrated in some of the Menæa with this Stichos on July 7;
πρὸς εὐστάθειαν καρδίας Εὐσταθίου,
καὶ πῦρ συρίζων ἠρεμοῦν πάντως ὕδωρ.

[3] S. Macarius is celebrated in the Western Church on March 10. It is singular that his name should not occur in the Eastern Menæa.

[4] Sozomen, H. E. II. 20. But later than the 12th century, Latin writers have been pleased to insert a certain S. Cyriacus as bishop of Jerusalem between Macarius and Maximus. He was, they say, advanced by Eusebius of Rome (who had been dead many years), and was a martyr under Julian the Apostate. The whole thing is a mere figment.

BOOK II.

THE GREAT SCHISM OF ANTIOCH:

FROM THE

DEPOSITION OF S. EUSTATHIUS,
A.D. 331,

TO THE

DEATH OF EVAGRIUS,
A.D. 392.

BOOK II.

1. ON the departure of Eustathius, great was the fer- A.D. 331.
ment at Antioch. The Catholics resolved to hold no communion with an intruded bishop, and accordingly convened their assemblies apart; the larger portion of the inhabitants wished for Eusebius of Cæsarea, and requested the Emperor's interference. That crafty person, who had sufficient opportunities of becoming acquainted with the internal state of the capital of the East, had no mind to exchange his present comfortable position for greater splendour accompanied by a seat of thorns. GOD forbid, he wrote to Constantine, that he should violate the canons which forbade translation! Many a priest must exist worthy of the dignity to which their kindness, rather than the good judgment of the citizens, had invited himself. He obtained his reward:—a fulsome[1] letter from the weak Constantine, which he has taken care to preserve, and great reputation as, in degenerate times, a staunch upholder of the canons. Constantine addressed another epistle to the Antiochenes, in which, while applauding their wish to possess Eusebius, he exhorted them not to rob another church in order to advantage their own. Another letter is addressed to Theodotus, Theodorus, Narcissus, Aetius, Alphæus, and the other bishops at Antioch;—the relics, apparently, of the council which had condemned S. Eustathius. Alphæus was of Apameia[2]; he had been at Nicæa, and we shall meet him again at the great Council of Antioch. Theo-

---

[1] Vit. Const. III. 61. [2] Le Quien. II. 911.

dorus[1] seems to have been of Sidon. Narcissus[2] was of Irenopolis, and a man of some note among the Arians; S. Athanasius tells us that he was thrice deposed by Catholic Synods. Theodotus[3] was of Laodicea, and a determined Arian; of Aetius I know nothing. These prelates are informed by the emperor that he is acquainted (partly by them, partly through Acacius, Count of the East, and Strategius, the imperial commissioner for the suppression of the tumults excited by the deposition of Eustathius) with the state of affairs at Antioch. It recommends two priests, Euphronius of Cæsarea in Cappadocia, and George of Arethusa, both ordained by S. Alexander of Alexandria, as well qualified for the vacant see. Euphronius did eventually succeed to it.

Eulalius, Patr. of Ant. XXV. Euphronius, Patr. Ant. XXVI. Placillus, Patr. Ant. XXVII. A.D. 333.

2. But the election seems to have been entirely free, for notwithstanding the recommendation of the Cæsar, one Eulalius[4] was elected. All that is known of him is, that he was an Arian, and that he survived only three months. He was followed by Euphronius[5], the Emperor's candidate, who held the see a year and a quarter. These two poor shadows passing, Placillus[6], an Arian of greater name, appears on the stage.

3. Having triumphed at Antioch, and to a certain extent established their party there, the Arians next resolved to carry Alexandria. For this purpose the Council of Tyre with its sixty prelates was convoked, and those proceedings, which terminated in the deposition of Antioch, and the tem-

---

[1] Le Quien. II. 812.

[2] Le Quien. II. 897. Nicetas Choniates, v. 7. He signed at Ancyra and Neocæsarea, and was at Philippopolis.

[3] Le Quien. II. 792. This man has had a singular fate. Deceived by the eulogy pronounced on him by Eusebius (VII. 32), V. Bede and Adon inserted him in their Martyrologies, and Baronius thence placed his name in the Roman Martyrology. But *Saint* Theodotus was a vigorous Arian; claimed by Arius himself at once as his chief partizan, and sufficiently exposed by Theodoret, H. E. v. 7.

[4] My numbers of the patriarchs of Antioch henceforth differ from those of Le Quien by one; as he, following S. Jerome, counts Eusebius as bishop of that see, merely because a strong party wished to have him.

[5] Euseb. Vit. Const. III. 62. Theodoret, I. 22.

[6] So S. Jerome calls him. Sozomen names him Placetus: but in another place (H. E. III. 5.) Plautus.

DEDICATION OF S. SEPULCHRE'S CHURCH.

porary triumph of Arianism, I have related at large in the history of Alexandria. Athanasius took refuge at Cæsarea Philippi; the bishops, summoned by Constantine to Jerusalem, in order to dedicate the basilica of the Holy Sepulchre, now complete, obeyed the command, and were conveyed to the city in carriages belonging to the State. Arrived there, they found a considerable number of prelates awaiting them; a vast assembly of all ranks had come up to the festival; and the gorgeous character of the building, united to the splendour of the office itself, must have made this an epoch in the æsthetical history of the Church. Pity only that here, as on other occasions, her truth was trampled under foot when her external beauty was at the highest! The greater part of the prelates present at the solemnity seem to have been men disposed to go with the wind; the few leading spirits were those of the Arianising party: Eusebius of Cæsarea, Ursacius and Valens from Thrace, Eusebius of Nicomedia and Theognius. There were, however, men of a different stamp; as for example, S. Alexander of Thessalonica,—a determined opponent of heresy; and S. Milles[1] of Persia, whose glorious martyrdom I shall ere long have occasion to record.

The bishops are summoned to Jerusalem.

4. Eusebius, who was present at the Encænia, has left us a gorgeous, though somewhat confused description of the new basilica[2]. The rock itself, which had been sanctified to all ages by the Three Days' Repose, seems to have been pared down, and encrusted on the exterior with marbles and such substitute for enamel as the art of the age afforded. We read of the great court, cloistered on three sides, the church forming the fourth, or eastern. The height and length were of as yet unrivalled magnitude; the interior, lined with marbles of different colours; the exterior of stone, but so admirably polished, and so marvellously fitted together, that it might well be mistaken for marble. Three gates, turned to the east, gave admission; the long nave had double aisles; the piers were apparently square, the vaulting gilt. The apse was surrounded with twelve piers, after the number,

[1] Sozomen, H. E. II. 13.   also Willis's *Architectural History*,
[2] Vit. Constantin. III. 34—39. See   p. 116.

says the historian, of the apostles; the capitals were of silver, a special gift of the Emperor. The external covering was of lead.

5. Of the act of dedication we have no account; perhaps, strictly speaking, there was none. The days of the festival were employed in sermons and expositions; those of the bishops who laid claims to learning[1]—and Eusebius hints that a certain prelate who afterwards related the proceedings was none of the least distinguished—explained the mystical depth of Holy Scripture; others, whose taste led them to more worldly subjects, panegyrized the Augustus; others, who felt themselves unequal to such tasks, offered the unbloody sacrifice for the stability of the throne, and for the peace of the Church. This dedication took place on or about the 13th of September, then, as still, the festival of the Holy Cross.

6. Well for all had the solemnities ended here; but Arius presented himself to the assembled fathers, demanding re-admission to their communion. He with Euzoius had memorialized Constantine in the city of Byzantium, then rising under a thousand architects to be the mistress of half the world. The Emperor graciously received a petition which, in effect, constituted him the final judge of doctrines, approved of the protest it contained against useless definitions, the ' *Consubstantial*' being one of these;—was pleased with the heretic's declarations—as decided heretics never fail to declare—that he believed the teaching of Holy Scripture on the point;—and finally, sent him to Jerusalem, with a civil *congé d'élire*, reception and Communion being substituted for election to a see. It would be interesting to know how the few Catholics in the assembly behaved. Marcellus of Ancyra was not there—at least not when this business was debated: S. Milles, as coming from so great a distance and speaking another language, might have been unacquainted with the subject-matter of the debate; but what did Maximus do? He had been at Tyre, and had there been saluted by S. Paphnutius with the bitter question: "Did we not

[1] Lib. IV. 45, 46.

ARIAN DOMINATION. 99

"each suffer mutilation for our LORD, and is one now in the "seat of the scornful?"—and, better instructed, had remained firm to S. Athanasius: what he did at Jerusalem no records exist to tell. The Council, however, was again broken up by Constantine, who summoned it to Constantinople. The Arians, instead of obeying the order, dispatched six deputies, fiercely bigoted to their own communion, to the imperial city. They there deposed Marcellus of Ancyra, and there also witnessed the awful death of the arch-heretic Arius. But these things are beyond our present scope.

7. The baptism and death of Constantine, the threefold division of his empire between Constantine the younger, Constans and Constantius; the murder of the former by his brothers, and the deep wound which the Church sustained by the death of so zealous a Catholic, the entire absorption of Constantius into the Arian sect, and the death of Eusebius of Cæsarea, remotely connected with our immediate history, bring us to the most celebrated Council which Antioch ever knew.

8. The nominal occasion, as so frequently during that age was the case, was the dedication of the magnificent church commenced by Constantine ten years before. At least ninety bishops were present, of whom we *know* sixteen to have been Eusebians, or semi-Arians. The Metropolitans on both sides were these: Of the Catholic party, Marcellus of Ancyra, whose orthodoxy remains an open question to this day, and who was bitterly accused by semi-Arians, and by some Catholics, of a modified Sabellianism: Agapius[2] of Seleucia, metropolitan of Isauria; he had been at Nicæa: *Council of Antioch, A.D. 341*[1].

[1] Every ecclesiastical student is aware that the very learned Belgian, Emanuel à Schelstraate, who was a canon of Antwerp in the 17th century, published a monograph on this Council under the title of "Sacrum Antiochenum Concilium nunc primum auctoritati suæ restitutus." His immediate object was the somewhat quaint one of procuring its confirmation by Innocent XI. It is a book marvellously full of learning; and though, I think, failing to shew that the council was not an Arian, or rather Eusebian conciliabule, affording the greatest assistance to the historian of that synod.

[2] In some MSS. he is called, in the Nicene list, Agapetus: but the same prelate was undoubtedly in both councils.

7—2

Magnus of Damascus, of Phœnicia Secunda: he had also been at Nicæa; Aitallahas[1] of Edessa, of Osrhoene, and Mennachos of Bostra, of Arabia: of both of whom the same thing may be said. Besides these, there are three bishops who have since been reckoned among the saints: S. James of Nisibis: S. Paul of Neocæsarea: and S. Theodulus of Trajanopolis[2], at that time a simple bishopric, afterwards metropolis of Rhodope.

9. The Metropolitans who were of the Eusebian party, were: Gregory, the intruded patriarch of Alexandria: Placillus, patriarch of Antioch: Dianæus[3] of Cæsarea, exarch of Patris, a good but weak man, by whom S. Basil was baptised, and held in great respect by that saint. Theodorus of Heraclea[4], exarch of Thrace, also a good man, though sadly mistaken in siding with the semi-Arians; praised by S. Jerome as an elegant commentator on Scripture, and whose notes on the Psalms[5] we still possess: Eusebius of Nicomedia, Acacius of Cæsarea in Palestine, of whom we shall hear much more: Maris of Chalcedon, and Patrophilus of Scythopolis, names of infamy: Theophronius[6] of Tyana, metropolitan of Cappadocia Secunda: Alpheus of Apamea[7].— Among the other bishops, I may notice Macedonius of

---

[1] At Nicæa he is called Etholius, also Etholicus, in Schelstraate's list Ætherius. The Chronicon Edessenum gives us his right name: which, compounded of *Aiti*, "he brought," and *Aloho*, "God," comes pretty near to *Deusdedit*. He built the south side of the cathedral of Edessa, Assem. B. O. I. 394.

[2] Schelstraate leaves his see uncertain; but (cf. Le Quien, I. 1190) there is no reasonable doubt that he is that Theodulus whom S. Athanasius mentions in his Epistle to the Monks, and again in his Apology for his flight, as falsely accused, and narrowly escaping with life. Socrates (H. E. II. 26) seems to say that he did afterwards die a martyr.

[3] He is called Danius in the list of Schelstraate, who does not seem to have been aware of his history.

[4] Le Quien, I. 1103.

[5] Published in his Catena of Greek fathers, by the Jesuit Corderius.

[6] Schelstraate has strangely inscribed this bishop among his list of Catholics. Whereas, in the diptychs presented by Euphratas of Tyana in the 5th General Council, his name is omitted on account of his heresy. Le Quien, I. 396.

[7] He also is reckoned by Schelstraate among the Catholics; but the position we have already seen him occupy in the deposition of S. Eustathius renders it next to certain that he was an Eusebian.

Mopsuestia, who had been a confessor under Diocletian, and who was one of the few whom the party could boast[1]; Mark of Arethusa, who at first one of the deepest dyed of the semi-Arians, and apparently not far removed from pure Arianism, gradually drew nearer and nearer to the Catholic Faith, *though he never professed it*, and suffered a most fearful and glorious martyrdom under Julian the Apostate: the eastern Church reckons him among[2] the saints: Eudoxius of Germanicia, a determined semi-Arian, but a learned man[3], whom we shall find subsequently bishop of Antioch, and then of Constantinople. George of Laodicea, originally a proselyte of Alexandria, who appears at this time[4] to have been little better than a pure Arian: but who afterwards attached himself to the semi-Arians, and was subsequently in the communion of S. Cyril of Jerusalem:—he was a learned man, and had written well against the Manichæans[5]: Eusebius of Emesa, at this time not uninfected with semi-Arian sentiments, but afterwards one of the ablest theologians, and best esteemed commentators[6] of his age. It is to be observed that Macarius of Jerusalem, acknowledging himself to have been previously deceived by the Arians, refused to be present, and that Julius of Rome sent no legate to the Council.

10. There is no doubt that, during the whole of the Synod, both parties—or, to speak more correctly, all three parties—communicated with each other: and the Emperor Constantius seems to have played much such a part, though with far less worthy intentions, which was afterwards assumed by Sigismund of Germany at the Council of Constance. They first agreed on a formula of faith, which seems to have been intended as a basis of communion, and which ran thus:

[1] He is called so with great emphasis by the prelates of Philippopolis, in their letter to Daretus of Carthage.
[2] March 29. The greater part of Mark's life is ingeniously left by the Synaxarion. The Stichos is pretty :

Επαγρυπνήσας πρῶτα πολλαῖς αἰκίαις,
ὕπνωσε Μάρκος θεῖον εἰρήνης ὕπνον.
[3] See S. Niceph. Callist. ix. 14.
[4] Le Quien, ii. 791.
[5] S. Epiph. Hær. lxvi. 21: Sozomen. H. E. iv. 24.
[6] Sozomen. H. E. iii. 6. S. Hieronym. Script. Eccles.

"We have neither been followers of Arius—for how, being bishops, should we follow a presbyter?—nor have we received any other faith than that which we have acquired from the beginning. But, having been investigators and provers of his belief, we have rather received him than followed him. And ye shall know from that which is now said: for we have learnt from the beginning to believe in One GOD of all, the Maker of, and provider for, all things intelligent and sensible: and in One Only Begotten SON of GOD, existing before all the ages, and remaining together with the FATHER that begat Him: by Whom all things were made, both visible and invisible: who also in these last days descended, and received flesh of the Holy Virgin: and having accomplished all His Father's counsel, that He suffered and arose and ascended into Heaven; and sitteth on the right hand of the FATHER; and that He cometh to judge the quick and the dead, and remaineth King for ever. And in the HOLY GHOST. And if it is meet to add it, We believe also concerning the Resurrection of the Flesh, and Life Everlasting."

11. This formula, then, was drawn up at the commencement of the synod by the Arianising bishops, and was intended to be, and actually received as, a passport to the communion of the Catholics. The terms are carefully selected from Scripture, and from Scripture only; there is no assertion, but neither is there any condemnation of the *Homoousion:* and we cannot wonder that, fuller consideration pending, the Catholic prelates, to whom it was earnestly recommended, received it. But a certain suspicion continuing to attach itself to the Eusebian party, from the omission of the Consubstantial, they hit, with all the ingenuity which characterized their clique, on a formula which could not, they thought, be rejected by their opponents, while it contained nothing obnoxious to themselves. Their new creed was attributed—and apparently with truth—to the martyr S. Lucian, of whom I have already spoken. Whatever might have been the sentiments of that saint, had he lived after the Arian controversy had broken

out, and whether he is rightly or wrongly charged with inclining, at least, to a belief which would afterwards have seemed semi-Arian—it is clear that no blame can attach to him for not employing the term *Homoousion,* at a period antecedent to the Council of Nicæa; the rather (as we have seen) that term had been actually condemned by a Council of Antioch against Paul of Samosata. The new document was as follows.

12. "We believe, in accordance with Evangelic and Apostolic tradition, in One GOD the FATHER Almighty, the Creator and Maker of all things; and in One LORD JESUS CHRIST His SON, the Only Begotten GOD, by whom all things were: begotten of the FATHER before all worlds: GOD of GOD: whole of whole: only of only: perfect or perfect: King of King: Lord of Lord: Living Word, Wisdom, Life, Very Light, Way of Truth, Resurrection, Shepherd, Gate, inconvertible and unchangeable, the immutable Image of the Divinity, Essence, and Power, and Will and Glory of the FATHER. The First-born of all creation: Him that was in the beginning with GOD, the WORD-GOD (according to that which is said in the Gospel: *and the Word was God*): by Whom all things were made, and in Whom all things consist; Who in the latter days came down from above, and was born of a Virgin, according to the Scriptures; and became Man; the Mediator of GOD and men; and the Apostle of our faith: and the Prince of Life: as He saith, *I have come down from heaven, not to do Mine own Will, but the Will of Him that sent Me:* and suffered for us, and rose again for us on the third day: and ascended into Heaven, and sat on the Right Hand of the FATHER: and shall come again with glory and power to judge the quick and the dead. And in the HOLY GHOST, Who is given for comfort and sanctification and perfecting, to them that believe: as also our LORD JESUS CHRIST commanded His disciples, saying: *Go ye, and disciple all the nations, baptising them into the name of the Father, and of the Son, and of the Holy Ghost:* manifestly of the FATHER, as being verily FATHER; and of the SON, as being verily SON; the names not being employed

loosely, nor idly: but signifying in very exactness the peculiar Person, and Order, and Glory of those that are named: so that in Person they are Three, but in agreement, One. Having therefore this faith before GOD and CHRIST, we anathematise every heretical heterodoxy. And if any one teaches at variance with the wholesome faith of the Scriptures, saying that there is or was a time or age before the SON of GOD was, let him be anathema. And if any one says, that the SON is a creature as one of the creatures, or a production as one of the productions—and not as the Holy Scriptures have handed down to us regarding each of the aforesaid things—or if any one teaches aught else, or evangelises at variance with that which we have received, let him be anathema. For we truly and manifestly both believe and follow all things which have been handed down by the Divine writings, and by prophets and apostles."

13. This creed, whatever authority it might derive from the name of S. Lucian, seems not to have been satisfactory to the Synod. Accordingly Theophronius, bishop of Tyana, and consequently metropolitan of Cappadocia Secunda, made another attempt, which appears to have been received with greater applause. This formula was conceived in the following terms:

"GOD knoweth, whom I call as a witness upon my soul, that I thus believe: in GOD the FATHER Almighty, the Creator and Maker of the universe, of Whom are all things; and in His only begotten SON, GOD the WORD, Might and Wisdom, our LORD JESUS CHRIST: through Whom are all things; begotten of the FATHER before the worlds; perfect GOD of perfect GOD, and existing with GOD in hypostasis: but in the latter days descending, and born of the Virgin according to the Scriptures. Who was Incarnate, suffered, and rose again from the dead; and ascended into heaven, and sat down on the right hand of His Father: and coming again with glory and might to judge the quick and the dead; and Who remaineth to all ages. And in the HOLY GHOST, the PARACLETE, the Spirit of Truth: Whom also by the prophet GOD promised to pour forth upon His Servant;

and the LORD promised to send to His Disciples, and also sent, as the Acts of the Apostles witness. And if any one teacheth, or believeth in himself, aught in opposition to this faith, let him be anathema; or [the doctrine] of Marcellus of Ancyra, or Sabellius, or Paul of Samosata, let him be both anathema himself, and all that communicate with him."

14. With these attempts, miserable indeed when compared to the simple and comprehensive majesty of the Constantinopolitan, or even of the Nicene Symbol, the creed-making of the Synod of Antioch came to an end. But the first anathema of the last creed requires that I should now enter into the history of Marcellus of Ancyra. This prelate, metropolitan of Galatia, distinguished himself in the first outbreak of the Arian troubles by his zeal for the Catholic faith. One Asterius, a sophist of Cappadocia, an apostate in the persecution of Diocletian, wrote a work on the Divinity of CHRIST, in which he expressed the broadest Arian tenets. Marcellus entered the lists against this person, and, judging from the testimony of impartial writers, expressed himself in a way which gave rise to a suspicion that he was infected with Sabellianism. The comparison is both interesting and instructive, which may be drawn between the Galatian bishop and S. Dionysius the Great. The latter, as I have shewn in the *History of Alexandria*, when Sabellius first began to propagate the poison of his doctrine in the Pentapolis—in attacking that heretic scandalised his Patriarchate by phrases akin to that which was afterwards Arianism, and expressly and pointedly denied the Consubstantiality of the SON. Marcellus, on the contrary, in attacking the Arian, did really, or was supposed to, give way to the Sabellian dogmas. His treatise was condemned by the bishops; first at Jerusalem, in the Synod of the Dedication, and afterwards at Constantinople. He was shortly afterwards, by the intrigues of the Eusebians, sent into exile.

Heresy of Marcellus.

15. On his return (how brought to pass we know not), he found his Church torn asunder by the intrusion of one Basil, an Arian bishop. Hence he betook himself to Antioch,

where, as we have just seen, he was condemned. On this he went to Rome, and presented his Confession of Faith to Julius I., by whom he was received as orthodox. The Eusebians, however, refused to acknowledge this sentence of Rome, and the question came before the Council of Sardica, and its rival conciliabule of Philippopolis. By the latter, Marcellus was again condemned as "an impudent Galatian, who had turned aside after another Gospel, and had mingled together the heresies of Paul of Samosata, Sabellius, and Montanus." The fathers of Sardica, on the other hand, absolved, and dismissed him with honour. Still, however, his see continued in the hands of the Arians, and he remained in the West. Photinus, bishop of Sirmium, had been his pupil; and the notorious heresy of this prelate undoubtedly tended to increase the suspicion which attached to Marcellus. He was at length dropped by S. Athanasius and S. Hilary, whose communion he had in vain endeavoured to secure; though the orthodox part of his own Church remained attached to him to the last. He seems to have departed this life A.D. 372, and it must have been in extreme old age, since he had subscribed the canons of the Synod of Ancyra fifty-eight years before.

16. It would be presumptuous to express a decided opinion as to the orthodoxy of Marcellus of Ancyra, after the learning which has been expended in considering both sides of the question. Schelstraate seems to have regarded him with almost a personal dislike: Baronius, though a little, in different parts of his annals, varying from himself, pronounces a more favourable, though still not an exculpatory, judgment; and the same thing may be said of Montfaucon in his diatribe *de Marcello Ancyrano*. Natalis Alexander inclines to the side of acquittal; and I think that truth, no less than charity, would bring us to that conclusion. It must be remembered that the confessions of faith which the bishop presented were never accused of heresy: it was only said—a thing always so easy to assert, and so impossible to disprove—that his heart did not go with his words. His condemnation, so far as it is implied in withdrawal of

communion—by Athanasius, is of less moment than at first sight it appears. Absorbed in the great battle he was fighting, that patriarch's was exactly the character to drop an individual for the purpose of assisting a cause. Marcellus had, undoubtedly, been suspended; a sense of injustice had probably not improved his temper; he seems to have be-become more reckless in his assertions after his acquittal at Sardica, and he was doing harm to the cause which Hilary and Athanasius would have laid down their lives to render victorious. S. Epiphanius is too inaccurate a writer to render his verdict of very great weight; while S. Basil's judgement is accounted for with ease. I have already had occasion to observe, that the leading minds of the Church have from the beginning divided themselves into two classes —the mystical and the rationalistic; the former, in its excess, Sabellian or Monophysite—the latter, Arianising or Nestorianising. Marcellus holds a marked place in the first class; undoubtedly the tendency of S. Basil's teaching—GOD forbid that I should seem, in saying so, to disparage in the slightest degree a glorious saint—was to the latter. The two, then, were from the first unlikely to agree; and if we remember the excessive jealousy which Basil evinced towards Roman interference, we shall still less wonder that he should incline to be unjust towards a protégé of Pope Julius, and of the Western Council.

17. We have now to consider the Canons of Antioch; which, whatever were the character of the prelates that composed them, form a not unimportant part of Church law. I. Renews the decree of the Council of Nicæa respecting the time of Easter. II. Has given rise, especially in these latter times, to much discussion. It excommunicates those who go into church, and hear the Scriptures, but after that refuse to communicate, κατά τινα ἀταξίαν. It has been endeavoured to shew that this canon forbids the habit of assisting at, without communicating in, the celebration. But, whatever particular reference might have been intended at the time, and whatever be the 'irregularity' referred to, a comparison with the 9th Apostolic Canon, on which it is

evidently based, and the unbroken tradition of all commentators, shews distinctly that it was not intended to forbid a custom which the East, no less than the West, has always practised. III. Forbids priest, deacon, and any one 'of the sanctuary,' if he shall leave his parish, and go into another diocese, so as to take up his abode there, there to celebrate; and if his Bishop shall recall him, and he shall refuse to obey, orders him to be deposed. IV. If bishop, priest, or deacon, having been deposed by a synod, shall, without absolution, continue to celebrate the Liturgy, he shall never be reinstated in his office. This canon was undoubtedly directed against S. Athanasius, who had, notwithstanding his so-called depositions at Tyre and Jerusalem, continued his episcopal functions; and it is this intention which has inflicted a deeper wound on the character of the council than any other of its proceedings. Yet, considered in itself, it is not unjust; and contemplating, as it does, a regular and organized system of appeals, till the appellant reaches that Œcumenical tribunal, which cannot err, it could not, except in a corrupt state of affairs, involve any mischievous effects. In fact it is only a repetition, as Balsamon has observed, of the 29th Apostolic Canon. It was quoted, by the eastern bishops, against Timothy the Cat; in Africa it was recognized by the Council of Hippo, in Portugal by S. Martin of Braga, in France by S. Cæsarius of Arles, and in Italy by Pope John II. So that, with whatever sinister intention it was carried at Antioch, it is now a part, and a very wholesome part, of the Code of Ecclesiastical Law. The Vth canon is again directed against schism; it condemns those presbyters, who, in defiance to the authority of their bishop, set up altar against altar; and concludes remarkably by calling in against such an one, should he obstinately persist, the secular arm. I am inclined to think that it was this canon which interested so deeply the feelings of Schelstraate in defence of the Synod of Antioch. VI. Those who are excommunicated by their own bishop, not to be re-admitted to communion by another, till they have first satisfied the former. VII. Strangers not to be received to communion without the letters termed pacific, or commendatory. VIII. Such letters cannot be given by country presbyters, except it be to the neighbouring bishop. IX. Defines the rights of metropolitans and bishops. X. Forbids Chorepiscopi to ordain to any ecclesiastical office but that of the subdiaconate. XI. Forbids, under pain of deposition, private appeals to be made to the Emperor by an individual bishop, or priest, without the privity and consent of the metropolitan and his comprovincials. This canon too was undoubtedly directed against S. Athanasius; but in itself it must be confessed admirable. XII. Is to much the same effect: that a clerk, condemned by a council, and seeking restoration from the Emperor, should be incapable for ever of returning to his office. XIII. Forbids one bishop to officiate in the diocese of another, unless requested. XIV. In case of the trial of a bishop, where the numbers for his condemnation or acquittal are evenly balanced, the metropolitan shall invite the prelates of a neighbouring province to decide the cause. XV. A bishop, unanimously condemned by his comprovincials, to have no appeal to the synod of another province. XVI. A bishop without a See, intruding himself into a see that has no bishop, without a "perfect council," to be ejected, though the people unanimously wish for him: a "perfect council," that in which the metropolitan is present. XVII. A bishop, elected and consecrated, but refusing to undertake his office, to be excommunicated till he shall consent. XVIII. But if prevented by the dislike of the people, or by any other cause, not his own fault, to be treated with all the honour due to, and to exercise, his ministry. The possible election of a bishop, who should be obnoxious to the people, in this canon, and the ejection of one (without any fault of his own), to whom they were attached, in the XVIth, shew a considerable variation from the primitive discipline as regards the election of bishops. XIX. A bishop only to be ordained in the presence of a provincial synod, summoned by the Metropolitan. XX. Provincial councils to be summoned twice in the year; once in the fourth week after Pentecost, once on the fifteenth of October. XXI. Forbids the translation of bishops. XXII. One bishop not to exercise any episcopal functions in the "parish" of another; if he does, to be punished by the provincial synod. XXIII. A bishop not to appoint his own successor. XXIV. Distinguishes, in case of a bishop's death, between his own property and the goods of the Church; so that his family may not, on the one hand, be impoverished, nor, on the other, the Church lose that which belongs to her. XXV. Gives the dispensation of Church property to the bishop; but with an appeal to the provincial synod.

18. These are the celebrated Canons of Antioch, which may be regarded, on the whole, as possessing the authority of the whole Church, by her adoption of them; though some, as for example, that against translations, have undoubtedly fallen into abeyance. Those who have undertaken to defend the authority of the Council itself, have proposed the hypothesis, that, when the Catholic bishops returned to their several homes, the Eusebian fathers remained, and turned the canons just made, and undoubtedly good in themselves, against Athanasius, whom they accordingly deposed. I confess that I can see no reason for such a belief. It would seem far more credible, that while the Arians did not possess an absolute majority in the council, they formed a very formidable minority; that the moderate party were ready to throw an individual overboard, in the vain hope of appeasing a troublesome adversary, and, by sacrificing a person, of maintaining a principle. Such proceedings we have seen again and again in our own times; and human nature was the same at Antioch in the 4th century, as it is among ourselves now. Certain it is that, in consequence of the 4th and 12th canons, the Emperor's ratification was procured to the deposition of S. Athanasius, and Gregory intruded at Alexandria, as I have related at length in my history of that Church. Thus ended the Council of Antioch.

19. While the diocese of Antioch was the scene of endless disputes between Arians and semi-Arians, and of the unfailing contest of the Church of GOD against both, Palestine was filled with the sanctity and miracles of another Antony.

S. HILARION.

Hilarion[1] was born at Tabatha, a little town in that portion of the Holy Land which had formed the tribe of Judah. Sent by his parents, who were idolaters, to Alexandria for the purpose of education, he there became converted to the true faith; and hearing much of the reputation of S. Antony, he sought him out in the desert, and became one of his disciples, and studied under him two months. There, wearied out by those who sought to be cured of their diseases, or who were possessed of devils, he returned to his own country. His father and mother were dead; he divided his property among his brothers and sisters, and then took up his abode in the desert, about seven miles from Majuma, in that which had once been the territory of the Philistines. Warned that the locality abounded with robbers, he opposed his poverty to their rapaciousness: "And if they take my life," said he, "death is the aim of my wishes." His earliest diet was a daily fast till sunset, and then a supper of fifteen figs: but finding that not even thus was he secured from the temptations of the flesh, he diminished his quantity of food, till he satisfied himself daily with six ounces of barley bread, a few wild herbs, and a farinaceous drink. He was frequently obliged to change his abode, compelled by the irruptions of the soldiers: his employment was basket-making, after the fashion of the Egyptian monks. His dwelling was so small as rather to resemble a tomb. His garments, a piece of sackcloth, which was never washed, and a sheepskin which he had received as a present from Antony. He had resided in the desert twenty-two years, when he first became celebrated for his miracles.

Birth of S. Hilarion, A.D. 292,

he retires into the desert, 307.

A.D. 329,

20. One of the first of these was the cure of the three sons of Elpidius, prefect, at a later period, of the prætorium. He, with his wife Aristæneta and these children, had been paying a visit to S. Antony; on their return, the youths were seized at Gaza with so violent a double tertian ague, that they were given over by the physicians. Their mother

his miracles

on the sons of Elpidius.

---

[1] See the relation of these particulars in S. Jerome's very entertaining life of the saint. From his long residence in Palestine, the biographer was in a position to speak of many anecdotes of this kind.

went to S. Hilarion, and conjured him, by that LORD Who in the same country had rebuked many fevers, to come and heal her children. The saint had resolved never to enter a city: but, overcome by her prayers, he accompanied her home. He prayed over the youths; and forthwith so abundant a sweat burst forth over their burning bodies, that they seemed three fountains: entire health followed. At Facidia, near Rhinocorura in Egypt, lived a lady of considerable property, who, blind from the age of ten years, had spent a large portion of her wealth among physicians, but to no purpose. "Had you given the same amount to the poor," said the saint, "JESUS CHRIST, the True Physician, would have healed you." He spat on her eyes, and immediately restored her sight. One Orion, tormented by a legion of demons was brought to him for cure; and, after the expulsion of his persecutors, came, with his wife and children, to the abode of the saint, in order to request his acceptance of rich presents. "Gehazi endeavoured to sell, Simon to buy, the gifts of the HOLY GHOST," returned Hilarion; "and do not you tremble?" "At least," pleaded the other, "take them for the poor." "You yourself can judge better than I can of their needs," said Hilarion; "the name of poverty is too often an excuse for avarice." And finding that the poor man remained disconsolate: "I do it for your sake, my son," he continued; "were I to act otherwise, I should offend God, and the legion of devils would return to their old dwelling-place."

A lady of Facidia.

Orion.

The horses of Italicus.

21. The story of Italicus is still more remarkable. A citizen of Majuma near Gaza, he was compelled, by the law of the land, to contend in a public chariot-race. His competitor, a duumvir of Gaza, dedicated his horses to the popular idol Marnas, "*lord of men:*" and the contest was generally regarded in the city as one between the true and the false GOD. Hilarion was at first unwilling to interfere: but when convinced that this was the case, he ordered a bowl of water to be brought, and drank from it; he then directed that the remainder should be sprinkled over the horses and their stalls. On the appointed day, anxiety was

at the height. The heathens insulted, with loud outcries, Italicus and his friends. But, the signal being given, his horses seemed to fly towards the goal, while those of his rival crept rather than raced; and even the Pagans cried out, "Marnas is conquered by JESUS CHRIST!"

22. The fame of S. Hilarion reached the ears of Constantius: and, having a favourite officer, a Frank by nation, among his *Candidati*[1], who was possessed by an evil spirit, he recommended him to consult the great hermit. Furnished with conveyance by the imperial bounty, the poor man arrived at Gaza, and applied himself to the Consular of Palestine for directions. A guard having been given him, and many of the inhabitants accompanying him from curiosity, they astonished the saint by the appearance of so numerous a band. Obliging the greater part to retire, Hilarion retained the Frank, his slaves, and brother officers. He thus interrogated the patient—who spoke no language but his own—in Syriac: and the replies were given in the purest dialect of that tongue. He continued the questions, for the benefit of the interpreters, in Greek:—and the demon answered that he had been forced to enter by art magic. "I care not," said Hilarion, "how thou didst enter! but now, "in the name of JESUS CHRIST, I command thee to depart." The Frank, in his ignorance, offered ten pieces of gold; Hilarion made him a present of a piece of barley bread: and, "of what value," asked he, "can gold be to those who are accustomed to food of this kind?"

A Frank Candidatus.

23. From Hilarion, the monastic life took root in Palestine, and if it never attained there the same importance in which it culminated in Egypt, it nevertheless produced marvellous fruits. He was accustomed[2] to visit all the monasteries in the late summer before the vintage, and was sometimes accompanied by as many as 2000 of his brethren. Before one of these visitations, he drew up a programme of his route, and of the places in which he intended to lodge: and the piety of the inhabitants provided for himself and his

His visitation of the monasteries of Palestine.

---

[1] Vit. Cap. 17.   [2] Cap. 20.

retinue, food as well as shelter. On one of these occasions he entered the town of Elusa in Idumæa: the townsmen were assembled in the temple of Venus, whom they adored in connection with the planet that bears her name. As they tumultuously crowded around him, and demanded his blessing—for he had delivered several of their fellow-countrymen from unclean spirits—"Only," said he, "believe in Jesus Christ, and I will visit you again and again." He traced for them the plan of a church, admitted a multitude to the catechuminate, and among these the idol priest himself, still wearing his garland of flowers.

Church of Persia. 24. I now turn to a most edifying subject, the great persecution under Sapor of Persia. Of the first introduction of the true Faith into that region, I have been able to say little; and the settlement of the various sees, of which we shall speak hereafter at more length, is in its commencement utterly unknown. Though the distinction of metropolitan jurisdiction was now only beginning to make itself felt, we see enough, through the darkness of early Persian history, to perceive that, next to Ctesiphon, the strength of the young Church *Shiraz.* radiated, as it were, from four nuclei. 1. SHIRAZ[1], in the very cradle of the kingdom, and which still retains the name of Farsistan. Here were the sees of Istakhr, the ancient Persepolis, and of Darabgherd; both, even at the present day, cities of considerable importance; to this also belonged the *Holwan.* island of Socotra, so famous for its export of aloes. 2. Holwan, on the eastern boundary of the territory of Irak, and *Mosul.* about a hundred miles N. E. of Bagdad. 3. Mosul, of which *Meru.* I shall have much to write hereafter. 4. Meru, as it is now called, then Maru, in the N. E. of Khorassan, a place now hardly marked in our maps: then the locality of a very flourishing church. At the period at which we have arrived, it was, I take it, the furthest advanced part of the Church in that direction. It was this Church which was now to undergo a tremendous conflict with Satan.

25. The throne of Persia was at this time filled by

---

[1] See Le Quien, II. 1247—1264. Assemani, B. O. III. 126.

Sapor, who was to make to himself a name scarcely second to that of Pharaoh or Antiochus Epiphanes, in the persecution of the Church. On the death of his father Hormuz, whom the Greek historians classicize into Hormisdas, the queen was left pregnant. If the future child were of the female sex, the house of the Sassanidæ would claim the crown; if the child were a male, it was to be expected that the loyalty of the magi would preserve for him the throne of his fathers. The consentient voice of the whole college of priests prophesied that a boy-king would be vouchsafed to the Persians. On this a royal bed was prepared with great pomp in the royal hall of the palace; and in the midst of the attendance of nobles, pontiffs and the most distinguished inhabitants of the metropolis, the diadem was[1] placed on the spot which might be supposed to conceal the future heir of the kingdom of Persia. It thus happened that, throughout his long reign of seventy years, the years of Sapor's royalty always preceded those of his birth. When he had attained the age of 18 he was incited by the magi to commence that persecution of the Christians which sent such an innumerable host of martyrs to glory. The names of 16,000 were preserved in the diptychs of the Persian Church; and it was well known that these were but a very small portion of those who fell for the true faith. The persecution did not indeed commence till the thirtieth year of the monarch's reign; but before that period many had here and there dispersedly laid down their lives for the sake of CHRIST. And it happens, remarkably, that none of the great histories of the Church have yet contained a detailed account of this persecution. To Baronius, to Fleury, to Cabassutius—even to that patient chronicler of martyrdoms, Ruinart—it was only known through Greek versions, themselves very imperfect always, and often very inaccurate. It was left to the munificence of Clement XI., to the enterprise of Elias Assemani[2], and to the learning of Stephen Evodius, of the same family, to render accessible to

Coronation of Sapor. A.D. 309.

The acts of the Persian martyrs

first correctly related by Stephen Evodius Assemani.

---

[1] Agathias, Lib. IV. circ. med. See also Gibbon, III. p. 135.

[2] For an account of these interesting negotiations, see the preface of Stephen Evodius to the Acta SS. Martyrum, pp. xxix—xxxiii.

the scholars of Europe the manuscripts which relate the endurance and the victories of these heroes of CHRIST. Whatever, therefore, the reader may find in the following pages which is not to be found in the great masters of Church history, is due either to that source immediately, or to enquiries originating in that source.

Anticipation of the great persecutions.

26. I have already related how, after the death of the wicked Papas, S. Symeon Bar-Saboe — "the son of the fuller"—succeeded to the throne of Seleucia. He must have seen, during the years of the childhood of Sapor, the efforts of the Magi directed to induce him to exterminate the very existence of the Church; and must have learnt that the young king was but too willing to obey their instructions. The first martyrs, however, so far as we know, did not suffer till two years after the Council of Nicæa. It would appear that, at the commencement of the persecution, apostasies were not unfrequent; nor, when we consider the character of Papas, does it seem wonderful that a low state of religion should have generally been prevalent. There

SS. Brich-jesus, Jonas, Zebinas, and companions.

was in the city of Beth-Asa, in the province of Adiabene (a province, the deep-seated Christianity of which I shall hereafter have cause to explain), and at no great distance from Mosul, two brothers, by name Jonas[1] and Brich-Jesus. Having heard that in the city of Hubaha an unusual number of apostasies had occurred, they determined themselves to travel thither, and to endeavour, so far as might be in their power, to strengthen their brethren. Their efforts were crowned with much success; and besides a larger number of confessors, they had the satisfaction of reckoning nine martyrs among their pupils: the names of the latter were Zebinas, Lazarus, Maruthas, Narsetes, Elias, Mahares, Abibus, Sabas and Shembaitas. The governor of the city, hearing of the arrival, and of the enthusiasm of the strangers, summoned them before his tribunal; and endeavoured at first with kindness to bend them to his will. Refusing to worship the sun, the moon, fire and the holy water, they were scourged with orange

---

[1] Assemani, Act. SS. Martyr. pp. 215—224.

boughs, from which, says the historian, the knots and buds had not been removed; and were then confined in separate prisons, under the idea that, if divided, each might be more easily overcome. Jonas was the first who was again called before the magistrate; and, on his second refusal, was scourged more severely than before; his weight being suspended in the mean time on a blunted point, put under the centre of the stomach. The annalist, who was present, and who seems to have taken down what he uttered, gives his word as follows: "I yield Thee thanks, GOD of Abraham, our FATHER, who didst of old time call him by Thy grace from this place"—the city in which he suffered was the ancient Ur of the Chaldees,—"and hast made me worthy by the mysteries of faith to know some few things out of many concerning Thee. And now I pray Thee, O LORD, give me to make good that which the HOLY GHOST of old time spake by the mouth of David: I will offer unto Thee fat burnt sacrifices with the incense of rams; I will offer bullocks and goats. O come hither and hearken ye that fear GOD, and I will tell you what he hath done for my soul." And one verse which seems to have been continually in his mouth was: "One thing have I desired of the LORD, that will I require." It were endless to go through with the torments by which this martyr of Christ was tried. It is said that being thrown into a caldron of boiling pitch, he came forth unhurt. Finally, he was cut in pieces, his remains being thrown into a well, and a guard of soldiers set over them to preserve them from the adoration of the Christians.

27. On this Brich-Jesus was set before the tribunal, and when desired to spare his own body: "It was not I who made it," said he, "neither will it be I that destroy it. GOD, who gave it to me, will restore it; will reward me and punish you." Hormisdatshir, one of the principal magi, forthwith gave orders that the martyr should be scourged, should then be stuck full of sharp reeds, and afterwards cast into a tank of liquid sulphur. The bodies of the martyrs were afterwards ransomed for five hundred drachmæ and

their silk vestments by an old friend, Abtushata. Their victory was gained on the 24th day of December, 327; and the details of their martyrdom were written by Isaiah of Erzeroum.

A.D. 327, Dec. 24.

28. We read no further details of any persecution during a space of twelve years. In the thirtieth of Sapor two bishops were called to the crown of martyrdom. These were Sapor[1] of Bethnicator, a small town on the river Capros, and Isaac of Bethseleucia, called also Carcha: they were accompanied by three others who appear to have been laymen— Mahanes, Abraham, and Symeon. The king was about to undertake a journey to Persepolis; but was wrought on by the magi personally to superintend the examination of the prisoners. Then, as all through the acts of the Persian martyrs, one cannot but be struck with their method of addressing those in authority; they seem to have endeavoured to aggravate, rather than to conciliate, and to state necessary truths with very unnecessary harshness. At the same time we must remember that their acts were, to a certain extent, dressed up to please the popular taste; and to this, rather than to any desire of their own to offend, it may be owing that one generally finds somewhat to regret in their replies during examination. We find from the questions addressed to Isaac, that even under Sapor church building went on. "How did you dare," enquired the monarch, "to erect any new temples?" "And when do you suppose," rejoined Isaac, "that I could find leisure for such a work?" This prelate was stoned to death: Sapor, committed to prison after being scourged, gave thanks to GOD for the victory of his friend, and two days after rejoined him in glory; dying, it was said, partly of his wounds, partly from the intolerable stench of the dungeon in which he was confined. Their followers were tried by even more cruel deaths. Mahanes was skinned alive; Abraham had red hot nails thrust into his eyes; and Symeon, buried to the waist in a pit excavated for that purpose, was shot to death with arrows.

Martyrdom of SS. Sapor and Isaac, bishops,

of SS. Mahanes, Abraham, and Symeon.

---

[1] A. A. S. M. I. pp. 226–280.

THE GREAT PERSECUTION.

29. I now come to the great persecution of Sapor; one of the four which may claim the chief place among those which the malice of Satan has excited against the Church: the other three being that of Diocletian; that of Huneric, the Arian in Africa; and that of Taycosama and his successors in Japan. Not to interrupt the thread of my narrative, I shall venture to go somewhat beyond the epoch which we have already reached; and shall for the present leave the schism of Antioch to maintain itself in its double succession, and S. Cyril of Jerusalem to free himself by degrees from the Arian teaching of his youth; while I tell of the noble deeds done by CHRIST'S servants in the far east. I have already said that S. Symeon Bar-Saboe was at this time Bishop of Seleucia and Ctesiphon, and primate with autocephalous power in the Chaldean Church. He, too, had been at Nicæa[1]; and probably the prerogatives of his see had been there acknowledged; though the thirty-third—others reckon it the thirty-eighth—Canon of that synod seems of very doubtful authenticity. After speaking of the Patriarchs, if the words be genuine, the fathers thus proceed: "Let the prelate of the see of Seleucia be honoured in a similar manner, which is in the region of the East, and is called Modain; and he shall be called by the appellation of Catholicos, and shall henceforth have the power of ordaining metropolitans." At all events he was a marked man throughout the whole Persian empire, and could hardly expect to escape unnoticed whenever the storm should burst. In this he was happy, that he was surrounded by so excellent a staff of suffragans. The martyrdoms of S. Sapor and S. Isaac we have already seen; that of S. Milles, whom we noticed on the dedication of the Holy Sepulchre, is to follow.

30. The acts of his martyrdom were written by S. Maruthas[2], who lived about eighty years later, but who had conversed with some of the actors in the scenes which he describes. I cannot commend his style; it abounds in figures of speech rather than in facts, and intersperses scenes,

---

[1] Assemani, Bibl. Or. I. p. 9. § XIV. Procop. Bell. Persic. II. 25. Le Quien, II. p. 1080, x.

[2] A. A. S. M. I. p. XLVIII. seq.

which ought to be told with the greatest simplicity, with the flowery eastern rhetoric. Instead of a pompous eulogy on Judas Maccabæus, and a comparison between that chieftain and the Bishop of Seleucia, I would rather have been informed what were the reasons which, in the thirtieth year of his reign, induced Sapor to commence so savage a persecution. Undoubtedly hatred to the Romans had a considerable share in influencing him; the persecution must be considered political as well as religious; the two nations hated each other with a border ferocity; and the ebb and flow of successes on both sides kept every feeling of ambition, emulation and rancour alive both in princes and people. Add, too, that S. James of Nisibis was he who, beyond all other, kept that border city firm in its allegiance to Constantius; in the two sieges which it had already suffered from the Persians, he was the soul of the defence, and in that which we have yet to relate, he was the defender of the place by miracle. Actuated then by the Magi on one side, to whom he owed his infant crown, impelled on the other by the natural hatred which a corrupt heart bears to a purer system, he was further incited by beholding his Christian subjects vassals in will of the Roman emperor, and resolved, at whatever expense of depopulation, to rid Persia of them root and branch.

31. The method by which he commenced the attack was not without its ability. He declared that all who were called by the name of CHRIST should be subject to a very heavy tax—our author has unfortunately not considered it worth his while to inform us of what kind. Symeon, in the name of his people, replied to this tyrannical edict. "CHRIST[1]," he said, "Who had freed the Church by His death, would not permit his people to bow the neck to such a yoke. While He remained their king, His servants were resolved not to

---

[1] A. A. S. M. I. p. 17. Stephen Evodius has a very long and angry note (17, p. 38) in defence of S. Symeon, and against Tillemont, who seems to me to take the Christian view of the subject. One can forgive a Syriac scholar some little warmth in defence of that great light of the Syrian Church: but for an ecclesiastical writer to accuse Tillemont, the first of Church historians, of inaccuracy and ignorance, is surely unpardonable.

contribute a tax which they neither could, nor ought to pay."
I confess that I cannot admire the spirit of this, which the
Syrian writers term the Golden Letter. It was not so that
the Apostles had learned CHRIST. Over their faith Cæsar
should have no power; the perishable dross of their earthly
goods,—if he demanded it, let it go. Certainly, the servants
of the poor king had no right to commence a virtual rebellion on such grounds. The king's indignation was, as might *S. Symeon resists,* be expected, violently excited; and, incited by the Jews, he
gave orders for the arrest of the archbishop, and two of his
priests, Ananias and Abdechala (if the Grecized form be
preferred, Hierodulus). Taken into custody in Seleucia, they *is apprehended;* were conducted to the king at Ledan, an episcopal city near
Susa. Here he again gave offence by refusing the accustomed adoration of the king—which, up to that time, it seems,
he had paid. He was urged by every argument to adore
the sun, but in vain. While we read the florid declamations
which S. Maruthas puts into the mouth both of the king and
of the archbishop, we cannot but wish that the authentic
reports, which bring a western martyrdom so vividly before
us, had been known in the East. The facts, no doubt, related
of the Syrian martyrs are authentic: the speeches must be
regarded as a spiritual romance. The archbishop was remanded to prison, when an eunuch, by name Guhshatazades, in rank an Arzabedes, or chief of the white eunuchs,
and formerly a Christian, saluted him. The archbishop turned
his face from an apostate: " If," said the wretched man,
" Symeon, once my friend, now turns from me, and refuses to *refuses to notice the* acknowledge me, because I have denied my LORD and his, *apostate Guhshata-* how shall I be received at the latter day by the GOD whose *zades,* faith I have thus betrayed?" Resolved, even now, to take
the kingdom of heaven by violence, he arrayed himself in
mourning apparel, and presented himself in the palace.

32. So flagrant a breach of etiquette could not but
excite the royal attention; and with the sarcastic observation that the delinquent could not plead—what it seems
could alone have been alleged with propriety—the death of
wife or child, he demanded the cause of these signs of grief?

122   THE PATRIARCHATE OF ANTIOCH.

who thereupon repents, and is put to death.

—"A conscience," replied the renegade, "which pronounces me unworthy of life." Of which speech, says the annalist, in almost English phrase, the king "could make neither head nor tail," and enquired more particularly into the occurrence. The truth was soon known; and Guhshatazades[1] was as quickly condemned to death. At his own earnest request the cause of his punishment was solemnly published; and this having been done, the old man was beheaded, says Maruthas, "on Thursday of the week of Azymes;" in other words, on Maundy Thursday. The happy news having been carried to Symeon, that prelate gave thanks to GOD, and besought Him to crown His goodness by so ordering his own

Martyrdom of S. Symeon, Ap. 14, 340,

martyrdom as that it should fall at the very hour of CHRIST'S sufferings[2]. Accordingly, at nine o'clock on the Good Friday, the bishop was summoned before the king, and, after a short examination, was condemned to be beheaded[3].

33. In this same city, Ledan[4], five bishops and ninety-nine priests or deacons, were kept in confinement. The

of SS. Gadinbes, Sabinus, Bolideus, John, John, and 99 others;

names of the former were: Gadiabes[5] and Sabinus, both of Beth-Lapitha; Bolideus of Pherath-Mesana; John of Carche-Mesana; and John of Hormisdadshir. To these Symeon addressed a few words of exhortation and encouragement, bidding them remember that "their resurrection would on

---

[1] Of this, as of all the Persian names, the Greek martyrologists make sad work; we have it in the Menæa, Chusdazat, in Epiphanius Scholasticus Usthazades; in Leo Allatius Isdes.

[2] This date, which is not unattended with great difficulties, seems to me, however, satisfactorily settled by Stephen Evodius, in the Introductory Notice to the Martyrdom of S. Symeon, A. A. S. M. I. p. 4, seq.

[3] S. Symeon is commemorated in the Menæa on April 17, with an ode by Joseph of the Studium, in which the acrostic is:

Στέφω, μάκαρ σε, Συμεὼν, μελῳδίαις
      Ἰωσήφ.

I cannot very much commend the composition. The title of the festival commemorates also Abdellas, i.e. Abdhaicla, a presbyter, Chusdazat, Phusek, and 1150 other martyrs. In the Roman Martyrology he is recorded on April 21.

[4] Ledan, the principal town of the Huzites, or Oxiani, was situated no great distance from Susa, between that town and Ahwaz, of which I shall have more to say: about lat. 34° 30′, long. 48° 30′.

[5] These are not mentioned by S. Maruthas, but in one of the Nitrian codices now in the Vatican, A. A. S. M. p. 41, note 24. Of S. Gadiabes we shall hear again.

that most holy day be buried along with them; that the LORD had been slain and was alive; and in Him their life was hid." After which, without any apostasy in their ranks, the hundred and four submitted themselves to the sword. Then came the turn of Symeon himself, and of his own more immediate companions, Ananias and Abdhaicla. The former evinced some signs of fear. On this a bystander, by name Phusek, by dignity a *Karugabar*, that is, Master of the Royal Workmen, cried out, "Have no fear, O Ananias! close your eyes but for one moment, and they shall open in the light of heaven." When the three had entered into rest, this brave man was hurried before the king, and condemned to perish in the most frightful tortures. With him received the crown his daughter, "a maiden of the covenant," that is, a consecrated virgin. of Phusek and his daughter.

34. On the same day a fresh edict was issued against the Christians, in terms of greater severity than before; and, from that time till the "Second Sunday in Pentecost," that is, till Low Sunday[1], not a day but added to the list of martyrs. The names of these glorious athletes seem already to have perished in the time of Maruthas; whence we may gather that they were probably of the lower class. Several of them were soldiers of the royal lifeguards; and one Azades, an eunuch of the palace, is especially commemorated as a glorious martyr. A fresh edict for persecution.

35. A still more illustrious confession followed. The queen of Sapor was attacked by an unknown disease—at least so the medical art of that age regarded her illness. The Jewish physician who attended her suggested that the attack was effected by the incantations of the sisters of Symeon, Tharba[2], a virgin dedicated to GOD, and of rare beauty, and Pherbutha, who, after having been married to a S. Tharba, V., and S. Pherbutha,

---

[1] See A. A. S. M. p. 50, note 3.

[2] This virgin martyr with her companions has no small fame in the Greek Church, and is commemorated on April 4, though not as the principal saint of the day; the mistress is here called Pherbutha. See also Sozomen, H. E. II. 11, and Ruinart in the Acta Sincera; but none of these had the advantage of being able to consult the original Acts, and inaccuracies are the necessary consequence.

nobleman of high reputation, was now a widow, and had bound herself by a vow of chastity. These two, with their servant, also consecrated to GOD, were arraigned before the judge. In vain they expressed the horror which all Christians entertained to the practice of witchcraft; in vain they quoted the divine laws by which it is forbidden; in vain they asked what injury they had to avenge, who believed that their dear brother had been sent by the sword of the headsman from death to life, from sorrow to joy, from a vale of misery to a paradise of immortality. They were remanded to prison; where Tharba received an offer of life for herself and her companions, if she would become the wife of the judge by whom they had been questioned. This offer being rejected with scorn, the three martyrs were led to the place of punishment. Each of them, after being stripped of her garments, was tied to two posts, erected for that purpose, and cut into fragments; and between these yet reeking portions the queen, by the prescription of the magi, was led, followed by the whole of the forces then in the city. She shortly after perished miserably[1].

36. In the same year another illustrious martyr glorified GOD. Milles[2], whom we have already seen present in the Council of Jerusalem, was born at Maheldagdar, the principal town of Razichitis[3]; and a place of some importance. He followed, in his youth, the life of a courtier; and, while in that position, he received baptism. We find him first resident at Beth-Lapet (it is marked in our maps by its Arabic name of Ahwaz, more properly Suk-Ahuaz, *i.e.* 'the town of the Huzites,' or Oxii[4],) where he probably was instructed in

---

[1] In the Jewish faith, says Sozomen. The Menæa will have it that she recovered.

[2] The life of S. Milles has never yet been related in English; nor is it to be found, of course, in Baronius, Fleury, &c. The original Acts are in the A. A. S. M. Tom. I. pp. 66—79.

[3] Or, as the Arabs call it, Ramanitis: it lies between Susa and the Persian Gulf.

[4] The note 3, p. 80 of the A. A. S. M. is here particularly to be observed. Note: that the four ancient people, the Susiani, Oxii or Uxii or Husitæ, Chusæni and Elymæi all occupied the territory now called Khuzistan. Though Stephen Evodius always distinguishes them, I can hardly think that the Oxii, who (as he says, note 2

the faith by SS. Gadiabes and Sabinus, who, as we have seen, were resident in that city. Hence he removed to Elam, the head of the region called Ilamitis, or Elymaitica, on the Persian Gulf, and now forming a part of the modern Khuzistan; the seat of the Elamites mentioned as present at Jerusalem on the day of Pentecost. Here, it would seem, he went through the inferior orders, and especially distinguished himself by his sermons; but, in process of time, he was raised by S. Gadiabes to the episcopate, and became Bishop of Susa. *he becomes bishop of Susa:* Here, however, he was ill-received, and worse treated; and at length left the city, after denouncing GOD'S extreme vengeance on its impiety. Only three months had elapsed, when a conspiracy having been formed in it against Sapor, that monarch dispatched a sufficient military force, with a body of three hundred elephants, against the rebels; and Susa was laid in ruins. Hence, carrying nothing with him but a copy of the New Testament, Milles visited Egypt, *is exiled;* with the especial intention of seeing Ammon, a favourite disciple of S. Antony. Here he remained two years; and, on his return, led for some time an eremetical life, in company with a certain monk, whom he found thus engaged. He next paid a visit to S. James of Nisibis, whom he found *goes to Nisibis;* busy in the erection of the church which is standing at this day; and on his return to Adiabene, sent that holy prelate a considerable weight of silk, as a contribution to defray his expenses. Hence he paid a visit to Ecbatane, then suffering under the tyranny of the Catholicus Papas, to which I have already alluded[1]. In Maisan[2], whither he next bent his steps, he found the petty prince of the country suffering from a severe disease, which, for two years, had made him a prisoner to his house. "Return," said Milles to the messenger, "enter the chamber of thy lord, and proclaim aloud, *his miracles,* 'Thus saith Milles: In the name of JESUS of Nazareth be thou healed, rise, and walk.'" The messenger obeyed; and perfect health followed. Several other miracles of his in the

---

of the same page) were the same as the Husitæ, are really different from the Chusæi.

[1] See Book I. § 95.
[2] Or, as the Latins call it, Mesene. It is now Bosra or Bassora.

same place, are related by the biographer. While thus engaged, Hormisdas Guphrez, governor of the province, and a man of intolerable pride, arrested our prelate, together with Abrosimus a priest, and Sinas a deacon, and sent them to the tribunal at Maheldagdar. Here they were twice scourged, and then imprisoned for some time, till the commencement of the ensuing year. Brought then before Hormisdas, and his brother Narses, who were prepared for a hunt on a grand scale, but wished first to dispose of this, Milles[1] was stabbed by the two brothers, and died, predicting their fate, at the same hour on the following day. The priest and the deacon were stoned. The next day, on the very same spot where S. Milles had breathed his last, Hormisdas and Narses, who had been, by one of the accidents of the chase separated, met in pursuit of the stag, galloping furiously in different directions, and pierced each other mortally. The bodies of the three martyrs were buried in a hill-fort named Malcan—thenceforth, it was observed, secure from the attacks of the Sabæans.

his arrest,

and death, Nov. 5, 341.

Fate of his persecutors.

Martyrdom of S. Shahdust, B. of Seleucia;

37. The place of S. Symeon Bar-saboe was filled by his nephew Shahdust[2]. Born at Beth-garma, he was sent by his uncle to Nicæa, to represent him in the synod; and now succeeded in the episcopate, after a vacancy of three months. It is said that he beheld his predecessor in a vision, who

---

[1] See Sozomen, H. E. II. 14. S. Miles, or, as he is there called, Milles, is celebrated in the Roman Martyrology on April 22; in the Menæa on Nov. 10, but not as the principal saint, with this Stichos:
Μίλος ὁ ἐπίσκοπος σὺν μύσταις δύω
τριπλοῦν ἔλαβε τὸν θρόνον ἐν τῷ πόλῳ.

[2] A. A. S. M. pp. 84—92. It is the same whom Le Quien calls Sadost: (O. C. II. 1108). He is commemorated in the Menæa on Oct. 19, with this Stichos:
Σαδὼθ ὁ θεῖος τὴν κάραν τμηθεὶς ξίφει
Θεοῦ Σαβαὼθ νῦν παρίσταται θρόνῳ
Δεκὰς δεκαπλῇ μαρτύρων συμμαρτύρων
καὶ δὶς δέκα θνήσκουσι πληγέντες ξίφει.

But by some mistake the same martyr is again commemorated under the name of *Sadoc*, on Feb. 20. When we remember the developments of recent Ultramontanism, and more especially some authorized Franciscan devotions in connection with the Portiuncula, it is singular to read in Assemani the following: "Præterea nec ab hæresi quam S. Sciahdusto impingit ipse purgatur, quum eundem S. Martyrem exhibeat de se dicentem, *Quicunque Deum in nomine meo invocaverit. salutem inveniet:* in solo namque J. C. nomine invocari posse Deum, et salutem invenire, docet ex Evangeliis Catholica Ecclesia."

informed him that his own martyrdom was at hand, and exhorted him to play the man for the name of Christ. With 128 companions he was arrested and imprisoned for five months, besides being more than once during that period horribly tortured. At length, condemned to be beheaded, they were led, heavily fettered, to the place of punishment; and there gave up their souls to GOD, while singing the 43rd Psalm. The scene of their triumph was Beth-Lapeth, or Ahwaz.

38. About the same time, an abbat of eminent piety, named Barsabias[1], resident somewhere near Istakhr, the town which sprang up from the ruins of the ancient Persepolis, was accused, with ten of his monks, to the governor of that town. After suffering divers torments, they were condemned to lose their heads; and, while the bloody tragedy was acting, a magi, with his wife, happened to pass. Struck by the calmness and courage with which the abbat, himself reserved to be the last victim, animated the rest; and seeing, as he affirmed, a cross of light that shone over the bodies of each of the martyrs, the traveller professed himself a Christian on the spot, and suffered with the others. *of S. Barsabias, abbat:*

39. At Shaharcadata, a city in the province of Bethgarma, the bishop, Narses[2], and a disciple, Joseph, were arrested, and carried before the king. He was at the moment in a caravanseray called Septa; and, after a few questions, ordered them to capital punishment: a vast number of people witnessed the unconquered courage of their deaths. Two bishops in the territory of Beth-Seleucia sealed the faith with their blood; John, slain at Beth-Haserta, by command of the ruler of Adiabene; Sapor, who sank under the miseries of a dungeon. Another bishop, Isaac, was put to death at a caravanseray, which took its name from Seleucus Nicator. In the same territory, at Hulsar, Isaac, a priest, was stoned; *of S. Narses, B. of Shaharcadata; of SS. John and Sapor, bishops,*

---

[1] A. A. S. M. I. pp. 92—96.
[2] A. A. S. M. I. pp. 96—102. Inaccurate accounts are given by Sozomen, H. E. II. 13, and in the Menæa, Nov. 20. Still, thanks to the labours of Stephen Evodius, my own pages contain the fullest account that ecclesiastical histories have yet given of these glorious athletes of JESUS CHRIST.

and others. Papa, pastor of a village called Helmin, was slain at Galul; Uhanam, a young clerk, was stoned by matrons, calling themselves Christians, compelled by threats of the most fearful tortures, if they refused to play the part of executioners; Guhshatazades, an eunuch in the service of the governor of Adiabene, was killed by an apostate priest—his name Vartranes. The little town of Lashuma sent four laymen to the noble army of martyrs: Sasannes, Mares, Timæus, and Zaron. Near this place a noble matron, by name Bahutha, and six virgins, Tatona, Mama, Mazachia, Anna, Thecla, and Danacha, received the same crown; the four former outside a little town called Burcatha, or by others Hevara. A fig-tree sprang up on the scene of their triumph, the fruit of which was held to be possessed of supernatural medical efficacy. Many years afterwards, a Manichæan, envious of the glory of the martyrs, rooted it up. He was immediately seized with a particular species of plague—called by the Persians the lion's breath—from which many of that sect died. Sapor, about the same time as the last-mentioned martyrdom, happening to pass through the province of Beth-Garma, put to death three other virgins—Abiatha, Hathes, and Mamlacha[1].

Fifth year of the persecution: an innumerable host of martyrs.
40. So came on the fifth year of the persecution. Does the recital of so many names, and a story so little varied by any striking features, weary my reader? Besides the feeling that those names which have been so gloriously enrolled in the book of life ought also to be precious on earth for ever, I would have him bear in mind that in no English work has any account of these saints hitherto appeared; that the brief annals of the Saporean persecution given even by such writers as Baronius, Fleury, Tillemont, and Ruinart, are necessarily very imperfect, and equally incorrect, taken as they are from the Greek Acts, instead of the authentic Syriac. The proceedings in the case of the most illustrious among them are related, in most cases, with more or less accuracy; but the very names of any but the brightest stars in

---

[1] This virgin martyr is in the Roman Martyrology on Oct. 17, under the name of Mamelta, and under that of Mamelcht in the Menæa on Oct. 5.

this constellation of saints would be looked for in vain in any, even the largest, Church History.

41. We have seen how many of the martyrs were natives of Adiabene. It would seem that, at this time, the greater number of the inhabitants of that country were Christians. In the first century, Helena[1], then Queen of that province, gave her name to CHRIST, and her son Izates, with most of his successors, had held the same faith. Hence the worship of the true GOD had taken deep root in that part of Persia. Daniel, a priest, and Uarda, or as the name might be more properly translated, Rose[2], a consecrated virgin, after suffering the worst of torments during three months—their feet having been bored with sharp irons—were kept in freezing water for five days, and then beheaded. From the same province one hundred and twenty Christians, nine of whom were consecrated virgins, the rest ecclesiastics of different ranks, were cast into prison in a filthy dungeon at Seleucia. Here they received such comfort and assistance as the times allowed from one Jardundocta[3], a noble Christian matron, a native of Arbela. Nor was she less earnest in exhorting the weaker among them to constancy, than she had been in supplying their bodily necessities; and, on the morning which admitted them into glory, she commended herself to their prayers, made preparation for their honourable interment, and was privileged to see them victorious.

Adiabene a Christian province.

A.D. 344, Feb. 21.

Courage of Jardundocta.

42. In the sixth year of the persecution, Barbasimen[4], a nephew of S. Simeon Barsaboc, and who had succeeded his cousin Sciahdust in the see of Ctesiphon and Seleucia, was delated to Sapor. Sixteen of his clergy, priests or deacons, or of inferior orders, were arrested with their prelate. For eleven months they were kept in the strictest confinement; and then removed to Ledan, near Ahwaz, the place which I have before mentioned. I still notice, in the examination of these martyrs, the same overbearing forwardness which I have lamented, either in S. Simeon himself,

A.D. 345, April 21. S. Barbasimen, B. of Seleucia, Martyr.

---

[1] Baron. Annal. 44, LXVI.; Sozomen, H. E. II. 12.
[2] A. A. S. M. I. 103.
[3] A. A. S. M. I. 106.
[4] Le Quien, II. 1109; A. A. S. M. I. pp. 110—117.

or (which I had rather believe) in his biographer, S. Maruthas. Their death followed as a matter of course; and the see of Seleucia and Ctesiphon was vacant for twenty years.

43. A fresh edict against the Christians accompanied, or followed, this martyrdom. A vast number fell throughout the various provinces; but their names had been lost, even as early as the time of our annalist; only then to be known when they that have lost their life for HIM shall keep it unto life eternal! A curious fact is elicited by the next martyrdom of which we have a detailed account. There was one James[1], parish priest at the hill of Sciahla, who resided there with his sister Mary, a "daughter of the covenant." These were arrested by Narses Tamsapor, a violent persecutor apparently, and by him commanded to feed on some preparation of blood. This was, as yet, forbidden by the whole Catholic Church, as it is to our own day in the East; and rather than violate a ceremonial canon, the brother and sister submitted their necks to the axe. Their execution was entrusted to one Mahdades, an apostate noble, who beheaded them with his own hand at the hill of Dara by the Euphrates.

44. At this time, one Paul was parish priest at the little town of Casciaz. (It is impossible to avoid the conclusion that, at the commencement of the persecution, this part of Persia, the modern Kurdistan, Khuzistan, and Louristan, must have been almost entirely Christianized—the bishops so numerous; the priests apparently stationed in every village of importance; the consecrated virgins so numerous. So far as can be judged from the light thus obtained, I cannot imagine that Adiabene, the Elymæi, and Susiana, were a whit behind Lydia or Cappadocia in the open profession of the faith.) This man was rich; and, on account of his wealth, was accused to Narses Tamsapor, of whom I have just spoken. In making their arrangements to catch the priest, the police arrested five "daughters of the covenant;" by name[2], Thecla, Mary, Martha, another Mary, and Anna. The wretched priest—rather, it was thought, for

---

[1] A. A. S. M. I. 122.   [2] A. A. S. M. I. 123.

the purpose of securing his earthly pelf than from any other reason—abjured CHRIST. Tamsapor was much disgusted, having hoped that Paul's money, on its possessor's firmness in his religion, would accrue to himself. In order therefore, if possible, to deter the priest from apostasy, he appointed him the executioner of the consecrated virgins; hoping that a task of such infinite disgrace would induce Paul to retract his abjuration. But Iscariot betrayed the LORD for silver; and Paul stooped even to this unutterable disgrace for lucre. The virgins, from the hand of a lictor, received each one hundred stripes, and were then given over to their late priest to be slain. "And are we," they said, "to be made a sacrifice by those very hands at which so lately we received that Holy Thing, the Sacrifice and Propitiation of the whole world?" But so it was; and the very hands that had consecrated His Body, who is the King of the virgins, now beheaded the virgins of the King. But so great a crime did not, even in this world, go unpunished. Narses was resolved on obtaining the money, which had been the original source of the whole evil; and on that very night his guards, entering the prison, murdered the miserable apostate. A.D. 346, June 6.

45. The persecutions by no means ceased with their deaths; but as no more martyrdoms have been related during the lapse of the next eight years, I shall for the present leave the affairs of Persia, to return but when further events shall call us thither. But during all this time, the war between Sapor and the Romans was being carried on with various vicissitudes of fortune. Nisibis[1], the bulwark of the Roman empire since the days of Lucullus, had in 338 been besieged for sixty, in 346 for eighty, days; but had repulsed with ignominy the Persian arms. Four years after the martyrdoms which I have just recorded, Sapor again formed the siege. This place, now reduced to a population of three hundred families, of which twelve only are Christians (Jacobites without an altar and without a priest), was then in the height of its glory. Surrounded by a triple wall, The three sieges of Nisibis. Present condition of that city;

---

[1] See Gibbon, III. 142; Julian Orat. III.; Spanheim, p. 188; Theodoret, II. 30; Badger, I. 66.

and enclosed by a deep ditch, its fortifications however were of far less value than the skill of its governor, the Count Lucilianus, and the desperate courage of its people—hating, as they did, the Persians with more than border hatred. The attack had continued more than a hundred days, when Sapor resolved on a method of assault which reminds us of the vast resources of those eastern monarchs; their contempt of human suffering, their command of human labour, and their power over the elements themselves.

its third siege, A.D. 350.

48.* At this time an attempt was made to introduce the Faith—or rather to spread the knowledge of Christianity—in Arabia. I have already related the mission of S. Frumentius, and the rich fruits which it produced in Ethiopia; out of emulation, it would seem, the Arians resolved on a mission to the other side of the Red Sea. The Homeritæ[1], settled in the extremity of Arabia the Happy, by the sea shore, called themselves descendants of Abraham by Keturah, and observed the rite of circumcision. A large number of Jews had sought refuge in this country. Constantius despatched a magnificent embassy to its prince, requesting permission to build three churches, at his own expense, in those parts where the Romans were most frequently called by commerce. Two hundred horses of a most valuable breed were sent as a present, and were graciously received. The spiritual interests of the embassy were given in charge to Theophilus, a native of the Isle of Diu, who had been sent in early youth as a hostage to Constantine, and had embraced the monastic life at Constantinople. He had been ordained deacon by Eusebius of Nicomedia; and, having given himself to the Arian party, was by them elevated to the episcopate, and charged with the regulation of ecclesiastical affairs in the East. The mission had considerable success. The prince of the Homeritæ erected three churches at his own expense: one at Aden, one at his capital, Dafur, and one at the mouth of the Persian Gulf. Hence Theophilus visited his native

Mission of Theophilus the Arian

to the Homeritæ.

* [There is here in the MS. a *lacuna* of two sections intended apparently for the completion of the narrative of the siege, and some notice of S. James of Nisibis, who was present at it. Ed.]

[1] Le Quien, II. 663; Baronius 354, XII. &c.; Philostorgius ap. Phot.

island, Diu, twelve hundred years later to be so-famous in Portuguese history for its double siege, and from thence other parts of India. Would that we had fuller accounts of the Christian peoples whom he there found! All we know is, that he corrected some trivial errors: among them, the custom of sitting during the lection of the Gospel. Theophilus then visited Ethiopia, and the preaching of Frumentius; and, returning to Constantinople, was received with great honour by Constantius; he afterwards lived a bishop without a see, in literary ease and luxury, leaving missionary labours to those whose vocation they were.

49. In Armenia the Faith of CHRIST spread and prospered. S. Gregory the Illuminator, armed with the secular as well as with ecclesiastical power, divided his native country into nine bishoprics; giving the territory which bordered on the Euphrates to one Alcinus, the region known by the name of Mesemrius to Euthalius, and appropriating seven other provinces to seven of his most faithful ecclesiastics. But, even in the Illuminator's own time, it was necessary, from the rapidly increasing number of the faithful, to subdivide these dioceses. As old age grew upon him, he resigned the pastoral care to his son[1], S. Rostaces, who seems to have been present at Nicæa, and also governed the Church of Armenia for some short time after his father's death. But boldly rebuking the wicked life of Arsaces, King of Armenia, he obtained, from the vengeance of that monarch, the crown of martyrdom. He was succeeded by Varbanes, who held the see for three years only.

Armenia. Proceedings of S. Gregory the Illuminator.

S. Rostaces, II. Cath. A.D. 335.

A.D. 337.

50. We left the Arian Placillus in the chair of Antioch. Of his deeds there we hear nothing: he held the see twelve years—a time of deep affliction for the Catholic Church. At the very conclusion of his episcopate, or it may even be at the commencement of that of his successor, another Arian[2] council was held at Antioch. In this assembly the Creed was drawn up which has usually gone by the name of *Macrostichus*, the "long-lined," on account of its unwieldy

Arian council of Antioch.

---

[1] Le Quien, I. 1373.
[2] Sozom. H. E. II. 10; Socrat. H. E. II. 15.

prolixity. It was a preeminently "safe" symbol—no doubt considered a happy *Via Media* by the moderate men of the day, and all the expressions were Scriptural. It is not worth transcription from the[1] pages of S. Athanasius or of Socrates: its more salient points were these. The SON was said to be *like* the FATHER; but not a word of essence or substance. It was declared not safe to assert that the SON had been produced from non-essence to existence: but why?—because Scripture nowhere asserted it. The SON is not created so *far forth* as to be like other created things. This document was sent into the West by Eudoxius of Germanicia, Martyrius, and Macedonius of Mopsuestia.

Stephen, Patr. XXIX. of Antioch, A.D. 345,

51. On the death of Placillus, he was succeeded by a more decided partisan of Arius, Stephen by name[2]. He had been a priest in the time of S. Eustathius, and having been suspended for some crime, had endeavoured, but in vain, to induce that saint to restore him to his office. He was the highest in rank of the seventy eastern bishops who

leader at the conciliabule of Philippopolis.

appeared at the Council of Sardica; and was leader in the secession which, fixing its head-quarters at Philippopolis, there became a mere Arian conciliabule and excommunicated S. Julius of Rome, the great Hosius, and other leading prelates at Sardica. My subject does not call me to enter into the history of these synods: I need here only remark that on the conclusion of the Council of Sardica, another Catholic Synod was held at Milan, in which a document was drawn up, addressed to Constantius, and praying him to re-establish S. Athanasius and S. Paul, and to procure the deposition of Stephen. The latter had already, together with seven other chiefs of his party, been excommunicated at Sardica. This address, backed by a recommendation from Constans, Emperor of the West, was sent to Antioch, where Constantius was then temporarily residing, by Vincent, Bishop of Capua, and Euphratas of Cologne. With them, as legate

---

[1] He gives it in his work on the Synods, and it is also copied by Socrates, who assigns a sufficiently forcible reason for its non-reception in the West.

[2] Sozomen, u. s.; Le Quien, II. 711.

from Constans, went Salianus the prætor, a man of tried virtue.

52. Stephen, a man apparently of the most abandoned character, bethought himself of a stratagem to ruin the reputation of these bishops, the desperate nature of which shews the extremity of the danger of him who contrived it. A young man named Onager, from his vile and audacious character, charged himself with the execution of the scheme. Having learned where the house was in which the bishops were to lodge, and having bribed the servants[1], he next made an arrangement with a prostitute of the city, and desired her, at a certain hour, to accompany him to the episcopal lodgings. Concealing a large party of his friends near, at the time appointed he led the unfortunate creature into the house—the doors having been purposely left open by the treachery of the servants, and desired her to go straight forwards, and to enter the room to which she should first come. In that room slept Euphratas of Cologne, the elder of the legates. He, waking in the dark, and hearing a woman's voice, thought it a diabolical illusion, and called on JESUS CHRIST. The woman, for her part, was equally astonished, expecting to find some young and dissolute citizen, when she discovered herself in the chamber of an aged prelate. In the midst of the disturbance, Onager and his ruffians burst in; but finding that the woman, in her terror, had revealed the truth, they made their escape undiscovered. Morning came, the whole city was in an uproar; and the more so since Easter was at hand. The bishops would have been satisfied with an ecclesiastical judgment; but Salianus, if with less charity, perhaps with more common sense, demanded a civil tribunal. The clerks of Stephen, who were implicated in the affair, were put to the torture; but, without enduring it, confessed at once. The mistress of the prostitute (for these poor creatures were almost always slaves) pointed out Onager as the prime mover in the plot, and the whole conspiracy was laid bare. This produced some

Emissaries from Constans at Antioch, A.D. 348.

Abominable stratagem of Stephen;

its discovery.

---

[1] This story is related by S. Athanasius in his epistle Ad Solitarios; by Theodoret, H. E. II. 9; and by S. Nicephorus, H. E. IX. 23.

impression on the mind of Constantius; the banished priests and deacons of Alexandria were recalled, and it was expressly forbidden to persecute those who in that great city held for S. Athanasius.

Stephen is deposed. Leontius, Patr. xxx. of Antioch.

53. Nothing remained to the Arians but to throw up the cause of Stephen, who was accordingly deposed. In his place a Phrygian[1], by name Leontius, a disciple of the martyr S. Lucian, was raised to the see. This man, by the canons of Nicæa, was incapable of consecration. He had, like Origen, made himself an eunuch, but under circumstances far more disgraceful than those of the other well-meant, though mistaken, action. He had seduced a young woman named Eustolium, though he asserted her purity; but, finding that it would be a bar to all his hopes of preferment were there anything suspicious in their relation, and yet unwilling to give her up, he hit on the device I have just mentioned, intending to preserve his character while he yet retained her. For this action he was deposed from the priesthood; but having been of great use to the Arians, they now advanced him to the chair of Antioch. He professed to be a man of moderate views; he endeavoured to persuade the Catholics to accord him their communion, but unsuccessfully. For they still continued to regard Eustathius as their lawful bishop; held their assemblies apart, though not allowed to use any of the city churches; and

The Eustathians hold their assemblies apart.

were generally known by the name of Eustathians. The schism thus commenced lasted, as we shall see, for sixty years; and, however melancholy to relate, is, as will appear, not without corollaries of the greatest importance in Ecclesiastical History.

Commencement of Aetius.

54. Whatever might be the wishes of Leontius for union with the Catholics, he soon lost all chance of attaining his end by ordaining Aetius deacon. To trace the former history of this wretched man by no means falls within my scope; he had long led the life of a charlatan and mountebank; and then, giving himself up to theological enquiries,

---

[1] Theodoret, II. 10; Le Quien, II. 712; Sozomen, H. E. III. 19.

became the most extreme of the Arians. The appearance of this new leader was, though not immediately, yet the virtual dissolution of the heresy: the semi-Arians, shocked at the abyss of impiety which seemed opening before them, began to return to the Catholic Faith; a general split took place; the better among the heretics were received into the fold, the worse became Aetians; and ere very long those who were not Homöusions became Anomæans. But this was not to be yet. *[he is deposed from the diaconate.]*

55. By far the greater part of the priests of Antioch had joined the party of Arius; and it would seem that those who remained firm to the Catholic Faith were not men of great talent or high reputation. At least it is certain that the leadership of the Antiochene Catholics was, at this time, in the hands of two laymen—Flavian, of whom we shall hear more, and Diodorus[1]; the latter, a disciple of S. Sylvanus of Tarsus, whom I have already mentioned, and in process of time to be bishop of that place, had studied at Athens, was a man of most ascetic life, and well versed in theology. These two friends assembled the Catholics by the "confessions" of the martyrs, and did their utmost to keep all firm to the Faith of Nicæa. Leontius dared not, from the great number of Catholic laymen, forbid their assemblies, though he ceased not to bewail in his soft, unreal way, the separation of so large a portion of his beloved flock on a mere hair-splitting question of words. The Arians affirmed that to these laymen was the Doxology, as it is now used, due; and say that till then it had been,—"Glory to the FATHER in the SON and the HOLY GHOST," or "*in* the SON *by* the HOLY GHOST." But it is far more probable that the latter was an Arian innovation, and the first the original use of the Church. Of Leontius it was observed, that all that could be heard of his own *Gloria* was: "Now and ever and to ages of ages." There are some who affirm that the present alternate method of chanting is due to Flavian; taught by him to Antioch, and from Antioch spread over the whole *[Flavian and Diodorus, leaders of the Catholics. Change in the Doxology.]*

[1] Philostorgius, II. 13; Theodoret, H. E. II. 24.

Church. Others attribute it to S. Ignatius the Apostolic, derived by him from inspiration. But, in all probability, it was not the alternate verse and response that came[1] from Antioch, whether the invention of these or of apostolic times; but rather the original use of the so-called Antiphon, a clause intercalated between each two verses of every Psalm.

56. Shortly after the appointment of Leontius to the vacant throne of Antioch, Gregory, the intruded prelate at Alexandria, was called to his account, having been murdered by his flock. On this, Constantius, having no longer any excuse for the prolongation of the banishment of S. Athanasius, and threatened by his brother with civil war had the exile continued, gave him permission to return. I have related the events connected with this triumph of the Catholic Faith, in my History of Alexandria. The great Confessor, in obedience to the Emperor's decree, took the way of Antioch[2], where he was received by Constantius with great apparent civility. In that city he carefully abstained from the communion of Leontius, while he communicated constantly with the Eustathians, in their private places of assembly. Constantius took occasion to request from Athanasius the grant of one church in Alexandria for the Arians: "Willingly," replied the Patriarch, "if Leontius will allow one here to be the property of the Eustathians." The concordat was declined by the leaders of the heretical party. "We," said they, "can hope for no great success in Egypt while Athanasius lives; whereas to give his followers a standing-point here were to increase their influence, already threatening our own." Leontius, who occasionally communicated with the partisans of Flavian and Diodorus, was aware that his courtesy to them was the best safeguard of his own flock. "When this snow shall have melted"—it was his wont to say—"we shall have abundance of mud."

---

[1] See the very able preface of Cardinal Thomasius to his edition of the Psalter, in the 2nd volume of his collected works.

[2] See the whole history of these proceedings, told with much spirit in the 2nd Apology.

57. S. Athanasius took his way to Alexandria by Jerusalem. Here Maximus[1] welcomed the illustrious exile; and summoned a council to ratify his return. All the bishops of Palestine were there; and, with the exception of those noted ringleaders of the party, Acacius of Cæsarea and Paleophilus of Beth-shan, all received him with outward courtesy at least, many probably with real joy. Those who had written against him excused themselves as having done so under compulsion, and requested him to accept their apology. The Synod addressed an epistle to all their brethren in Africa and Egypt, more especially the presbyters and deacons at Alexandria; in which the fathers expressed their thankfulness for the restoration of Athanasius, and recommended him very heartily to the love and the duty of his flock. It is signed[2] by Maximus of Jerusalem, Aetius[3] of Eleutheropolis, S. Arius, otherwise Macarius[4], of Petra, Theodorus, of an uncertain see, Germanus[5], probably of Neapolis, Silvanus[6] of Ashdod, Paulus and Patricius of uncertain sees; Elpidius and Germanus, of whom the same must be said; Eusebius[7] of Gadara, Zenobius of an uncertain see, Peter[8] of Jamnia, and another Paulus, Macrinus, and Claudius, of whom nothing is known.

He is welcomed at Jerusalem by S. Maximus.

Council of Jerusalem, A.D. 349.

58. It was probably this open sympathy with Athana-

---

[1] Apolog.—Ad Solitar.—Socrat. H. E. II. 24.

[2] These names are given by S. Athanasius himself in his Apology: the sees, so far as I give them, I have collected with much trouble from incidental notices: they are specified in none of the usual histories.

[3] He is mentioned by S. Epiphanius, Hæres. 40: as the detector of the heretic Eutactus, the leader of the so-called Archontæi, a branch of the Gnostics.

[4] Perhaps the name Macarius was assumed when the original appellation of this bishop had become so ill-sounding to Catholic ears. He is mentioned several times in the 2nd Apolog. and is in the Roman Martyrolog. for June 20, where we learn that he suffered much from the Arians and died in Africa, whither he had been exiled by them. I do not find his name in the Menæa.

[5] If the Germanus who signs in this council were Bishop of Neapolis, we find him at Ancyra in A.D. 314, Neocæsarea in the same year, and Nicæa. Le Quien, III. 647.

[6] He also had been at Nicæa. Le Quien, III. 659.

[7] Le Quien, II. 597.

[8] This prelate also was at Nicæa. All who sign the Council of Jerusalem here, had signed at Sardica also, with the single exception of Macrinus.

sius that induced Acacius and Patrophilus to procure—by what artifice we know not—the deposition of Maximus[1]. This prelate, who, could we forget his fall at Tyre, would deserve to be reckoned a worthy occupant of the see of S. Ignatius, appears to have died shortly after his removal. The death of Constans, and consequent freedom of Constantius to declare himself more openly, probably emboldened these wicked men to take the necessary steps, as they also gave rise to the general persecution which broke out over the whole Church, exiled Athanasius anew, and sent S. Paul of Constantinople to glory. The character of Maximus himself I can hardly sum up better than in the words of Touttée: "If any one is willing to believe that this prelate was free from the common error of his brethren at Tyre,—that forsaking Athanasius in his exile, for which they together apologized on his return, I shall not hinder him. Yet it must be remembered that he had been present at the Synod of Jerusalem in the same year as that of Tyre, in which Arius and his followers were received to communion without penitence. Whether he opposed himself to such a breach of all ecclesiastical law, is uncertain; Sozomen affirms that Marcellus of Ancyra was the only bishop who refused to be present. Again, he was one of those who condemned that bishop, both at Jerusalem and in Constantinople. He is said by Sozomen to have abstained from assisting at the great Antiochene Council of 341, through sorrow at the manner in which he had been cajoled so as to condemn Athanasius. Yet he gave no public adhesion to that Confessor till his return to Palestine." On the whole, it is not a very bright character, and Maximus disappears from my pages without any great sorrow on my part.

59. The Arians could find no one whom they thought more likely to meet their views, and to assist their party, than the priest Cyril[2]—afterwards to gain a worthier name

---

[1] S. Maximus is reckoned by the Western Church among the saints. His name is not in the Menæa.

[2] Here, once for all, let me acknowledge my great obligations to the life of S. Cyril, prefixed to the edition of his works by Touttée, with the Dissertations at the end of the Biography.

in the Church. Raised to the priesthood about the year 345 by S. Maximus, he had by him been put in charge of the catechetical classes; a work in which he greatly distinguished himself. He was consecrated[1] by Acacius of Cæsarea, whose see still held metropolitical rank in the province. It is not surprising that S. Cyril's biographers have endeavoured to slur over the unhappy way in which he reached the episcopate; at the same time if we suppose[2] him inclined to semi-Arian views, we need not wonder that, as the future developed itself, he should gradually have been led back to the true faith. There was a report that Maximus on his death-bed—for by some the story of his exauctoration seems to have been held a fable—had designed one Heraclius as his successor; and that Cyril, by fraud, procured the nullification of that appointment. There seems, however, no real ground to imagine any fraud in the transaction; and if Cyril opposed a nomination which was contrary to the discipline of the Church, he surely deserves praise, rather than blame, for his zeal.

60. His promotion was[3] yet of recent occurrence when

Touttée was one, and not the least brilliant, of the constellations of S. Maur. The "Death of the Predestinate" carried him off at the age of 41: or he would probably have left a name to be ranked with the Le Quiens and Renaudots. I am also indebted to the biography of S. Cyril by Constantine Cartogorius, pp. 216—266 of the 2nd volume of his Philological History.

[1] Touttée does not profess (p. xviii.) to settle the question whether S. Maximus were deposed or not. S. Jerome says that he was removed by death: Socrates and Sozomen agree in his deposition. Later writers of course simply copy from one authority or the other.

[2] Touttée naturally endeavours to make his hero blameless. But in truth, we must be content to believe that S. Cyril, at the time of his accession, was a good specimen of the better sort of semi-Arian.

[3] The history of this apparition is given in the saint's letter to Constantius. It is also mentioned by these writers: S. Jerome in his Chronicles—of which, however, I say with Touttée, *quam tamen auctoritatem non usquequaque certam libenter agnosco;* Philostorgius, who, as an Arian witness, deserves great weight, Socrates (H. E. II. 28), Sozomen (H. E. 4, 5), and the Chronicon Alex. Of these, Sozomen mentions S. Cyril's letter, and that fact is enough to silence reasonable scepticism. Gibbon's account is amusing enough: " Cyril immediately"—that is after the battle of Mursa, as if the two events had any connection—"composed the description of a celestial

a remarkable phenomenon occurred, which the saint shall describe in his own words. He is addressing the emperor Constantius, to whom he wrote a letter on the apparition. "In these holy days of Holy Pentecost," *i.e.* the period between Easter and Whitsunday,—"on the 7th of May, about the third hour, a huge cross, fabricated of light, appeared in the sky over holy Golgotha, and stretched to the Mount of Olives; not seen by one or two persons only, but most evidently manifest to the whole population of the city. Nor, as we might have thought, did it pass away swiftly after the manner of a phantasm, but was seen, visibly to the eye, for many hours above the earth; while the blaze that glittered forth from it was brighter than the solar rays......So that the whole city forthwith ran in crowds to the holy church, struck at one and the same time both with terror at the divine vision and with gladness: youths and elders, men and women, all ages, even girls dwelling in the retreat of their own apartments; citizens and foreigners, Christians and Gentiles who had come together from different regions." This marvellous apparition has, of course, been called in question by Protestant writers; but after all, the only question seems to be, whether the epistle which records it be Cyril's or not. It is ascribed to him by writers almost contemporary; it bears every evidence of his style[1]; and the only possible circumstance which might seem to render its authenticity doubtful is the ascription of praise to the consubstantial Trinity with which it concludes. At the same time, were we to grant that Cyril had not yet given in his adhesion to the Homöusion, nothing is more likely than that some zealous

Miraculous appearance of the cross, May 7, A.D. 351.

cross, encircled with a splendid rainbow." This rainbow is the infidel's own invention, that he may presently be able to suggest "some particular appearance of a solar halo." The apparition is kept in the Menæa, as the principal celebration of the day, with a canon by S. John Damascene,—not first-rate. The stichos is:

σταυροῦ παγέντος, ἡγιάσθη γῇ πάλαι·
καὶ νῦν φανέντος, ἡγιάσθη καὶ πόλος.

[1] Especially in the Cyrillian pet-word, ἐνεργεία· in the phrase, as applied to our LORD, οἰκείοις τιμίοις αἵμασι; and in the particular kind of parenthesis, impossible to be described but so well-known to the students of S. Cyril. See Touttée, Prologium, p. 346, VII.

copyist inserted the whole passage in which it occurs; a passage which hangs but loosely on the general narrative, and might be removed from it without casting any slur on the authenticity of the letter itself. The arguments in favour of the miracle will, however, find their best place in a note.

61. While the Arian and Catholic parties were striving throughout the world for the mastery and the fate of the Church hung, to all eyes save to those of the LORD of the Church, in the balance, Cyril was governing the flock committed to him, and composing those works which have made his name immortal. One glance at the stormy annals of the period, and we will again return to Jerusalem. The murder of Constans, that great supporter of the Catholic cause, the deposition of Vetranion, and the decisive victory obtained over Magnentius in the battle of Mursa, left Constantius at liberty to give the rein to his Arian predilections. Now followed the Council of Sirmium; the accession of Liberius to the see of Rome; the Synod of Arles; the renewed banishment of S. Athanasius; the increased violence of the persecution; the exile of Liberius, S. Hilary, S. Eusebius of Verceil, and S. Lucifer; while, to add to the miseries of the Church, Julian the Apostate became Cæsar. Then came the fall of Hosius; who thus, from one of the most illustrious of saints, became one of the most miserable among penitents; and that of Liberius, which entailed the loss of the maiden-purity of the see of Rome. Yet, as if to cheer the Church in the hour of her deepest sorrow, S. Gregory of Nazianzum and S. Basil first appeared on the scene; while S. Hilarion, whose miracles in Palestine we have heretofore seen, now passed over into Egypt, to console the Catholics there, lamenting at once the exile of S. Athanasius and the death of Antony.

Glance at the progress of Arianism.

62. In such miserable times it was that our Cyril took the helm of the Church of Jerusalem into his hands. Of his episcopate there we have singularly few memorials: one accredited reference is made by S. Basil to the multitude of pious persons in Jerusalem when he visited the Holy City in A.D. 357; while the liberality which the prelate

A.D. 351.

displayed in a great famine to the poor, for whose benefit he even sold the plate of his church, was afterwards turned into a charge against him. But he had not long been raised to the episcopal dignity before he was involved with Acacius of Cæsarea in a sharp contest regarding metropolitical rights. We are not to imagine, in the obscurity which has settled down over the controversy, that Cyril arrogated to himself the rights of a metropolitan over the province of Palestine. No document which remains gives the least hint of such an ambitious step. Jerusalem was indeed, in process of time, to acquire far greater dignity than even this; but that time was not yet ripe. It would seem that the bishop merely stood out for those privileges which the seventh canon of Nicæa had somewhat vaguely conferred upon it. Acacius, a professed Arian, was not likely to hold the canons of Nicæa in any great respect; and perhaps it was his having to substantiate their authority on one point, which rendered Cyril more amenable than he had been at his accession to their decisions on all. It would seem most probable that an autocephalous prelature was all that the Bishop of Jerusalem claimed; and certainly, if the canon of Nicæa implies anything, it cannot well involve less than this.

63. It seems, however, that not only on this ground, but on a charge of heresy it was that Acacius founded his attack on Cyril. *What* charge of heresy is not clear; but probably that of holding the Consubstantiality of the SON of GOD. For two years the metropolitan summoned the bishop to appear before his tribunal; a summons of which Cyril took no notice. During these years he appears to have attended the Council of Melitine in Armenia. The obscurity which has settled down over that Synod allows us to make out that it was the scene of a struggle between Arians and semi-Arians, in which the former triumphed; that Cyril allied himself with the latter, and thereby probably increased the odium under which he laboured from the heretical party. Eustathius of Sebaste, a Homöusian, was deposed; but by the influence of S. Basil maintained him-

Circ. A.D. 355.

self at his post. Shortly afterwards, Acacius of Cæsarea summoned a council of the bishops of his province. There were present—that old heretic, Paleophilus of Beth-shan, Eusebius of Sebaste, a semi-Arian, Eutychius, who had succeeded Aetius at Eleutheropolis, a semi-Arian, but afterwards to become a Catholic, Peter of Hippus, and Charisius, who had succeeded Silvanus at Ashdod. It has been thought by some that these were all the prelates who were present: whether this be so or not, it was at all events a very small Council. The charges against Cyril were those of insubordination, heresy, and the having parted with the church ornaments, as said before, to relieve the poor in famine; and on them he was deposed. Appealing to a larger Council, Cyril, who was obliged to leave Jerusalem, went to Antioch, which he found without a prelate,—Leontius being just dead. On this he continued his journey to Tarsus, where he was most hospitably received by the Bishop Sylvanus, and became a popular preacher among his flock. Acacius wrote to remonstrate, but to no effect.

64. S. Cyril's visit to Antioch may be a reason for our turning thither. On the death of Leontius, Eudoxius of Germanicia, an Arian, was, by the intervention of the eunuchs of the palace, raised to the vacant see. He was at the time in Europe; and it would seem his elevation was effected without the voices of those prelates who had a right to be consulted; and of whom George of Laodicea and Mark of Arethusa are especially mentioned. He also was a disciple of S. Lucian, and most assuredly, as we find one after another of the pupils of that martyr fallen into heresy, we cannot but think that, though himself Catholic in intention, there must have been something heterodox in his method of teaching, if not in his doctrine itself. Eudoxius was born at Arabissus in Lesser Armenia: his father being, originally, a man of profligate life, but afterwards—at least if we may trust the Arian Philostorgius—a martyr. His own heresy had been so early declared, that S. Eustathius had refused to admit him into the ranks of the priesthood. We have already seen him present at the

great Council of A.D. 341, in the character of Bishop of Germanicia. Afterwards we find him charged with the commission of being the bearer of the Macrostichus to Constans in the West. There we find him in the Councils of Philippopolis Sirmium and Milan. Shortly after the latter synod he returned to the chair of Antioch.

65. Thus pure Arianism seemed triumphant in the city where the disciples were first called Christians. But still the Eustathians maintained their separate assemblies; and now also the semi-Arians, indignant at the ultra tenets of Eudoxius, began to separate themselves also from his communion. Aetius, who had fled into Egypt when deposed from the diaconate, returned, and was well received by Eudoxius. The bishop was a complete voluptuary in his habits of life; and Aetius was everywhere invited as his parasite. Outrunning as he did the general belief of Antioch, Eudoxius thought it well to summon a Council, which he did as soon as possible after his accession. Very few attended it, and those few only the purest Arians, such as Acacius of Cæsarea and Uranius of Tyre. Here the *Homöusion* and the *Homoiousion* were equally condemned, but not even so was Aetius re-established in the diaconate.

A.D. 354. 66. We now return to Persia, where the persecution was still raging. There was, in the city of Arbela, a deacon, by name Barhadbesciabas, who had distinguished himself by his zeal in encouraging and comforting the confessors. Arrested by the especial command of Sapor, he was most cruelly tortured in the presence of the king. In the midst of his sufferings, Sapor tempted him with offers of life and honour, on condition of worshipping fire and water. These having been rejected, the brave deacon was remanded to prison, under sentence of death. According to the infernal practice of Persian vengeance, the execution of that sentence was committed to Ughæus, a Christian layman of good reputation, a native of Tahal, now himself thrown into prison for having refused to adore the sun. This man, though retaining the name of a believer, was not proof against the threats of immediate death; and having in vain endeavoured to be-head Barhadbesciabas, he transfixed him at length with a sword. The apostate, it is said, met with a frightful punishment. The arm with which he had struck the fatal blow swelled to so enormous a size, as to compel him to a reclining posture; and, at length mortifying, ended his miserable existence.

67. The operations of Sapor against his Roman rival now claim our attention. A languid border warfare was succeeded by a negotiation between—on the part of the Persian monarch, his satrap Tamsapor, on that of the Emperor, Musonianus, prætorian prefect, and Cassianus, governor of Mesopotamia. An arrogant letter, which Ammian has preserved, having been despatched by the Brother of the Sun and Moon—so the King was termed in it—to Constantius, Sapor declared himself ready, instead of asserting his undoubted rights to the possession of all the territory that lay east of the river Strymon in Macedonia, to content himself with the surrender of Armenia and Mesopotamia; and, these provinces having been ceded to him, he was, he said, willing to settle the conditions of an equitable and lasting peace. Constantius returned an answer which, unless the historian falters, does credit to his temper. It was his great desire to conclude a durable peace with Persia, but the terms now proposed could hardly have been different were the Roman legions annihilated by the arms of Sapor. True the eagles had known occasional defeats; but, it must ever be remembered, the general conclusion of each war had been favourable to the Cæsar. Three ambassadors should at once be despatched into the East: might their efforts be successful in the establishment of a cordial understanding between the two great nations!

68. Sapor, it is said, was determined in his rejection of reasonable offers by the counsel of Antoninus, a refugee from Rome. The ambassadors—a count, a notary, and a sophist, were sent back unheard; while a second and more honourable embassy was basely detained in captivity and threatened with death. On this, while Sapor with the flower of his troops advanced towards the Tigris, troops were moved

up from all quarters to the support of the legions already defending the Roman Marches; and among these Ammianus Marcellinus held an honourable post, which has thus enabled him to present us with a lively picture of the whole war.

69. From an eminence on this side the Tigris the Roman officers beheld the whole plain of Assyria alive with men, horses, and elephants. The enemy was about to form a bridge over the river; and every night distant flames, in various quarters of the horizon, told the rapine and cruelty of the bands of light infantry. In the main army, Grumbates, king of the Chionites, an aged and illustrious chief, held the place of honour to the right. Sapor himself, conspicuous by the purple, commanded in the center; while the left wing obeyed the orders of the king of the Albanians, those Georgian tribes who more immediately border on the Caspian. "Strike a bold stroke,"—such had been the advice of Antoninus; "do not waste your strength and dally away time in ignoble enterprises; press forward bravely, and Antioch is yours." But though the Roman forces fell back, they so wasted the country that forage for the invading army was not to be found; the fords of the Euphrates were rendered impassable by stakes and calthrops; and an attempt to take the usual route by the bridge of Thapsacus was frustrated by a heavy freshet of the stream. Under these circumstances it was resolved to track the river to its infant stream, and there to cross. Directing his course somewhat to the right, Sapor was informed that two Roman forts, Reman and Busan, lay in his direct route; that a vast amount of treasures were stored in each; and that in one of them, a woman of singular beauty, the wife of one Craugasius of Nisibis, had taken refuge. Summoning these places to surrender, he obtained their instant submission; and having sent for the lady of whom he had heard, he gave her a safe conduct to her husband, hoping, as Ammian suggests, to induce the inhabitants of Nisibis, hitherto so resolute against yielding to his attacks, to take a more favourable view of his character. There were also, the same historian informs us, certain virgins, dedicated to the Christian service, according

to the custom of that religion; these also he treated with all possible courtesy, ordering that they should be conveyed to any spot which might seem best to themselves.

70. Advancing hence, he passed Nisibis without assault, being too well acquainted with its strength to imagine it reducible by a *coup-de-main*. But as he marched under Amida, he resolved to try whether a summons might not terrify it into a surrender. The reply was an arrow which, had it not glanced from the monarch's breast, would have ended his conquests with his life. Such an insult was too great to be overlooked; and on the next morning, Grumbates, advancing at the head of a picked body of his own troops, demanded the instant surrender of the place as the atonement of so sacrilegious a defiance. There was the twang of a balista from the wall; and the only son of Grumbates fell dead on the plain. "The city," said Sapor to the disconsolate father, "shall be the funeral pile and the monument of your dear son."

71. Amida, now known as Diarbekir, and sometimes as Kara-Amid, *Black* Amida, from the colour of its basaltic rocks, stands on the western bank of the Tigris, and was a stronghold of Christianity, being the metropolis of Mesopotamia. Previously to the siege we are acquainted with the name of but one of its prelates, Simeon, who was present at the Council of Nicæa. An artificial bend of the river encircled the place on the East; and seven legions had been lately sent to reinforce the ordinary garrison. The fortifications had been strengthened and increased; and a very large arsenal of military engines here established. Fortunately for history, Ammian himself was one of the officers charged with the defence of this most important place; and his account of the siege is the most spirited piece of writing, in my judgment, which is to be found among the works of Roman historians. Sapor resolved on a general assault. The nations who followed him were thus arrayed. To the east of the city, the spot where the prince had fallen, and opposite to that which is now called the Bâb-Mardeen, were the Chionites, burning to revenge their fallen leader. To the

north, arrayed against the Bâb-ool-Jebel, the Albanians; to the west, by the Bâb-oor-Room, the Segestans, the bravest of the Persian forces, who protected themselves by a line of elephants; to the south, by the Bâb-ool-Jedeed, the Vertæ, who appear to have come from Beloochistan.

72. The besieged fought with the courage of despair: especially two Gallic legions who had followed Magnentius, and had been sent into exile here. The walls echoed with the shout of "Constantius Cæsar!" the advancing forces replied with "Sapor Pyroses!" "Sapor Saansaan!" Balistæ, catapults, and other military engines thundered against each other the whole day; and tardy night alone separated the combatants. While those who had borne a part in the conflict were attending to their wounds or renewing their strength with food or sleep, the Gallic legions, who could not understand fighting behind walls, and who had been terribly in the way all day, made a vigorous sally, from whence, Ammian naïvely says, "they returned with diminished numbers." We may imagine the Christians crowding the great church (one of the largest in Asia, if we may judge from its remaining ruins), and asking the protection of the Almighty on the Roman arms. One cannot, however, but regret to have been left in ignorance of the name of the metropolitan.

* * * * * *

[I leave in all its baldness the abrupt termination of Dr Neale's Manuscript; both because it would require his graphic pen to complete the abridgement of Ammian's narrative as he has commenced it; and because, however interesting, the siege of Amida has really very little bearing on the History of the Patriarchate of Antioch[1]. It may here be mentioned that the Manuscript has reference numbers to notes as far as section 63: but the notes themselves were either never written, or have been lost. The last note (viz. that on p. 142, 1) is numbered in the MS. 85, but the references were continued up to 96. ED.]

---

[1] The story may be read in Ammianus Marcellinus, Lib. XIX. Capp. VI—IX.

THE
PATRIARCHS OF ANTIOCH.

THE
PATRIARCHS OF ANTIOCH.

By CONSTANTIUS,
PATRIARCH OF CONSTANTINOPLE.

---

1. PETER the Apostle first administered the Episcopate of Antioch for eight years, then leaving Euodius as his successor in that office, he departed into Upper Asia to the Jews in the Dispersion, that he might deliver the doctrine of the Gospel to them; and since Antioch first received the chief Bishop, surely she should rather have the Primacy, forasmuch as Peter was Bishop there before he was in Rome.

2. EUODIUS, (A.D. 53), in the time of Claudius Cæsar was consecrated Bishop of Antioch, by Peter, for those of the Hebrews who believed; when they who of old had been called Nazarenes and Galileans were first called "Christians" in Antioch. He having presided for fifteen years in all, was adorned with a martyr's crown in the year A.D. 68.

3. IGNATIUS, called also Theophorus, succeeded him, being ordained Bishop for those of the Gentiles who believed;

---

[1] No attempt has been made to check the names and dates of the Patriarchs in this list up to the middle of the fourth century, to which date Dr Neale has carried down his history of the Patriarchate. From that period a few notes have been inserted by the Editor to verify, or, more frequently, to correct the chronology of Constantius by that of Le Quien, which appears to be much more accurate. See more in the Introduction.

he, having tended the Church of Antioch two and thirty years, was commanded by Trajan to be exposed to wild beasts, and sent as prisoner to Rome. Being then brought on his way through Smyrna he wrote divers epistles (of which seven are genuine) confirming the faithful in godliness. When he had now arrived in Rome and heard the roaring of the lions, burning with a desire to suffer, he said, "I am the wheat of Jesus Christ, and I pray that I may be ground by the teeth of the wild beasts, that I may be found a pure loaf." Thus becoming the food of lions, he received the blessed consummation. After a vacancy of some months,

4. HEROS was advanced to this Apostolic Throne, and having guided the Church for twenty-six years departed to the Lord, and was succeeded by

5. CORNELIUS in A.D. 127. He continued Bishop twenty-four years, after whom

6. HEROS II. received the helm in the year 151. He died after an Episcopate of eighteen years, and was succeeded by

7. THEOPHILUS in the year 169. He was descended from the Hebrews, but by constant reading of the holy Scriptures he attained the knowledge of the truth, and became a Christian. He was well read in Greek literature, as is proved by his three books to Autolycus, a learned Gentile and a lover of the truth. Having governed the Church of Antioch piously for twenty years, he departed this life, and was succeeded by

8. MAXIMIANUS, or Maximinus, in the year 188. After four years he died, and was followed by

9. SERAPION in the year 192. On his death, after an Episcopate of 20 years, there succeeded

10. ASCLEPIADES in the year 212 A.D. After eight years he died, and was followed by

11. PHILETUS in A.D. 220. After reigning twelve years he died, and

12. ZEBINUS, or ZENOBIUS, was ordained in A.D. 232. On his death, after eight years, there is raised to the Throne

13. BABYLAS, the holy Martyr, in A.D. 240, who, after an

THE PATRIARCHS OF ANTIOCH. 155

Episcopate of thirteen years, was, on account of his Confession of Christ, crowned with a Divine Crown of Martyrdom under the Emperor Numerian. This athlete was succeeded by

14. FABIUS in A.D. 253; who, after governing for three years, died a martyr's death, and was succeeded by

15. DEMETRIAN in the year 256, on whose death, after seven years,

16. AMPHILOCHIUS, or according to others MACARIUS, was appointed in the year 262. After four years he ended his days, when the throne was invaded by

17. PAUL OF SAMOSATA, the heretic, in the year 267. This accursed one said that there was in the Godhead one Hypostasis or Person, and pretended that the Son of God was One ănd Christ another; whence he professed also in Christ two natures different one from the other, and wholly without communication one with the other. Having been convicted and condemned as a blasphemer by the Synod assembled in Antioch against him, he was deposed and ejected from the Episcopate, after having tyrannised eight years. The followers of his heresy were called Paulians or Samosatians. The Fathers of the above-mentioned Synod, after the fall of Paul, ordained,

18. DOMNUS, A.D. 270. He was adorned with all the virtues that become a Bishop. After three years he departed to the Lord, and

19. TIMÆUS succeeds to the Service of this Church in 273. He died after four years, and his successor was

20. CYRIL, in the year 277. Having presided twenty-two years, he departed this life, and

21. TYRANNION is raised to the Episcopal Office in the year 299. He directed the Church of Antioch nine years, and was then exalted to a Martyr's Crown, when

22. VITALIUS was consecrated in the year 308. He presided six years, and had for his successor

23. PHILOGONIUS, in the year 314; on whose death after nine years,

24. PAULINUS, Bishop of Tyre, according to Eusebius, was advanced in the year 324, but according to Sozomen

ROMANUS; one or the other of whom having ruled about eight months, died and left as his successor

25. EUSTATHIUS the Great, Bishop of Berrhœa (Aleppo) of Syria, whom the first General Council assembled at Nicæa in A.D. 325 confirmed by its universal suffrage. He, being a champion for the truth against Arius and an advocate for godliness, was deposed under false charges by the Pseudo-Synod assembled in Antioch by Eusebius of Nicomedia, and the Arian Bishops of his party, and was sent an exile to Illyria. But when his innocence of the unjust accusation was ascertained, he returned again to his own throne, and was again sent into banishment by Constantius, and a third time by Valens; during which last banishment this thrice blessed man departed this life in a certain city of Thrace; having worthily governed the Church of Antioch in quiet for seven years, and accomplished the remaining years as an object of invective and in exile until A.D. 364, when he died. After the unjust deposition of Eustathius, the following, who were infected with the leprosy of Arius, were elected.

26. PAULINUS of the year 332, tyrannises six months and dies.

27. EULALIUS in the same year, tyrannises five months and dies.

28. EUPHRONIUS, A.D. 333, tyrannises one year and some months and dies.

29. PLACENTIUS, in 334, tyrannises seven years and dies.

30. STEPHANUS, in 341, tyrannises four years and dies.

31. LEONTIUS, in 345, tyrannises five years and dies. In his time the divine Eustathius again occupied the throne, but for a short time; when he was again banished by the Arians. After this invader of the Episcopal Throne of the Church of Antioch another invader intrudes into the Throne after the divine Eustathius,—

32. EUDOXIUS in 350, on whose expulsion[1] the Church of

---

[1] He was deposed by the Council of 160 Bishops, assembled in Tracheia, i.e. Seleuceia of Cilicia, A.D. 359. Socrates II. 39, Sozomen, IV. 22.

Antioch was deprived of a pastor[1]; wherefore those of the party of Arius, thinking him to be of the same opinion with themselves, requested the Emperor Constantius to appoint to the presidency of the Church of Antioch

33. MELETIUS the divine. Therefore being elected he was summoned to Antioch from the Bishopric of Berrhœa in Syria, which he then held. Being thus raised to the Throne, in the year 354[2], he delivered to the multitude both by deed and word the true rule of doctrine concerning the Holy Trinity; for exhibiting three fingers of his hand, and then drawing in two, and leaving the one, he gave utterance to this memorable expression: τρία τὰ νοούμενα, ὡς ἑνὶ δὲ διαλεγόμεθα[3]. On which the followers of Arius, disgusted as having been deceived, falsely accused the man to Constantius as Sabellianising, and he was banished to his own country, Melitene [in Lesser Armenia], when they immediately substituted in his place their sympathiser and advocate

34. EUDOXIUS, A.D. 354[4]. On his deposition and banishment as a voluptuous flatterer and evil-doer, another wild boar is brought in by the Arians for the devastation of the Vineyard of Christ in the person of

35. ANNIAS or AMMIANUS, in the year 357, on whose death another Arian invaded the Throne—

36. EUZÖIUS in the year 360[5]; but in the year 362, when Julian the Apostate had issued a permissive decree for the Bishops who had been banished by Constantius to return to their own sees—advisedly, for this end, that he

---

[1] Le Quien, Oriens Christianus, Tom. II. col. 713, reckons Eudoxius 31st in the succession, and places Anianus between Eudoxius and Meletius, on the authority of Nicephorus and Theophanes. They assign him 4 years; according to Socrates and Sozomen, ll. cc. he was elected by the Council, but never sat.

[2] This date is corrected by the fact that the Council of Antioch, was held in 361.

[3] The words, which defy translation, omitted by Sozomen, Hist. Eccl. IV. 28, are supplied by Theodoret H. E. II. 31.

[4] Eudoxius and Annias are omitted by Le Quien, l. c. col. 713.

[5] Reckoned 34th in the succession by Le Quien, l. c. He had been degraded from the diaconate, together with Arius, by Alexander, Bishop of Alexandria, and is called by Theodoret "a champion of Arian impiety." H. E. II. 31.

might bring the Orthodox Bishops into collision with the Arians by contentious disputations, and so advance the cause of idolatry by such skirmishes—the holy Meletius returned to Antioch, and found the faithful doubly divided; for the Eustathians having, on account of the all-praiseworthy Eustathius, kept aloof from the others from the beginning, assembled by themselves. In like manner the adherents of the holy Meletius, separating themselves from the Arian party, performed their sacred Services apart; so that while the confession of the faith among the godly was indeed one, their disposition towards their Rulers alone separated them. In these circumstances, on Euzöius departing this life, another Arian was substituted; viz.

37. DOROTHEUS, A.D. 370[1]. But before this, the Synod assembled in Alexandria under the great Athanasius (after his return to his own throne under Julian the Apostate), proposed to bring together the Churches as far as possible to a general agreement. So it seemed good that Lucifer of Caralis, the learned Metropolitan of Sardinia, a champion of the Nicene faith, should proceed to Antioch of Syria. He then having arrived at Antioch, and seeing the above-mentioned division of the Orthodox, in order to put an end to the schism, consecrated as Bishop of the Orthodox the leading presbyter of the party of the divine Eustathius—

38. PAULINUS, A.D. 371. He failed however in his object, and widened the breach between the godly. Under the Emperor Valens, the holy Meletius was a third time driven away from his Throne, and condemned to exile in Sebasteia; but during the reign of Gratian, Meletius again returned to Antioch, in the year 373, and found the Church still divided into three: one of which bodies Dorotheus, the Arian, ruled after Euzöius; while the Orthodox were ranged, part under Paulinus, and part under Meletius; but about the year 380, under the law which Gratian and Theodosius the Great

---

[1] Le Quien, O. C. col. 714, reckons him with Meletius and Paulinus under No. 35, and identifies him, on the authority of Philostorgius, with the noted Arian Bishop of Heracleia in Thrace. He is called Theodorus by Sozomen, VI. 57.

published against the heretics, the governor Sapores, who was sent to carry out this law throughout the whole of the East, having come to Antioch, expelled as heretical

39. VITALIUS, in the year 376, who, after the death of the Arian Dorotheus, had been consecrated Bishop of Antioch; but, in order to put an end to the schism, he compelled the two parties, divided under the Orthodox Meletius and Paulinus, to come to terms of unity. But seeing Paulinus opposing himself to this arrangement, and the holy Meletius remaining quiet without opposition, he confirmed the latter in the Bishopric and departed. In the year 381 the holy Meletius was present with the rest at the Second General Council. During its session, Meletius having fallen ill at Constantinople, committed his spirit to the Lord[1] in the year 381, having ruled the Church in Antioch at intervals (owing to the persecutions which he endured) in all twenty-seven years[2]. In this Synod the vote of the majority prevailing, though opposed by the holy Gregory, with others of the wiser part, who judged that Paulinus alone should be recognised as Bishop of Antioch, they consecrated as Bishop—

40. FLAVIAN, the presbyter, in the same year. Paulinus having returned from Rome in 384, whither he had gone two years before, died at Antioch in 389; but before his death, not wishing that Flavian should be recognised, he ordained as Bishop of Antioch, on his own mere motion, one Evagrius, on whose death, two years later, Flavian alone reigned for twenty-two years; having worthily distinguished himself in this;—that having gone to Byzantium, in order to supplicate the Emperor Theodosius, he appeased his wrath against the Antiochines, who had inconsiderately broken the statue of his deceased wife, the pious and charitable Placilla;

---

[1] Meletius is commemorated in the Greek Church on the 12th of February. The stichus is:

Τὰς χεῖρας αἴρων Μελέτιος Κυρίῳ
Ταῖς χερσί σου τίθημι τὴν ψυχήν,
λέγει.
Δωδεκάτῃ Μελέτιος ἔδυ χθόνα πουλυβότειραν.

He was decorated by the encomiums of SS. Chrysostom and Gregory of Nyssa; the former of whom was baptized by him and ordained reader of the Church at Antioch, A.D. 367. Le Quien, O. C. col. 715.

[2] Nicephorus says 25 years. O. Ch. l. c.

on which occasion John Chrysostom, being a presbyter of Antioch, delivered those marvellous discourses on this subject, entitled "the Statues." After the death of Flavian,

41. PORPHYRIUS[1] was raised to the patriarchal Throne in the year 404. He, according to Theodoret[2], left many monuments of his philanthropy. Having occupied the Throne four years, he died, and

42. ALEXANDER[3], the divine, was consecrated in the year 408. His manner of life was in harmony with his priestly office[4]; and by his discipline and philosophy and life of self-denial, and by his fluency of speech and other graces with which he was adorned, he was able to put an end to the long and troublesome schism of the Eustathians and Meletians, and to attach them by agreement to the rest of the body of the Church. He was the first to insert the name of John Chrysostom into the ecclesiastical diptychs, after the blessed death of that holy man. Having adorned the throne for ten years, he departed to the heavenly country, and

43. THEODOTUS was raised to the throne in the year 418[5]. He was named "the pearl of wisdom." By his virtuous conversation and teaching he converted to the true doctrine of godliness all the followers of Apollinarius. Having governed the Church in a godly manner for nine years, he departed to the life that knows no decay, and was succeeded by

44. JOHN, in the year 427[6]. In his time, the third Œcumenical Synod was assembled in Ephesus (A.D. 431) against Nestorius the blasphemer; over which presided the divine Cyril of Alexandria,—who also was the representative of Celestine pope of Rome—and Juvenal of Jerusalem. But this John of Antioch, owing to delays, arrived at Ephesus after the deposition of Nestorius, and being vexed that he had been deposed in his absence, he separated with

---

[1] Reckoned 37th in succession by Le Quien, O. C. II. col. 718.
[2] H. E. Lib. v. cap. 35.
[3] 38th according to Le Quien, l. c. who places his accession in A.D. 413.
[4] Theodoret, loc. cit.
[5] Le Quien, who numbers him 39 (col. 720), makes him succeed to the throne in 421 or 422.
[6] Numbered 40 by Le Quien, col. 721, who dates his accession A.D. 428.

the other bishops of his party from St Cyril and the rest of the Synod, but through the exertions of the Emperor Theodosius the Younger, all were united in harmonious agreement with the exposition of the orthodox faith and the deposition pronounced against the blasphemer Nestorius. On which account the accursed man was banished by the order of the Emperor to the Egyptian oasis, where the divine judgment overtook him. John continued at the helm of the Church for fifteen years, when he died and was succeeded by

45. DOMNUS II. in 443, the nephew of John[1]. He was an upright man, but in that Robber's Council assembled at Ephesus in A.D. 449, when confusion had arisen, from intrigues contrived by Dioscorus patriarch of Alexandria, and violence had been used by the heretical Monophysite bishops, under the impious Dioscorus, the pious orthodox bishops were anathematized; together with whom was the excellent Domnus also, who after a godly pastorate of seven years died and was succeeded by

46. MAXIMUS in the year 450[2]. He came to the fourth General Council, assembled in Chalcedon in the year 451 together with the others, and was present with Juvenal of Jerusalem and the representatives sent by pope Leo III., striving with them against Dioscorus of Alexandria and Eutyches, whom they anathematized and deposed as introducing a dualism of Sons, maintaining that the Godhead is passible, and daring to think and to speak of a confusion in the two natures. Having presided over the Church five years he died and was succeeded by

47. BASIL in the year 456[3]; on whose death after three years,

48. ACACIUS follows in the year 459[4]. On his death after two years,

---

[1] He is reckoned 41st in the succession by Le Quien (col. 721 sqq.), who gives a very different account of him, and makes him succeed his maternal uncle in A.D. 441, for 7 years, when he was deposed for heresy, and returned to Palestine, where he had been a disciple of S. Euthymius.

[2] Le Quien says 449, and numbers him 42nd.

[3] Numbered 43 in Le Quien.

[4] 44 in Le Quien. Evagrius (lib.

49. MARTYRIUS in 461[1]. In his time, when Zeno, the son-in-law of Leo the Great, had been appointed General of the whole East, Peter the Fuller, presbyter of the Church of the Martyr Bassa in Chalcedon, attached himself to him, as sharing his sentiments; and being in Antioch he misbehaved against the patriarch Martyrius, and stirred up against him ten thousand troubles, by which Martyrius being extremely disgusted, resigned saying, "I withdraw from a disorderly clergy, a disobedient laity, and a corrupt Church, reserving to myself the rank of the priesthood;" and the throne was illegally usurped by

50. PETER THE FULLER, in the year 465[2]. This heretic from the first outset of his career exhibited his perverted sentiments concerning the faith; dividing the people of Antioch and introducing into the Tersanctus the words "Who was crucified for us:" but hearing of the sentence of banishment decreed against him by the Emperor Leo, he took to flight, and

51. JULIAN is ordained Bishop of Antioch, in the year 466[3]. But after four years, the same blaspheming Theopaschite resumed the throne a second time by command of Basiliscus, who had usurped the empire.

52. PETER THE FULLER (A.D. 474) who perpetually warring against the true doctrine by the addition to the Tersanctus, filled Antioch with tumult and slaughter, against those who did not receive it; but after one year, when Zeno resumed the kingdom, he deposed the Fuller by the decree of the Eastern Synod, in consequence of his having abetted Basiliscus in the matter of the Empire, and banished him to Pitsunda; and the heretic

53. JOHN II., surnamed Codonatus[4], ascends the throne in the year 475: but the Fuller, the author of disturbances,

---

II. cap. 12) records the destruction of Antioch by an earthquake during his occupation of the See.

[1] According to Le Quien (who reckons him 45th Bishop) in 460.

[2] Le Quien (col. 424) dates the first invasion of the throne by Peter,

A.D. 468, on the authority of Theophanes. He reckons him 46th, and 48th in succession.

[3] Le Quien says A.D. 471, and assigns him 6 years.

[4] 49 in Le Quien. He sat only 3 months. He had been appointed

craftily plotting again a third time invades the throne, by the permission of the Emperor Zeno, after the deposition of John in 477. Coming to Antioch, he again did much evil, such as the expulsion of irreproachable bishops, and the introduction of others, illegal ordinations, and such like, until by the judgment of the longsuffering God he was brought down to the tortures of Hades. After him,

54. STEPHEN II. the Pious[1], becomes bishop in the year 490; on his death after three years

55. STEPHEN III.[2] is raised to the throne in the year 493. He was slain by the heretics with sharp arrows after two years, as he was performing the liturgy at the altar[3], and is succeeded by

56. CALLANDION the heretic in 495[4]. On his deposition and banishment, the throne is occupied a second time by

57. JOHN CODONATUS, in the year 495. On his death, by

58. PALLADIUS, in the year 497[5]; he having presided over the see for eight years, dies, and the pastoral office is undertaken by

59. FLAVIAN II. in 505[6]. In the eighth year of his wise and gentle government, through crowds of heresies, the impious Eutychian

60. SEVERUS succeeds[7]. He had been expelled from a monastery lying between Gaza and Majuma, as an heretical blasphemer, and, coming to the Emperor Anastasius Dicorus, who was infected with the same heresy, he was appointed a noble, and by the use of flatteries and false accusations, he advanced so far, that by the command of

---

Bishop of Apameia by Peter the Fuller, but the citizens would not receive him.

[1] Numbered 50 in Le Quien, col. 726.

[2] 51, in Le Quien, col. 727.

[3] John Malalus (ap. Le Quien l. c.) says he was murdered by the clergy of Antioch, as a follower of Nestorius.

[4] Le Quien makes John II. (Codonatus) succeed Stephen III. (No. 52),

and Calandion to follow him (No. 53), in 482. He represents Calandion as orthodox. He held the see 4 years.

[5] No. 55 in Le Quien, col. 729, who dates his appointment A.D. 490.

[6] No. 56 in Le Quien, A.D. 498. He gives him 13 years.

[7] November, A.D. 512, according to Evagrius, as quoted by Le Quien, col. 731, who reckons him 57th in succession.

Dicorus, the keenest enemy of sound doctrine, he banished Flavian from the throne and sent him into exile to Petra, in Arabia, and himself ascended it by violence, being by nature active in mischief and an evildoer; he excited a great tumult in Antioch, shouting out in the churches anathema against the 4th General Council, being himself wholly full of anathema. But as for the orthodox monks and clergy, some of them he loaded with irons, and banished as convicts and malefactors; others he put pitilessly to death, and cast out their bodies to be food to the birds and wild beasts, and others he drowned in the river Orontes, which flows by Antioch, as not holding communion with him. Thus he tyrannised in the most savage manner for five whole years, until 518, when the pious Justinus came to the throne [1]. But Severus having learnt the imperial sentence against him, not merely of banishment, but of the loss of his tongue, as a "scoffer and blasphemer," escaped to Egypt, to those of like sentiments with himself. When he had been thus disposed of, the Warden of the Hostel of Eubulus,

61. PAUL II., is ordained in the year 518 [2]. He resigns after three years, and

62. EUPHRASIUS of Jerusalem was raised to the throne in 521. In the sixth year of his episcopacy, the great and renowned city of Antioch was destroyed by fire and an earthquake, which lasted six days, and its beauty vanished; it became the tomb of 250,000 inhabitants, the church built by Constantine the Great fell, and Euphrasius the bishop was buried in its ruins and died [3]. But the Emperor Justinus, deeply compassionating the calamity, and contemplating the restoration of the ruined city, sent as commissioner, in addition to others, the Count of the East, an excellent man adorned with zeal and learning, and with such heavenly grace of pity, sympathy, and philanthropy towards all the

---

[1] The Emperor Anastasius died July 9th, 517, and was immediately succeeded by Justin. There was, however, some delay in the appointment of a successor to Severus. Le Quien, col. 732.

[2] No. 58 in Le Quien, l. c.

[3] This calamity took place on Friday, the 29th of May, in the seventh year of the Emperor Justinus, A.D. 526, on the morrow of the Festival of the Ascension.

needy, that the people of Antioch, influenced by deep gratitude and desire, with the consent of the emperor, ordained him as their bishop—

63. EPHRAIM, surnamed Amadas, in 526[1]. During his patriarchate, after the death of Justinus, when Justinian the Great was emperor, two years after the first calamity, another earthquake occurred at Antioch in the year 528, the earth being shaken incessantly by the space of an hour, so that the buildings restored by Justinus, and those repaired by the Antiochines, and the very walls of the city were levelled with the ground, and 4870 of the citizens were buried in the ruins of the buildings. At this time flourished in Syria the wonder-working Simon Stylites, who recommended the surviving inhabitants to write on the lintels of their houses the words "Christ is with us—Stand!" and in fact the earthquake ceased. Wherefore, by order of Justinian, the name of the city was changed from Antioch to Theopolis (the City of God), a title well becoming this city, since in it first the Disciples and followers of the Gospel were called Christians. Having adorned the throne for twenty years, Ephraim was exalted to the heavenly mansions, and

64. DOMNUS III. was consecrated in the year 546[2]. He was present in the fifth General Council, assembled by Justinian the Great in Constantinople, in the year 553. Having presided over the Church of Antioch for fifteen years, he migrated to the Lord, and a learned man of the monks of Mount Sinai was advanced to the throne,

65. ANASTASIUS the Sinäite, A.D. 561. In the ninth year of his episcopate, certain of those who rejoice in iniquity, falsely accused him to the then Emperor, Justinus the younger, of malversation of the property of the church and of recklessly wasting it[3]; but the emperor, giving credit to the

---

[1] Le Quien says 527, and reckons him 60th in the succession. Following Nicephorus he assigns him 18 years, and places his death in A.D. 545.

[2] He had been head of an Almshouse near Lychnis, or Lychnidus, in Illyricum. He had come to Constantinople on business, and was presented to the Emperor Justinian, who at his first interview appointed him to the See of Antioch. Le Quien, col. 734.

[3] The real cause of his troubles, as

falsehood, ejects from the throne the godly man, venerated throughout the whole East for his holiness and wisdom, but substitutes for him one not inferior in virtue and knowledge,

66. GREGORY, in the year 571[1]. He having been exercised in monastic discipline from his earliest youth, and rapidly advanced to the highest degrees, had by order of Justinus undertaken the presidency of the monastery of Mount Sinai, and from this was raised to the priestly throne of God's city, Antioch. He excelled in understanding and virtue and obtained wide renown for poetry, as an excellent composer of hymns. Having governed the church for twenty-three years amidst many trials and conflicts, he departed to the heavenly mansions under the Emperor Maurice, and

67. ANASTASIUS the Sinäite again occupies the throne in the year 594[2]. Having again adorned the church by his virtues and doctrine until the year 599, this thrice happy father of the church migrated to heaven, leaving writings full of all kinds of divine grace, when another

68. ANASTASIUS II. succeeds to the throne. He resembled the former, as in name so in monastic discipline, and in vigorous efforts on behalf of the faith. Having governed the church for ten years[3], he was put to death in the market-place, with many others, in the insurrection raised by the

---

narrated by Evagrius and Theophanes, may be seen in Le Quien, col. 735. He reckons him 62, and 64 in the Patriarchal succession.

[1] Reckoned 63rd Bishop by Le Quien, col. 736. This Gregory was known to John Moschus, who says he was conspicuous for his alms, his oblivion of injuries, his tears, and his great compassion towards sinners. Evagrius gives a full account of his troubles and of the false accusations of which he was the victim. Hist. Eccles. lib. v. 18, and vi. 7.

[2] This date is fixed by Evagrius, whose history concludes with the death of Gregory and the restoration of Anastasius, and terminates, as he tells us, in the 12th year of the Emperor Maurice (lib. vi. cap. 24), i.e. A.D. 594.

[3] The annals of the Church of Antioch after the martyrdom of Anastasius II. are conflicting and confused. The authorities cited and followed by Le Quien make a vacancy in the See of from 22 to 31 years, i.e. from A.D. 607 to 638. O. C. II. col. 738.

THE PATRIARCHS OF ANTIOCH. 167

Jews in Antioch, after he had been shamefully mutilated and exposed: after the death of this holy martyr in the cause of Christ,

69. GREGORY II. succeeds in the year 610, on whose death,

70. ANASTASIUS III. follows in 620. After eight years he dies, and

71. MACEDONIUS becomes patriarch in 628[1]. After twelve years' episcopate he migrated to the Lord, and was succeeded by

72. GEORGE in the year 640[2], and on his decease after fifteen years,

73. MACARIUS the Monothelite invaded the throne in the year 656[3]. On the assembling of the sixth General Council under Constantine Pogonatus in 680, Macarius was sent for to Constantinople, where he was ordered by the emperor and the synod to give an exposition of his faith. This he did, but would by no means profess two wills and operations in Christ, "Not even if he was to be cut in pieces and cast into the sea." On his thus remaining immoveable and unchangeable in his heterodoxy, professing one will and operation in Christ, the holy fathers of the Council pronounced against him the deposition and anathema. After his condemnation and banishment,

74. THEOPHANES is ordained in the year 681[4]. Having governed the church for six years he died, and the presidency of the Church of Antioch was assumed by

75. SEBASTIAN or STEPHEN in the year 687[5]. Having

---

[1] Le Quien omits Gregory II. and Anastasius III., and places Athanasius doubtfully next before Macedonius, whose succession he dates, after Eutychius, A.D. 640. He reckons him 67th in the list of Bishops, coll. 739, 740.

[2] Dated A.D. 645 or 646 by Eutychius; but even this would appear to be too early, as Macedonius was still living in A.D. 655. Le Quien, l. c.

coll. 741, 2.

[3] He is numbered 69 by Le Quien, l. c.

[4] 70 in Le Quien, col. 743. He was present at the sixth General Council and subscribed its definitions.

[5] In place of Sebastian, Le Quien substitutes Alexander II. (No. 71), and Thomas (No. 72), but the dates are much confused.

continued in the throne three years, he departed hence, leaving as his successor

76. GEORGE II. of Sebasteia in the year 690[1]. He with the other patriarchs was present, and became a fellow-worker with them in the Canons which were decreed in the General Council assembled under Justinian Rhinotmetus in Constantinople, in the year 692, and in the Trullum of the imperial palace, entitled the Quinosext, which supplied the deficiency of the Canons of the fifth and sixth Councils[1]. Having shepherded the people of Antioch for five years, he departed to the Lord and was succeeded on the throne by

77. ALEXANDER II. in the year 695. He, together with many other Christians slaughtered for Christ, ascended to the heavenly glory, adorned with a martyr's crown, in the seventh year of his patriarchate, in the persecution raised by the Arab Caliph Oumeyeid[2]; on whose martyrdom, as the Mussulman generals forbad an election, the throne of Antioch continued in a state of widowhood forty years, until the year 742, when the governor of Antioch, under the authority of the Caliph Moavia, being much attached to a monk, told the people of Antioch, that if they chose him, they would be permitted to have him as the patriarch of their church, which had already been in widowhood so many years. The Antiochines, therefore, considering this to be of God, ordained him, by name

78. STEPHEN (742), the fourth of that name in the succession of the patriarchs of Antioch[3]. On his death, after six years, the presbyter of Edessa succeeds him—

79. THEOPHYLACT, in the year 748. He being emi-

---

[1] He had been present also in the 6th General Council as representative of the Patriarch of Jerusalem, being then priest-monk of Sebaste. Le Quien, c. 744, who numbers him 73.

[2] Le Quien dates the vacancy in the patriarchal throne from the death of George II., and places Alexander II. before him. (See above, note 5, p. 167.) From A.D. 637 to A.D. 742 the Moslems were in occupation of Antioch: during which time the Patriarchs seldom resided there; and for the last 40 years the succession was suspended.

[3] In Le Quien's list the 3rd of that name. He numbers him 74th in his Catalogue.

nent in sanctity, fell asleep in peace, after fourteen years[1], under Copronymus, and when the Abbasseid Caliphs ruled in Syria; and is succeeded by

80. THEODORE in the year 767[2]. In his time, A.D. 783, the seventh General Council was assembled in Nicæa of Bithynia, for he, with the patriarchs of Alexandria and Jerusalem through fear of the Caliphite Rulers, who then governed that country, acted in the Synod through two presbyter monks, John and Thomas, whom they sent as their representatives. He having performed patriarchal functions twenty years,

81. JOHN IV. was raised to the throne, in the year 797. He it was who, as has been said, was sent with Thomas to the seventh holy Œcumenical Synod as the representative of the entire eastern ecclesiastical Diœcese. On his death, at an advanced age, after thirteen years,

82. JOB succeeded in the year 810[3]; presided sixteen years, and had for his successor

83. NICOLAS, in the year 826[4]. He reigned eight years, when

---

[1] Theophanes assigns him 10 years, another (Arabic) authority 18 years. Le Quien, col. 745 (no. 75).

[2] Le Quien, after Theophanes, says A.D. 751, and assigns him 23 years, col. 746 (no. 76). On the same authority, and that of Eutychius, he makes Theodoret the successor of Theodore in 787. They omit John IV.

[3] Eutychius says in the 1st year of the Caliph Al-Mamun, i.e. A.D. 818, and assigns him 30 years. Le Quien, col. 747. He places Christopher (no. 79) between Job and Nicolas, but admits that this is probably an error, as Eutychius has no notice of him.

[4] The differences between our author and Le Quien, who relies chiefly on the authority of Eutychius, are so numerous, both as regards the names and order and dates of the Patriarchs for the next century, that it seems better to represent the latter in a tabular form which may be compared with the text. Or. Ch. II. coll. 748—751.

Number.	Name.	Accession.	Length of reign.
80	Nicolaus I.	A.D. 847	22 years
81	Stephanus.	869	1 day
82	Theodosius, al. Thaddæus.	869	22 years
83	Eustathius II.	Uncertain.	
84	Simeon I.	891	12 years

84. SIMEON was ordained in the year 834, who accomplished six years, and had for his successor

85. ELIAS in the year 840, who presided twelve years; to whom succeeded

86. THEODOSIUS in the year 852; who, having presided over the throne eight years, left as his successor

87. NICOLAS II., A.D. 860. He died in the eighteenth year of his patriarchate, and was followed by

88. MICHAEL in 879: when he had ruled eleven years he died, and

89. ZACHARIAS was promoted in the year 890. On his departure hence after twelve years,

90. GEORGE III. is advanced to the throne in the year 902. He presided fifteen years, when he died, and

91. JOB II. is raised to the throne in the year 917. He continued on the throne twenty-two years, and falling asleep in the Lord,

92. EUSTRATIUS succeeded in the year 939. After a patriarchate of twenty years, he departed to the life that knows no decay, when

93. CHRISTOPHOR followed in the year 960. In 966[1] the Arab Rulers in Antioch having learnt, that the most noble Emperor Nicephorus Phocas was advancing with a large army

Number.	Name.	Accession.	Length of reign.
85	Elias II.	A.D. 903	28 years
	Throne vacant for 4 or 7 years.		
86	Theodosius II. (pr. Stephanus)	A.D. 936	
	[He was living when Eutychius closed his Annals, A.D. 937.]		
87	Theodoretus II.	Uncertain.	
88	Agapius I.		
89	Christophorus *Martyr* (in whom the two lists again concur).		

[1] Le Quien, l. c. says A.D. 968. The Synodicon, recited in the Greek Church on "Orthodox Sunday," is the authority for the names and order of the 10 successors of Christophor; but Le Quien doubtfully inserts Eustratius (No. 90) next to Christophor, without any countenance from the Synodicon.

for the deliverance of this renowned city of the East, and suspecting the patriarch of having written to summon him, put him to death as a traitor, in the most barbarous manner, and threw his body into the Orontes which flows by. The Christians found and reverently buried it. After the death of this holy martyr, the City of Antioch being occupied by the Imperial armies, by common consent

94. THEODORUS II. is consecrated, who having governed the Church in a godly manner under the Emperor Nicephorus and John Zimiskas for the space of ten years, died; and, according to the petition of the Antiochines, preferred to the Emperor Basil II. (Porphyrogenitus, surnamed also Bulgaroctonus), the Bishop of Berrhœa in Syria (Aleppo) is promoted to the patriarchal throne,

95. AGAPIUS, A.D. 977[1]. The Emperor had raised him to the throne of Antioch on his promising to preserve immoveable his fidelity and that of the Antiochines. But after ten years of the presidency of Agapius, when the Emperor had conquered, overthrown and put to death the rebel general Peter Phocas, he unexpectedly found, in the baggage of Phocas, a letter of the patriarch of Antioch, in which he approved his rebellion, and encouraged him in it. As a punishment for such gross ingratitude, Basil did nothing else, except to carry him off and detain him in a monastery at Constantinople where he received sustenance from the Emperor; and having administered the throne seven years in all, he gave in his voluntary resignation. After this

96. JOHN V.[2], the Registrar of the Great Church, is raised to the throne, by the choice of the Church, confirmed by the Emperor Basil, A.D. 995. He, having governed the Church for five years, died, and

97. NICOLAS III. is advanced to the see, A.D. 1000. On his death, after two years,

---

[1] Elmacin, in his Saracenic History, as cited by Le Quien, dates his accession A.D. 985, and says he was deposed after he had presided 12 years.

[2] The third of that name according to Le Quien, who reckons him 93rd in succession.

98. ELIAS II. presided in the year 1003. On his death, after seven years,

99. GEORGE LASCARIS succeeds, who changed his name to THEODORE II. in the year 1010, being the sixth year of the Emperor Romanus Argyrus. He lived five years, and on his departure hence,

100. MACARIUS the Virtuous is ordained, A.D. 1015[1]. He was patriarch eight years, and on his departure to the Lord,

101. ELEUTHERIUS the Good is consecrated, in the year 1023. After a pastorate of five years he dies, and

102. PETER, the most holy and learned, is raised to the see in 1028. He was a zealous defender of the Faith, and sent letters in defence of orthodoxy to the Pope of Rome, the Archbishop of Aquileia, and Michael Cerularius of Constantinople; and in the Synod assembled by the Emperor Constantine Monomachus[2], and the fore-named patriarch, he was present, nobly contending with the others to put a stop to the corruption of the sacred doctrines and Canons, which was perpetually being increased by the Bishops of Rome. Having discharged the office for twenty-three years he departed to the Lord.

103. JOHN VI. succeeds in the year 1051[3]. He continued in the administration of the throne eleven years, when he died, and was succeeded by

104. ÆMILIAN, A.D. 1062[4], on whose death, after thirteen years,

---

[1] In the Synodicon the order is, Theodore, Basil, Peter, Theodosius, Nicephorus, John. In Le Quien thus: (96) Theodosius III., (97) Basil II., (98) Peter III. (whose accession he dates in A.D. 1053), (99) Theodosius III., (100) Æmilianus, (101) Nicephorus, (102) John IV.

[2] A.D. 1054, which proves that this author has antedated this Patriarch's death at least, probably his accession also. He signified his accession to Pope Leo IX., who only came to the throne in 1049. Le Quien, who reckons him 98th in order, dates his accession A.D. 1053.

[3] Le Quien, following the Synodicon, ignores John, and transposes Æmilian and Theodosius II. whom he reckons III. Or. Ch. II. col. 755.

[4] The Byzantine historians relate that the Patriarch Æmilian was instrumental in raising to the imperial throne Nicephorus Botaniates, on the deposition of Michael Ducas in A.D. 1078. Le Quien l. c.

105. THEODOSIUS II. is advanced, in the year 1075. Having sat for nine years, he departed hence, and

106. NICEPHORUS was advanced[1] in the year 1084. He was surnamed the Black. Having reigned less than six years, he died, and

107. JOHN VII.[2] was raised to the throne in the year 1090. In his time, Antioch was taken by the Crusaders, after a siege of eight months, in the year 1099. It had been enslaved before this, A.D. 1086, having fallen under the power of the Turks, whose General was Malec-Shah, the Governor of Persia. With the permission of this same Governor of Persia, Suliman bore sway by conquest and subjugation from Antioch nearly as far as the Hellespont. But it fell under his power on account of the insurrection which was contemplated against the Emperor Alexius Comnenus, by the perjury of Philaret, who derived his descent from the Armenians, and was unfortunately at that time Duke of Antioch, in order that thus he might secure the friendship and protection of the Turks, as being of the same religion. But his son, not enduring the disgrace of the treachery contemplated by his father, and sympathising rather with Suliman, who then governed Nicæa, than with Alexius, brought him up for the reduction of Antioch. The Latin Crusaders, then, having possession of Antioch, the throne experienced another widowhood, since the pope consecrated and sent false patriarchs of Antioch for the space of fifty-five years. In the year 1154 the Emperor Manuel Comnenus invaded Cilicia with a great army, and from thence made an expedition to Antioch in Syria; but the prince Renaud de Chatillon, who then governed Antioch for the Crusaders, constrained by fear, hastened to meet the Emperor in Cilicia with much servile humility, and journeyed with him to Antioch; but when the Emperor had entered the city with much tumult and pomp, the before-named prince Renaud, holding the enamelled stirrups of the Emperor's horse, Manuel made him renew, in

---

[1] By the Emperor Botaniates, in the year 1089, according to Le Quien, l. c.

[2] The 4th of that name, according to Le Quien, who reckons him 102nd in the succession.

addition to other engagements, the broken promise given to his grandfather Alexius the Emperor, that there should be an orthodox patriarch of Antioch, having the same honours as the Latin patriarch[1], upon which, by permission of the Emperor,

108. JOHN IX.[2] is raised to the throne of Antioch in Constantinople A.D. 1155. He had before been a monk, distinguished for his virtues, in the monastery of the Archangel Michael, situated in the islet Oxeia, in the Propontis. John came to Antioch, and after governing the Church four years departed to the Lord, and

109. EUTHYMIUS is promoted in the year 1159, on whose death, after five years,

110. MACARIUS II. succeeds, A.D. 1164. He survived but a short time, and was succeeded by

111. ATHANASIUS, in the year 1166[3]. Before, however, he was ordained and inducted another had been elected to this throne in Constantinople, viz., Soterichus, surnamed Panteugenus, a man excelling in wisdom and eloquence all others of that time. But before he had been consecrated, there arose at Constantinople a dogmatic question, the originator of which was a certain Basil, a deacon monk, whose office it was to expound the sacred Scriptures in the Church; to whose opinion Soterichus adhered, holding "that one and the same Son of God both became a sacrifice, and, together with the Father, received the Sacrifice." On which a Synod was assembled, presided over by the Patriarchs of Constantinople and Jerusalem, in which were condemned both Basil and other learned men agreeing in this opinion—who main-

---

[1] Le Quien mentions this article of the treaty, but adds, on the faith of John Cinnamus, that Baldwin, king of Jerusalem, prevailed with the Emperor to annul this article, col. 758.

[2] Between John IV. (No. 102) and John V. (No. 104), Le Quien introduces (103) Theodosius IV. or Theophilus, on the very doubtful authority of a Catalogue of the Patriarchs of Antioch, then lately written by Athanasius patriarch of Antioch, and by him placed in the Vatican Library. For this Athanasius see below, No. 150.

[3] Le Quien, ignoring Euthymius and Macarius II., makes (No. 105) Athanasius II. immediately to succeed John V., col. 759.

tained that, if one were sacrificed and another received the Sacrifice, two natures were introduced—among whom was also Panteugenus, who was deposed from his nomination to the throne of Antioch. After Athanasius had held the patriarchate fourteen years he died, and was succeeded by

112. THEODOSIUS III., A.D. 1180[1], on whose death, after two years, followed

113. ELIAS III., in the year 1182. He likewise exercised his ministry for two years, when

114. CHRISTOPHER II. succeeded in the year 1184; but, after the death of the Emperor Manuel and the brief reign of his son Alexius, whom Andronicus Comnenus, the usurper of the Empire, strangled to death, when everything was full of trouble and confusion and all kinds of political commotion, the Crusaders in Antioch, thinking the opportunity favourable to their designs for the violation of all the obligations in regard to the patriarch given by them to Manuel, removed the Patriarch Christopher out of the way, by secret murder, some months after his arrival in Antioch. After his lamentable death the then Emperor, Isaac Angelus, set up in his place

115. THEODORE IV., Balsamon, in the year 1185[2], who, through fear of the Latins in Antioch, did not choose to set eyes on the throne to which he had been elected. He was a learned man and well versed in Canon Law beyond any of his time, as is manifest from his writings. But the Emperor Isaac, desiring to raise Dositheus of Jerusalem, who was his familiar friend, to the Œcumenical throne, and seeing that the Canons did not suffer such a translation, makes secret advances to Balsamon, and pretends that his wish was to translate him, on account of his piety and wisdom, and knowledge of the laws, from the Church of Antioch to the Œcumenical Throne, but

---

[1] Between Athanasius II. and (No. 107) Theodore Balsamon, Le Quien places only (No. 106) Simeon II. on the authority of a letter published by Baronius, from George, Metropolitan of Corcyra, to Simeon, Patriarch of Antioch, A.D. 1178. Or.

Ch. II. col. 759.

[2] Le Quien post-dates his appointment A.D. 1193, but states that, according to another authority, he sat from 1186 to 1214, according to others till 1203.

that he shrank from the translation as being contrary to the ancient Canons. Theodore, being dazzled by this glory and honour, undertook that all should be accomplished. A Synod was assembled, and the question of translation proposed, when Theodore, having smoothed away the difficulty of the Canons and solved the doubt as to the hindrance, found himself tricked, for he remained at Antioch, while Dositheus, of Jerusalem, was promoted to the throne of Constantinople[1]. When Theodore had held the patriarchate fourteen years he died, and was succeeded by

116. JOACIM[2], in the year 1199, on whose death, after 20 years,

117. DOROTHEUS[3] succeeds in 1219. He died after 26 years, and

118. Simeon II.[4] is promoted in the year 1245. When he had reigned fifteen years,

119. EUTHYMIUS II. is ordained in the year 1260, being the fifth of those who were patriarchs of Antioch only in name. He survived till 1268, and in his time the Mameluke governors of Egypt, having conquered Syria, besieged and destroyed Antioch also, taking it out of the hands of the Latins, who had held possession of it 161 years. These

---

[1] Le Quien narrates this same story on the authority of the Byzantine historian, Nicetas Choniates, in his Life of Isaac Angelus, lib. II. num. 4. Or. Ch. II. col. 761.

[2] This must be the Patriarch who was deposed by the Latin Patriarch of Jerusalem, under instructions from Pope Innocent III. (cir. A.D. 1214), as an intruder in the See. Or. Ch. 762.

[3] Le Quien (No. 109) supposes this Dorotheus to be identical with Hierotheus in the Vatican Catalogue of Patriarchs, but the lists are very confused. If the date in the text is correct this must be the Patriarch, who, in conjunction with Germanus II., of Constantinople, held a conference in that city with four envoys of Pope Gregory IX., on the subject of the union of the churches; and who afterwards (A.D. 1238) excommunicated the Pope with the whole Roman Church and Curia. Matthew Paris, p. 407. Le Quien, O. C. II. col. 763.

[4] No. 110. Simeon III., in Le Quien, who inserts (111) David between him and (112) Euthymius, after whom, on the authority of Nicephorus Callistus, the following:—
113 Theodosius V.
114 Arsenius.
115 Cyrillus II.
116 Dionysius I.
117 Cyrillus III.
118 Dionysius II.
119 Sophronius.

Mamelukes, shewing themselves more tolerant than the Latins, gave permission to the orthodox Christians to elect a patriarch. They accordingly chose

120. THEODOSIUS IV. in the year 1269. He held the patriarchate seven years, when he died and was succeeded by

121. THEODOSIUS V. in the year 1276, on whose resignation[1], after nine years,

122. ARSENIUS, called the Hagiosymeonite, succeeds in the year 1285. On his deposition, on account of certain misdemeanors, a schism arose among the Christians concerning the succession to the throne, and Cyril of Tyre is chosen by the Cilicians, but by the more powerful Antiochenes

123. DIONYSIUS of Pompeiopolis[2], in 1293. When he had presided over the church for twenty-five years,

124. MARK is appointed his successor in 1308[3], on whose departure hence, after thirty-four years,

125. IGNATIUS II. occupied the throne in 1342[4]. While he was administering the Church, Pachomius invades the throne by foreign intervention, but Ignatius retired to Cyprus: after two years this intruder and transgressor is ousted, and the legitimate pastor, Ignatius, after a patriarchate of eleven years dies in Cyprus, and

126. MICHAEL II. is elected in the year 1353[5]. He

---

[1] He had favoured the union of the Greeks and Latins, which the Emperor Michael had brought about (A.D. 1277); but on the accession of Michael's son Andronicus (A.D. 1282), who was unfavourable to the union, Theodosius, fearing his displeasure, fled to the Latins, who still held some towns on the coast of Syria. Or. Ch. col. 765.

[2] Pachymeres, a contemporaneous authority, cited by Le Quien, says the very reverse: that the Cilicians chose Dionysius, the Syrians Cyril of Tyre. O. C. col. 765.

[3] Between Dionysius and Mark, Le Quien, on the authority of Joseph Assemani, inserts (120) John VI., col. 766.

[4] He was present in a synod of bishops at Constantinople in 1344, where the errors of the Palamites (Quietists) was condemned. But when John Cantacuzene, who favoured that fanatical sect, was raised to the throne, Ignatius was deposed, and subjected to severe persecution, which did not terminate with his life. Le Quien O. C. col. 767.

[5] Le Quien says in A.D. 1370, and assigns him only 9 years. Assemani introduces another Mark before Pachomius, O. C. l. c.

died after a patriarchate of sixteen years, and after his death,

127. PACHOMIUS succeeds in the year 1386[1]. He departed hence after seven years, and

128. NILUS[2] succeeds A.D. 1393, on whose demise, after eight years,

129. MICHAEL III. is advanced to the throne as his successor, A.D. 1401. He was the son of Michael, who after his widowhood became monk and archbishop of Bosra, and was kinsman of the before-named Michael II. He witnessed the devastations, massacres, and pillages of Tamerlane throughout Syria, who plundered also the property of the throne of Antioch. On his death, after nine years, he is succeeded by

130. PACHOMIUS II.[3] in the year 1410. On his death, after one year,

131. JOACIM II. of Antioch is advanced in the year 1411. On his decease, after fifteen years,

132. MARK III. succeeds, A.D. 1426. He died after ten years, and

133. DOROTHEUS II., Bishop of Deina (Seidanayia), occupied the throne of Antioch in the year 1436. In his time was assembled that notorious pseudo-synod in Florence[4]. He, together with Philotheus of Alexandria, and Joacim, patriarch of Jerusalem, assembled a council in Jerusalem in 1443, in which they condemned that pseudo-synod as a spurious and illegal meeting of evil-doers, and annulled and anathematised its acts as impious, violent, and tyrannical; deposing, together with Metrophanes, the Latinising patri-

---

[1] Our author's figures are at fault here; but whether in the dates of the patriarchs or in the length of their episcopate there is not sufficient light to determine. I can but follow the text, without attempting to correct it.

[2] So called also in Assemani's Arabic list. Apparently the Nicon of Le Quien, whom he numbers 128, and introduces between Pachomius II. (127), and Michael II. (129) l. c. col. 768.

[3] Pachomius III., according to the Vatican Catalogue, followed by Le Quien, who numbers him 130.

[4] Dorotheus was represented in the Council of Florence by Isidore Metropolitan of Kieff (who subscribed the Decree of Union in his name), and by Mark of Ephesus. Le Quien O. C. col. 769.

arch of Constantinople, those also who had been ordained by him. But about the year 1450, under our last emperor, Constantine Palæologus, Dorotheus, together with the patriarch of Alexandria, and Theophanes, who had succeeded Joacim as patriarch of Jerusalem, coming to Constantinople, assembled a council in the Church of S. Sophia[1], and deposed in like manner Gregory of Mamma, who had succeeded Metrophanes as patriarch of Constantinople, as being also a Latiniser; they appointed in his stead Athanasius the Orthodox. This synod also condemned again the Council of Florence, as opposed to the seven Œcumenical Councils, as abominable, deceitful, and tyrannical; and received with tears the repentance of the bishops and clergy who had joined in that pseudo-synod and subscribed its acts. This Dorotheus having governed the Church of Antioch for eighteen years, died, and was succeeded by

134. MICHAEL IV.[2] in the year 1454. He survived eight years, when he died, and the throne was occupied by

135. MARK IV. in 1462, on whose death, after fourteen years,

136. JOACIM III. succeeds to the presidency of the Church of Antioch, A.D. 1476, and on his death, after seventeen years,

137. GREGORY III. is elected. He lived eighteen years, and, on his death,

138. DOROTHEUS III. is advanced, in the year 1511. After presiding twelve years, he was deposed, on canonical accusations, by the three patriarchs, Jeremiah I. of Constantinople, who had come to Jerusalem as a pilgrim to the holy places, Joacim of Alexandria, who had been summoned thither, and Dorotheus of Jerusalem. He was succeeded by

139. JOACIM IV. in 1524[3]. On his death, after thirty years, there succeeded

---

[1] Dorotheus subscribed the Acts of this Council in the name Ananias —the Hebrew equivalent for his Greek name. Le Quien l. c.

[2] The order in Le Quien's Vatican list is 134, Michael, (whom he identifies with Mark), 135 Theodore V., 136 Michael IV., 137 Dorotheus II., 138 Michael V., 139 Dorotheus III. Assemani's Catalogue more nearly corresponds with our Author.

[3] Le Quien continues his list on

140. MICHAEL V. in 1555. After twelve years the Damascenes ejected him from the throne in an unprincipled manner, under a false and bitter accusation, and sending for

141. JOACIM V., Bishop of Tripoli, advanced him to the patriarchate in the year 1567. But on this there arose a struggle between them—Joacim sitting in Damascus, and Michael in Apameia, his own country. This contest lasted some years, until Michael, on his return from Constantinople a second time, fell sick on the way and died at Rhodes in the year 1582. But Joacim, after journeying through Wallachia, Moldavia, and even Little Russia, for the exigencies of his throne, on his return to Damascus was struck with blindness, on which the Damascenes compelled him, against his will, after ordaining as priest and bishop a noble citizen, a deacon-monk, administrator of the patriarchate, to substitute him also as his successor in the patriarchate; on this he departed in disgust with the Damascenes and went to Egypt, where he died, after having administered the throne well for eighteen years in all, until the year 1585. But he who had been substituted in his place,

142. DOROTHEUS IV., having governed the Church for twelve years, died [1]. The candidates for the patriarchate being many,

143. ATHANASIUS III., Bishop of Chabranium, was preferred in 1598, in consequence of a promise that he would pay off the arrears of the tribute paid by the Christians of Damascus to the sultan. But, as years passed on, and the patri-

the authority of his Vatican MS. as follows: 140 Joachim IV., 141 Michael VI., 142 Macarius II., 143 Joachim V., 144 Michael VII., 145 Joachim VI., 146 Joachim VII., formerly Bishop of Emesa, according to the Vatican Catalogue; named Benzaiada, in Assemani's list; who subscribed the Acts of the Synod of Constantinople (A.D. 1593), conceding patriarchal rights to the Metropolitan of Moscow. Le Quien l. c.,

col. 772. If this were so, our author's Chronology is, as usual, at fault; since he makes him die in 1585.

[1] Le Quien places his death in 1610. He reckons him 147th in the order of succession. 148 Athanasius III., whose death he assigns to 1619. 149 Ignatius III. 150 Cyril IV. brother of Athanasius, whose murder by the Turks he believes was instigated by his rival Ignatius!

arch deferred from time to time the payment of the arrears, on the plea of insolvency, the Damascenes no longer enduring such a pretext, came to words, quarrelling for a long time with the patriarch, and at last, in consequence of his obstinacy, they brought a public accusation against him, until the Government, being annoyed at this logomachy, delivered Athanasius to prison, as not having kept his promise and pledge; on which Damascenes alone, without the knowledge and consent of the other Christians of the throne, elected another patriarch of Antioch, viz. the Bishop of Sidon,

144. IGNATIUS III., but suspecting an opposition from the Clergy and other Christians to this independent election of theirs, they sent him to Constantinople to receive his promotion from Timothy, the then patriarch, in 1614; but in the same year, after the return from Constantinople of Ignatius thus advanced to the throne, Athanasius being released from prison, went to Tripoli in Syria, where he died; but his brother Cyril, Bishop of Chabranium, in revenge for the treatment his brother Athanasius had met with, availing himself of the powerful intervention of foreign aid, was advanced to the patriarchate in Tripoli, by the bishops of Epiphaneia, Emesa, and Arcadia, against their will; which ought not to have been done, because, in consequence of this invasion of the throne, violent conflicts broke out—a great and most desolating schism between the throne and the Christians; Cyril being vigorously incited against Ignatius, under the protection of Cyril Lucar, patriarch of Constantinople. But while (not induced thereto by repentance) he alone proposed to the civil power the assembling of a General Council, in which he of the two should be sole patriarch who was determined by the Council, he was cast into prison, and miserably put to death by the Government; and Ignatius alone remained administering the throne. He having been patriarch for fourteen years, in the midst of troubles and invasions, on his journey from Sidon to Beyrout was murdered on the road by brigands. After this, by common consent, the virtuous Bishop of Berrhœa of Syria (Aleppo) was chosen, who, on his election to Antioch, changed his name from Meletius to

145. Euthymius III., A.D. 1629. He, having ruled the Church in a manner well pleasing to God for two years, departed this life, having, before his death, chosen as his successor his deacon-monk, Meletius of Chios, as a virtuous man, who, on his consecration to the episcopate and his advancement to the patriarchal throne, changed his name also to

146. Euthymius IV.[1], A.D. 1631. He, having governed the Church for sixteen years, died, and left, as his successor, the Metropolitan of Berrhœa of Syria (Aleppo), who, having been a secular priest had, after his widowhood, adopted the monastic life; a man adorned with virtue and learning, viz.,

147. Macarius III., A.D. 1647[2]. In consequence of the invasions and losses incurred by the events that happened concerning the aforesaid Cyril, the throne had been reduced to dire necessity and penury, by reason of which this patriarch was compelled to undertake foreign expeditions in quest of assistance. Accordingly he came to Constantinople, and went thence to Wallachia and Moldavia, and from thence passed through Poland and Little Russia to Moscow in the year 1562, while Alexi Michaelovitch reigned; who both received him honourably and contributed to the necessities of the patriarch. On this he returned with gratitude to his throne, and reduced the debt; but in the year 1666, being summoned by letters of the aforesaid Emperor Alexi, addressed to the four patriarchs, requesting their judgment in the matter of the accusations against Nicon, Patriarch of all Russia, on account of his presumption exceeding all bounds, violating

---

[1] He is called Eutychius of Chios in Assemani's list, followed by Le Quien (col. 773), who reckons as follows:—
151 Euthymius II.
152 Eutychius.
153 Macarius.
154 Cyril, V.
155 Neophytus.
156 Cyril, 2nd time.
157 Athanasius IV.
158 Cyril, 3rd time.
159 Athanasius, 2nd time.
160 Seraphin.
161 Cyril.
162 Sylvester.
—O. C. Tom. II. cols. 774—776.

[2] Le Quien says in 1643, in which same year he was at Constantinople, and subscribed the "Confession of the Eastern Church," by Peter Mogila, in common with the other Patriarchs, Parthenius of Jerusalem, Joannicius of Alexandria, and Paisius of Jerusalem.

his duty and allegiance to the Emperor himself, assuming worldly power, and exhibiting intolerable arrogance;—on this account it was resolved by a Synodical decree at Constantinople, that Paisius of Alexandria, and our Macarius of Antioch, should go to Moscow. Accordingly, journeying by land, they passed through the Diocese of Theodosiopolis (Ersroum) in the patriarchate of Antioch, through Georgia[1] and Astrakan, and came to Moscow, where, in conjunction with the Russian bishops, they condemned Nicon, and deposed him from the patriarchate; but the patriarch of Antioch, returning from his second journey to Damascus, paid off the remainder of the debt on the See, restored and beautified the patriarchal church with sacred vessels of great price, which he had brought with him, erected the patriarchal palace, and did other good works. He departed to the Lord after a patriarchate of thirty-eight years; but the Damascenes, from their attachment and love to the blessed man, remembering the good works he had done for the throne, with one voice elected a grandson of the ever-memorable man, and son of Paul, son of the Patriarch, the monk-deacon Constantine, who was in his twentieth year. On his ordination and advancement to the see, he changed his name to

148. CYRIL III. in 1686. But certain agitators, not considering that Grace, seeking out the worthy, supplies their deficiencies, would not receive him, although, young as he was, he possessed the eloquence and intelligence of an old man. They wrote therefore to the Great Church, accusing Cyril as being under the canonical age and incompetent; and proposing Neophytus of Chios, bishop of Epiphaneia, as qualified and worthy; but the Church, persuaded by their arguments sent for him, and advanced him to the throne and sent him forth.

149. NEOPHYTUS, A.D. 1688, having arrived at Damas-

---

[1] It was on this journey that he baptized an innumerable multitude of Georgians of all ages: for the ignorant priests in that country had used only the chrism, and not baptized them at all with water. Or. Ch. col. 774.

cus, his presence gave rise to tumultuous scandals and to terrible schism among the Christians, until Neophytus having consented that Cyril should perform his functions, and that he should receive Laodiceia, which Cyril conceded to him, went and remained quiet there, where after a short time he died. On this Cyril again undertook the administration of the throne alone in the year 1691. But after some years, the prince of evil, who sorely tried that throne, not enduring the repose and calm of the Church, stirred up a new storm of troubles against it through the Christians of Aleppo. They sent to Constantinople without the knowledge of Cyril, and procured an order and decree that

150. ATHANASIUS IV. should be ordained and appointed patriarch of Antioch, A.D. 1700. When this had been done, as it ought not, the miserable scandals, divisions and injuries became worse than the former; but the most terrible thing of all was, that the destruction wrought by the papacy began on this to advance with rapid strides throughout Syria; for Athanasius, perceiving that the party of Cyril was the more powerful, fraternised with the papal missionaries in Damascus, who promised him protection through the ambassadors at Constantinople; on which account Cyril also was compelled, in order to countcract his influence, to make friends with the same missionaries, who, availing themselves of this favourable opportunity, entered without hindrance into the houses of the Christians, sowing among them the teaching of Rome. Meanwhile, while these divisions and scandals were coming to a head, an arrangement was made by which Athanasius took the diocese of Berrhœa of Syria (Aleppo) and departed thither, but Cyril remained in Damascus as patriarch; but he having ruled the Church for some time longer in peace and quiet, all being subject to him, and himself being serviceable alike to all; having by his exertions corrected many injustices, which the Christians suffered from the Government; he departed hence in 1724[1], after a patriarchate of thirty-eight years. After his death Athanasius continued sole patriarch.

---

[1] Le Quien gives, as the date of his death, January $\tfrac{5}{18}$, A.D. 1720.

He lived four years longer in sorrow and repentance because that, through his friendship and toleration towards the popish fathers, he had become the cause that many of the orthodox in Damascus and Aleppo had revolted from the sacred traditions of their fathers and embraced the Roman doctrines[1]; miserably beguiled by the popish fathers,—who in the name of the pope granted indulgences and relaxations of the fasts to those who were by nature slaves of their bellies, and everything else besides which was forbidden by the orthodox Church of the East; but, seeing that he was unable to check or restrain the evil progress of these opinions, he died from despondency, but others say by poison administered to him by the papists. Having been patriarch only in name twenty-four years, but in fact for four years after the death of Cyril, before his death he left as his successor his former deacon, who however had with his consent left him, and was practising discipline in the Holy Mountain,

151. SILVESTER[2]. On reference being made by the Christians of Damascus to Päisius then Œcumenical patriarch and his synod concerning this succession, they sent for him from the Holy Mount, consecrated him Bishop, and advanced him to the throne of Antioch, A.D. 1728. He was a man of virtuous life, as having passed a considerable time in the hermitages on mount Athos, and was in consequence unworldly, simple in his habits, easily cheated, severely persistent in the rules of the sacred Canons, rigid and unbending. On this account he appeared unsuited for so high a spiritual rule in this world; for in addition to virtue, it is necessary that such an one should be a good manager, according to

---

[1] He was the author of that Vatican Catalogue of the Patriarchs of Antioch, of which Le Quien has made so much use. He was lately deceased in August, 1724. Or. Chr. col. 775.

[2] Le Quien inserts 160 Seraphin and 161 Cyril VI., between Athanasius and (162) Sylvester, who is the last in his list. His editor, however, states that there was no mention of the former in the Catalogues lately brought from the East, i.e. A.D. 1734. Cyril was avowedly a Latiniser, confirmed by the Pope; and Sylvester (styled a "schismatic!") was maintained in his see against him by the authority of the Porte, under the influence of the English—"agentibus Anglorum protestantium Primoribus." col. 776.

circumstances of the various human infirmities, performing the office of an evangelist with forbearance and patience, in meekness and condescension, shewing himself long-suffering and full of endurance; that thus he may gain, if not all, at least many of those who are deceived and rebellious. But this blessed man, on arriving at Aleppo from Constantinople on a Wednesday, and seeing fish on the table which had been prepared for his reception outside the city by the principal Christian inhabitants of Aleppo, in an ungovernable fit of passion, upset the table and violently reproved those leading Christians who had come out to meet him; paying not the slightest attention to their explanations,—that in consequence of the lack of fast meats in those parts, the patriarchs his predecessors, had, by way of ecclesiastical condescension, granted this indulgence. On his entrance into Aleppo, he not only shewed himself unbending to their earnest appeals on this subject, but excommunicated them in the churches as being guilty, through gluttony, of eating fish on fasting days. Not satisfied with this, he further accused them to the pasha of Aleppo as Franks and infidels; on which some of the most distinguished among them were apprehended, imprisoned and punished: but the sufferers, burning with hatred and vengeance, turned the attack by bribing the pasha, who was about to apprehend Silvester and punish him. When he had knowledge of this he fled to Laodiceia, but after his secret retirement, all the orthodox in Aleppo, with the exception of a very few, from their youth upwards have declared themselves papists, miserably withdrawing themselves from their mother, the Eastern Church, unto this day. After this, labouring and exerting himself much for the conversion of those Aleppines who had revolted from the pious doctrines of their fathers, and for others in Damascus, Beyrout and elsewhere throughout Syria, who had been carried away, separated from the truth and miserably bowed down to western innovation and doctrine; and through the missionaries sent from Rome, with plenary papal indulgences and relaxations of fasts; and other irregularities forbidden by the orthodox Eastern Church; and having used great exertions and gone to great expense in order to procure the expulsion of the false bishops, secretly brought into Aleppo by the Latinisers, and especially of one native agitator Seraphim, otherwise called Cyril, who became false patriarch and invaded for a time the throne by foreign intervention[1]; and having, for the purpose of meeting the great expenses which had reduced him to great poverty and distress, travelled through Wallachia, Moldavia and other parts, and endured much during the whole period of thirty-eight years of a patriarchate passed in the midst of so many toils and afflictions, distresses and dangers, labours and martyrdoms, he departed hence to the Lord, as having endured much, in the year 1776. After his death, as the bishops of the throne of Antioch could not agree concerning the election of a new patriarch from among themselves, they wrote to the Great Church, which took upon itself the government of the metropolitan see of Aleppo, so separating it from the patriarchate of Antioch, which was not able to rule it, owing to the inroads of the papists: and advanced to the patriarchate its metropolitan, whom thirteen years ago they had consecrated and sent; he was a native of Constantinople, and then residing in that city—

152. PHILEMON, in April 1766. He sailed to Beyrout and came to Damascus, from whence he passed through Emesa and Epiphaneia and came to Aleppo, where he consecrated as Metropolitan of Aleppo, by permission of the patriarch of Constantinople, Neophytus of Laodiceia, an

---

[1] This man, being affected with Roman doctrine, calling to his aid the violence and threats of a powerful chief of Mount Lebanon, was named Bishop in a certain cave, by Neophytus, Metropolitan of Beyrout, and an Armeno-Catholic Bishop brought from Lebanon, cursing and excommunicating him—instead of prayers! After this comedy, the accursed man, aiming also at the patriarchial dignity, this too was accomplished in this still more ridiculous and horrible manner. A certain Capuchin friar, a Roman missionary in Syria, breathed on him thrice saying..."By the grace and power given me by the Archbishop of Rome, I have this day appointed thee patriarch of Antioch." Thus the lawless supremacy and insolence of the papal see unblushingly despises the divine laws and Canons, shamelessly mocking at all that is sacred and holy for the sake of making one proselyte to Popery!

Aleppine, whom he had left as his Vicar during his absence. He departed thence to Laodiceia, where he fell ill and died, after a patriarchate of one year and two months; but after his death, the bishops, subject to the throne of Antioch, again could not agree concerning the election of a patriarch, as some wished for the bishop of Beyrout, others for Tyre and Sidon, and others for Tripoli. They wrote, therefore, to the Great Church, which, in order to put a stop to these divisions and scandals, consecrated the Protosyncellus of the Great Church, and translated him to the throne of Antioch.

153. DANIEL, a native of Chios, A. D. 1767, was a good man, and lowly minded. He repaired the patriarchal church in Damascus, which had fallen into decay, and the convent of nuns at Seidanayia, renowned throughout all Syria. There happened under him also many disputes with the Romanisers in Damascus; who, seeing his meekness, humility, and peaceable disposition, ceased not, as apostates from their ancestral piety, who had become messengers of Satan, to involve him in terrible troubles, concerning which he twice went to Constantinople and returned. After a patriarchate of twenty-five years, when old and in failing health he went a third time to the capital, and having chosen the bishop of Helenopolis, a Cypriote by birth, an exceedingly learned and high principled man, presented him to the Œcumenical Patriarch and Synod, saying 'this is my successor,' and having resigned the throne to him, he departed to his country, Chios. The aforesaid

154. ANTHEMIUS was advanced to the patriarchate in 1793. He, no less than his predecessors, struggled and contended, as far as he was able, against the attacks of the papists, who having become secretaries of the pashas throughout Syria, and thus obtaining power, seized both the monasteries and churches of the orthodox, whom they afflicted; inducing some by persuasion, some by force, and others by bribes and promises, to abjure the doctrines of piety and to embrace the novel teaching of Rome, in imitation of themselves. Having presided amid such conflicts and agitations

twenty-one years, he departed this life in Damascus; but on a reference of the bishops of the See, and the orthodox there to the Great Church,

155. SERAPHIM of Constantinople was advanced to the throne of Antioch, having been a titular bishop only, in the year 1813. He having succeeded to the position and troubles of his predecessors, and survived nine years and seven months, demised in Damascus on the 19th of February. After his departure to the Lord, a general requisition of the bishops of the See and of the Christians was sent to the Great Church, requesting Constantius, archbishop of Sinai, for their patriarch; but, on his declining, by no means wishing to accept the office, the metropolitan of Ancyra is raised to the throne—

156. METHODIUS, a Naxian by birth, in the year 1823, who is exercising the patriarchal office worthily up to this time, a man of high principles, kindly in his manners, adorned both with zeal for the faith and virtue; on which account he is held in respect and esteem by all in those parts. But what has he also endured in his conflicts for piety, muzzling and racking his Latinisers and apostate antagonists, who are styled Roman Catholics! besides which, by help from above, he has skilfully beaten off and dispersed the frauds and plots of those who are called Reformers and Missionaries, who have been introduced into Syria, and who are likewise plotting by all means against the faithful of the orthodox church; and confirming again, in the sound doctrine, those who have been deceived by gold and shaken in their religion. All these conflicts of his, though protracted to his old age, are rather the subject of more private history. Being a lover of the beautiful, but destitute of means, he thought of seeking assistance from the North, which he obtained, and with which, besides other works, he rebuilt from the foundations the ruined patriarchal Church, the only one in Damascus, adorning it and beautifying it in the most splendid manner[1].

[1] The catalogue of Constantius ends with Methodius; but the Editor of the Minor Works of Constantius, on p. 117, note (1), speaks of Methodius as

157. HIEROTHEUS, formerly titular Bishop of Mount Tabor, and the successor designate of the Patriarchal Throne of Jerusalem, commonly known as such under the title of ὁ Διάδοχος. On the death however of Athanasius, Patriarch of Jerusalem, in 1844, the Great Church of Constantinople, under the Patriarch Herman, sought to impose conditions and restrictions on the new patriarch of Jerusalem for the aggrandisement of the Church of Constantinople. Hierotheus resisted the usurpation, and maintained the liberties of the See of Jerusalem. On this account he incurred the displeasure of the Great Church, which instigated the Ottoman Porte not to confirm the appointment. A ready and effectual pretext was found in the fact that Hierotheus had been sent to Russia to collect alms and offerings for the Church of Jerusalem, and had, during his sojourn there, ingratiated himself with influential members of that Church, and become biassed with Russian proclivities. He was not allowed to assume the Patriarchal throne of Jerusalem, to which Cyril, then Bishop of Lydda, was elected. But shortly after this, on the death of Methodius, Patriarch of Antioch, he was elected to that See, and the Government made no objection. During his occupancy of the Patriarchal Throne he has been engaged, like his predecessors, in unavailing attempts to resist the encroachments of the Roman Propaganda, on one side, and of the Protestant Missionaries on the other. He took an active part in the proceedings of the General Synod of Constantinople in 1872, and subscribed the excommunication of the Bulgarians, on the ground of *nationalism*. By this act he incurred the displeasure of the Bishops and Clergy of his Patriarchate, who assembled in Synod at Beyrout and voted his deposition.

the "immediate predecessor of the present patriarch Hierotheus," whose biographical notice I supply from my own knowledge. See *Holy City*, Vol. II. pp. 544—547. G. W.

APPENDICES.

APPENDIX. I.

[I am indebted to my most revered friend Gregory, the very learned Metropolitan of Chios, for the following authentic records relating to the Patriarchal Throne of Antioch during the latter half of the 18th Century, extracted, for the most part, from the Archives of the Patriarchate of Constantinople, and obligingly communicated to me for the illustration of this Volume. G. W.]

By reading the following Ecclesiastical memoirs extracted from the Archives of the Great Church of Christ (i.e. Constantinople) you will obtain information concerning the encroachments of the Papists in the East, especially in the parts subject to the Patriarchal See of Antioch; the History of which you are publishing.

"The very holy Apostolic See of the Church of Antioch remaining without a Pastor, its ruler the venerable Kyr Philemon having departed to the better life, the Christians of that region and those living here in the capital—men entitled to consideration, and well acquainted with those parts, fearing lest some one favourable to the Latins should come in;—as the like was about to happen at another time, in our own days, when a double-named individual Seraphim or Cyril (one and the same man differently named) from among the well known Latinizers, thrust himself in by the help of money, got possession of the See and became the cause of a thousand evils and unspeakable destruction, expended and emptied the treasures accumulated from former ages and for the adornment of this Patriarchal See; also whatever sacred offerings and gifts there were he used for his misplaced desires and aims, and above all persecuted Orthodoxy and exalted and strengthened the cause of the heterodox and did besides many things which it were grievous to relate :—Having then foreseen such and the like events, those of that fold and we ourselves, entrusted with the general care and forethought for all the Churches; on account too of the Patriarchal Epistle, addressed to us by the late Kyr Philemon; who having fallen dangerously ill, and being unable to rise and to be cured of his disease, foreseeing the future and knowing the instability of man's nature, as a good steward, and governor of his flock, wrote to us with all details and with religious zeal, though in great apprehension lest some one of the Arabs should come in and strive to extinguish the bright flame of Orthodoxy.

He therefore named as his successor our Great Protosyncellus of the Apostolic and Œcumenical See, having chosen and appointed him as successor in preference to any other person residing either there or here in the capital. Moved by these claims and arguments our Great Church of Constantinople, in order to meet the probable evils (those, that is, resulting from the Papacy), thought to *secure* and *promote the welfare of the Orthodox fold of Antioch* by the wise zeal and firm hand of an orthodoxly-ruling Primate of that spiritual fold. Therefore according to the ancient order[1] of this Apostolic and Œcumenical See, after the death of either of the other Patriarchs, to receive and take upon itself the charge of Ephorus and Epistates of his successorship; moreover as general Overseer and Ephorus of all the Holy Churches of Christ, as Head of the whole body, bound to care for all its members and to watch over the common interest of all[2]—exercising this right the See of Constantinople, in consideration of *the written opinion* of the late Kyr Philemon, expressing his own desire with regard to our Great Protosyncellus Kyr Daniel, has decided to vote in accord and brotherly agreement with him: the most blessed Patriarch of Jerusalem Kyr Ephrem, our beloved brother and fellow-minister in the Holy Ghost, holding the same opinion, as did likewise the sacred assembly of Bishops present. First of all then this very Reverend Great Protosyncellus Kyr Daniel, already consecrated Metropolitan of Damascus, is declared worthy of succession to the See of Antioch; next to him, according to lawful order, we name the former Bishop of Brailov (in Wallachia) Kyr Zacharias, and thirdly the Bishop of Chios Kyr Nicephorus, whose names have been entered in this sacred act of the Great Church of Christ.

In the year of Salvation 1767. August 6th.

+ Samuel, Patriarch of Constantinople."

---

[1] According, that is, to the order in force since the capture of Constantinople, by which the Œcumenical See took upon itself the task of Epistates and Epoptes of the welfare of the other Patriarchal Churches, particularly in matters of succession by *consent* or *demand* of the Patriarchs and the Orthodox Christians subjected to them: this interference of the Œcumenical Patriarch in the matters of the other independent Churches was not an act of love of dominion, but of brotherly love required by the circumstances of the times. For, on account of the tyranny of the conquerors, and the unceasing attacks and conspiracies of the Papists, a greater *concentration* of power was requisite. Therefore this act (I repeat it) was no violation of the canons, but a temporary measure of conciliation and the fruit of Christian charity. (Remark made by ourselves.)

[2] This is a somewhat exaggerated expression.

ANOTHER MEMOIR.

"Our Holy Great Church of Christ and its most Holy Patriarchal and Œcumenical See holds it as its undoubted duty to protect, care for, and watch over all Christian communities, as the common mother of every holy Church and the most holy Patriarchal Sees representing them; according to the privileges long granted to her of overseeing them and correcting the fallen and those in need of raising. Since therefore she has found the very holy Metropolis of Aleppo (formerly subject to the most holy See of Antioch), and its Christian community in perturbation for many years past, on account of its subjection to the said Holy See of Antioch, its appeal was not received as long as it was subject to that See[1]. But the most blessed and Holy Patriarch of Antioch our beloved and much-esteemed brother in the Holy Ghost and fellow-churchman Kyr Silvester, seeing well and understanding by so many years' experience the impossibility of ruling this diocese of Aleppo as long as it remains under the government of his Holy See, of his own freewill and independent desire, having been of himself prompted so to act, wrote to this Holy See of Constantinople, both to the Patriarch then occupying it and to the sacred Synod of Holy Bishops, and by free voluntary resignation transferred and abandoned this very Holy Metropolis of Aleppo to the most Holy See of Constantinople; requesting that it should be taken and separated from its union with Antioch and united and subjected to the See of Constantinople. Having accepted this request, the Church of Christ, in order to settle the matters of that Christian community, consented to the demand of his Beatitude and to the written application made by him. Therefore we fellow-Bishops residing in Constantinople, by the desire and permission of our most holy and Reverend Superior and Lord the Œcumenical Patriarch Kyr Seraphim, having assembled in the venerable Patriarchal Church of the glorious Martyr Saint George Tropaiophoros, and having collected the canonical votes for the choice and election of a person worthy and meet to receive the Episcopal Government of this diocese of Aleppo, have selected, first, the very Reverend Protosyncellus of the very Holy Metropolis of Derkon, the Priest-monk Kyr Philemon[2], secondly the Reverend Priest-monk Kyr Theophilus, and thirdly the Reverend Priest-monk Kyr Hierotheus; whose names have been entered in this sacred Register of the Great Church of Christ, the year of Salvation 1757, November 6th of the Indict.

+ JEREMIAH, Bishop of Nicæa.
+ GABRIEL, Bishop of Thessalonica.

---

[1] The matter seems here to me somewhat unintelligible.

[2] He afterwards became Patriarch of Antioch. See the former Synodical Act. It was customary that the name of him who had the greater number of votes should be placed first in the Act.

+ Dionysius, Bishop of Adrianople,
having the proxies of my brethren
Kyr Gerasimus, Bishop of Heraclea,
Kyr Gabriel, Bishop of Nikomedia,
Kyr Samuel[1], Bishop of Derkon.
+ Auxentius, Bishop of Philippopolis,
having the proxies of the holy Kyr Meletius of Broussa.
+ Neophytus, Bishop of Ganos and its region."

The Patriarch Silvester requested the incorporation of the diocese of Aleppo into the Œcumenical See—although it was from the first canonically attached to the Patriarchal See of Antioch—in order to save it from the evils it was suffering at the hands of the Papists. Thenceforth this Metropolis, *with but little intermission*, continued under the jurisdiction and protection of the patriarch of Constantinople, containing only 120 orthodox households; its other numerous inhabitants having about 150 years ago been won over to Popery by the intrigues and wiles of the Jesuits.

In the extensive writings of Athanasius Ypsilanti (+1775) recently published by the Archimandrite Germanus Aphthonides of Sinai, bearing the title "Events after the Capture" (of Constantinople), you will find much relating to the Patriarchal See of Antioch.

Patriarchal and Synodical Act concerning the diocese of Aleppo.

"To care for, and, when possible, to assist the needs of the other most Holy Patriarchal Sees, our most Holy Patriarchal, Apostolic and Œcumenical See has ever held quite befitting to itself; but as for taking away their rights and profiting unjustly, this it *not only refuses to do, but even to hear of*[2]. For the first act is just and worthy of it; whereas the second is *on the contrary* unworthy and unbefitting the Patriarchal dignity. This is manifest from many other documents, as well as from the synodically attested Patriarchal and Synodical Act, concerning the very Holy Metropolis of Aleppo, published in the year of Salvation 1766, under Samuel Patriarch of Constantinople; for it is written in this Synodical Act :—

"The very Holy Metropolis of Aleppo, formerly and from the beginning subjected to the most Holy Patriarchal and Apostolic See of Antioch, in later times (the year of Salvation 1757) under the Patriarchate of the ever-memorable Silvester, on account of the troubles and disorders excited there by some evil-minded men, was declared by common decision, as a prudential measure, subjected and united to this our Patri-

---

[1] He became Patriarch of Constantinople, of whom see further.
[2] Mark this phrase well.

archal, Apostolic and Œcumenical See (but all this, as attested by the said writing, for expediency). Wherefore, after the death of the said blessed Silvester, the blessed Philemon having been translated from the Metropolis of Aleppo to the most Holy Patriarchal See of Antioch, that Patriarchal See (of Antioch) caring for the Metropolis of Aleppo as formerly its own, took upon itself the debt of 3000 piastres for it, and declared it free, and delivered from all debt. For this reason, and likewise because the former difficulties and troubles had ceased to exist, the said very Holy Metropolis of Aleppo was once more, by general agreement and approval of the Synod, restored and made subject to the most Holy Patriarchal See of Antioch, as it was before. But, on account of the necessities of the time, and on prudential considerations, the name of the Patriarchs of Constantinople continued to be mentioned there in the churches[1]. Meanwhile the successive Metropolitans of Aleppo are to be subject solely to the most Holy Patriarchal See of Antioch, and are to render to it the befitting honour, obedience, submission and reverence, and are to regard the ruling Patriarchs of Antioch as their lords."— These now are the contents of the said Synodical Act, and hence it is manifest how, in this case also, our most Holy Patriarchal Apostolic and Œcumenical See kept itself blameless, assisting *in brotherly wise* the Patriarchal See of Antioch in its difficulty and need concerning the said Metropolis of Aleppo; but never at all regarding it as its own property. Therefore now, by general agreement and Synodical decree, since the most Holy Patriarchal See of Antioch has from henceforth taken upon itself the debt of 3000 piastres, incurred by the Metropolis of Aleppo, and is still paying the interest thereof; and since by Divine help all troubling circumstances have disappeared, and in the Metropolis of Aleppo it has been voted that this very Holy Metropolis should henceforth and for ever be attached, as before, to the most Holy Patriarchal and Apostolic See of Antioch, and that in future the Metropolitan of Aleppo should be canonically consecrated by the ruling Patriarch of Antioch, and that they should recognise him alone as their Patriarch and Lord, obeying and submitting to him according to the law:—We do therefore by this Synodical Act declare, conjointly with the very reverend Bishops surrounding us, our honoured brethren and fellow-Churchmen in the Holy Ghost, that from henceforth in future time and for all ages the said very Holy Metropolis of Aleppo shall be, as before, subjected to and dependent on the most Holy Patriarchal and Apostolic See of Antioch, and that the Metropolitan of Aleppo is to recognise as his Patriarch and Lord the ruling Patriarch of the Most Holy Patriarchal

---

[1] This in order that the Papists, by whom the name of the Œcumenical Patriarch was more dreaded on account of his dignity and direct relations with the authorities, hearing this name pronounced by the Metropolitan of Aleppo, and taking him to be a dependent of the Œcumenical Patriarch, should be withheld from their violent acts against the Orthodox of the Diocese. The town of Aleppo is the formerly famous Berrhœa.

and Apostolic See of Antioch, to commemorate his canonical title, and to render to him all due and fitting obedience, honour and submission, as is meet and reasonable, according to the law. And whosoever of the Christians young or old (or high or low) whether of the clergy or the laity, of whatsoever station or rank he may be, shall dare in future to infringe or in any way to alter the present Synodical decree, such an one shall remain separated from God, and accursed, and unabsolved, and after death unshriven and condemned, and shall incur the eternal fire of Gehenna. These things then have been decreed and synodically confirmed. And as proof and sufficient warrant of the same, this present Patriarchal and Synodical Act (entered in the Sacred Register of our Great Church of Christ) is published and given to the Most Holy Patriarchal See of Antioch, in the month of January, 10th of the Indict 1792[1].

> NEOPHYTUS, by the Grace of God Archbishop of Constantinople, New Rome, and Œcumenical Patriarch.
> + GREGORY, Bishop of Cæsareia.   + SAMUEL of Ephesus.
> + METHODIUS of Heracleia.   + AGAPIUS of Cyzicus.
> + ATHANASIUS of Nicomedeia.   + JEREMIAS of Chalcedon.
> + GERASIMUS of Derkon.   + MATTHEW of Tornova.
> + ANTHIMUS of Broussa.   + MELETIUS of Larissa."
> + MACARIUS of Arta.

[1] The present Patriarchal and Synodical Act was published under the Patriarchate of Anthemius at Alexandria and Neophytus at Constantinople: for when Daniel, Patriarch of Antioch tendered to the Œcumenical See his resignation, on the 15th of December, 1791, as is proved by and entered in the sacred Register of the Great Church, then in the month of December, 10th of the Indict, Anthemius was appointed to the See of Antioch.

APPENDIX. II.

THE CHURCH OF ANTIOCH.

[The following Memoir of the Patriarchate of Antioch is translated from a Russian pamphlet, which was printed at Moscow in the year 1845, with a view to enlist the sympathies of the Orthodox of Russia in the Mission of Neophytus Metropolitan of Heliopolis and Mount Lebanon, who had come to that country with a commission from the Patriarch to collect alms for his impoverished Church. It contains some interesting historical notices: and a description of the actual state of the Patriarchate, in very characteristic language, and is therefore inserted. G. W.]

Within the walls of Moscow, in the Jerusalem Convent-yard, resides Neophytus, the Metropolitan of Heliopolis [Baalbek] and Mount Libanus, who is sent, with a letter from Methodius the Patriarch of Antioch, into our native country for the purpose of collecting alms in behalf of the poor See of Antioch, of establishing orthodox schools and printing-presses, of renovating the Church of S. Nicolas in Damascus, of repairing other old churches and monasteries, and finally of erecting various public buildings indispensable to the Christian residents.

The Church of Antioch, one of the blessed branches of the Orthodox Eastern Church, the eldest sister of our Russian Church, suffering under the heavy yoke of infidels, and oppressed by other persuasions inimical to ours, now, in the person of her Patriarch, extends her blessing hand to our Orthodox brotherhood which is strong, rich, independent, and prays for assistance! Shall we then turn a deaf ear to her plaintive cry? Shall we, happy and triumphant, refuse to stretch out our hand to her weeping and oppressed?

Wishing as far as possible, to induce our fellow-countrymen to take an interest in this appeal of the Church of Antioch, we have undertaken the duty to revive her holy traditions in their memory; to give them a short account of the chief events of her history, which will clearly prove how wonderfully she has preserved her orthodoxy against all possible temptation; to bring back to their mind her ancient connexion and all her most important relations with our native Country; and finally to represent to them her actual condition.

The See of the Church of Antioch derives its origin from the Apostle

Peter. He was the first that preached the Word of God here, wrought miraculous cures, established an Episcopate. Till his departure for Rome he resided for the most part either at Jerusalem or at Antioch. Treading in the footsteps of the Apostle Peter, the Apostles Barnabas and Paul laboured in Antioch : during a whole year they assembled in the church of that town, taught numbers of people, and their disciples in Antioch were the first to be called Christians, so that this blessed name originated in these parts and from Antioch spread over the universe. There is to be found to this day that gracious spring of water which was brought forth by the prayers of St Paul for the baptism of the Antiochians. It still bears the name of this Apostle.

St Peter, on quitting the See of Antioch, left in his place Euodius, to whom succeeded St Ignatius—the Bearer of God (Theophorus). There is a tradition which says that St Ignatius was that very child, whom the Saviour set in the midst of His disciples and, embracing him, said: "Verily I say unto you, that except ye be converted, and become as little children, ye shall not enter the Kingdom of Heaven. He that humbleth himself like this little child, is the greatest in the Kingdom of Heaven. He that receiveth this little child in my Name, receiveth Me."

Over the head of the infant Ignatius were these Divine words spoken. The holy Apostle St John the Evangelist received him as his disciple. Afterwards, by the advice of all the Apostles, Ignatius was ordained Bishop of Antioch. (See Menæa of the Saints, December 20th.) He first introduced into the Church-service the antiphonal singing.

It was he also that taught the Orthodox Christians to cross themselves with the three united fingers of the right hand to the glory of the Thrice-holy Consubstantial and Indivisible Trinity.—Fearlessly did he defend the Christians against Trajan in his own Antioch ; he was hence called to Rome, to be condemned to wild beasts in the Colosseum ; the incorruptible remains of his bones and of his heart, miraculously spared by the wild beasts, were gathered by the faithful and returned to the Church of Antioch.

In the second century public Divine Service in Antioch was performed in private houses. Theophilus, the 7th bishop of Antioch, seeing that the former houses could not contain all the faithful, gave up his own house for the public worship. In the time of Macarius the 16th bishop of Antioch, genuflexion was introduced in the church, on the day of Pentecost at Vespers.

The title of Patriarch first of all belonged to the Bishop of Antioch, even before the first Œcumenical Council, at which the Patriarchate of Constantinople was established. All greater and lesser Asia and all the countries of the East were at first under the jurisdiction of the Patriarch of Antioch. At the 1st Œcumenical Council in Nicæa, St Eustathius the 25th Patriarch of Antioch was present.—At the request of the Emperor Constantine, he consented to acknowledge Metrophanes

APPENDIX. II. 201

bishop of Byzantium as Patriarch and to cede to him all the parts contiguous to Constantinople. The Emperor promised the See of Antioch for this concession a yearly gift of 36,000 measures of wheat. Afterwards were conceded to the Patriarch of Constantinople the metropolitan dioceses, situated on the Asiatic side from the Bosphorus and Chrysopolis, now called Amidar, to Malatiah on the borders of Syria. At the 4th Council was established the Patriarchate of Jerusalem—and Maximus, Patriarch of Antioch, conceded to Juvenal the Patriarch of Jerusalem both the Palestines, which from the time of St Peter had been under the jurisdiction of the See of Antioch. Notwithstanding all those concessions there remained, in the year 553, during the reign of the Emperor Justinian, under the jurisdiction of the Patriarch of Antioch 153 Metropolitans, Archbishops and Bishops, besides the Catholici of Seleucia, as far as India, of Armenia, of Georgia and of the Northern part of Asia, which all became subject to Antioch. It is but since the 5th Council that the island of Cyprus ceased to depend upon Antioch.

Early did Antioch begin to wrestle with the persecutors of Christianity. In the time of Constantine the Great, and of Bishop Eustathius, Sapor, king of Persia, attacked Antioch, and many Christians became the victims of his persecution. Delivered from the Persian yoke by Constantine, Antioch began to extend the true faith into Georgia. In this country appeared a wonderful woman, St Nina, who taught the people Christianity. The king of Georgia and the people wished to be baptized: St Eustathius, by command of Constantine the Great, set off to Georgia, with the priests, with all the clergy and with Bacurius the heir to the Georgian throne; they brought the Georgian king sacred presents from Constantine, some monuments of the Lord's Passion[1], some relics of the saints, the images of the Saviour and of the Mother of God; they baptized the king and the people, ordained Bishops and Priests, established divine service, and by preaching accomplished the conversion of all Iberia to Christianity from the shores of the Black Sea almost to the Albanian mountains, and from the Caucasus to the Persian dominions.

In 341, the fourth of the local councils was held in Antioch, and therefore is called the Council of Antioch: wherein were constituted 25 rules concerning Easter, the Church communion among Christians and the duties of Bishops.

St Meletius, the 33rd Patriarch of Antioch, who attended at the second Œcumenical Council (381), is also renowned in the History of the Church for having baptized, and then ordained St John Chrysostom, sub-deacon, deacon, and priest, as well as for having consecrated the

---

[1] It was then that St Constantine sent to Georgia the nail from the holy cross, now preserved in the Moscow Cathedral of the Assumption. This nail was transferred to Moscow from Georgia by king Archiel in 1686.

Hierarch S. Basil Archbishop of Cæsareia in Cappadocia. Thus the representative of the Church of Antioch participated in the ecclesiastical preferment of two of the greatest teachers of the Church.

In 451, at the time of the 4th general Council held in Chalcedon, all Asia Minor went over from the Patriarch of Antioch to that of Constantinople. In 518 Antioch was destroyed by a dreadful earthquake, during which a great number of people perished and among them the Patriarch Euphrasius. The Governor, Count Ephraim of Amida, being sent by the Emperor Justinian to rebuild the ruined city, became a monk at the request of the people, and was raised to the Patriarchal Throne. It was in his time that Chozroes, king of Persia, destroyed all Syria and Antioch, and led many Christians into captivity: the Emperor Justinian conquered Chozroes and liberated the prisoners. Dreadful earthquakes continued in Antioch: the terrified people ran out of the city; but the Patriarch Ephraim forbade the inhabitants to quit it. He ordered every owner of a house to write over the gate: "May Christ be with us." The earthquakes ceased. In memory of this miracle, Antioch was called Theopolis—the City of God.

At the 5th Œcumenical Council in 553, held in Constantinople, was present Domnus the 65th Patriarch of Antioch. At the 6th Œcumenical Council of Trullum, held in 691, presided George, the 76th Patriarch of Antioch.

In the year 629, under the Patriarch Gregory, the Caliphs of Babylon began to extend their power over all Syria and Antioch. But in 742, El-Walid heir to the Caliph of Babylon, in the time of Stephen, the 79th Patriarch of Antioch, imposed a heavy and firm yoke on both these parts. It was he that forbade them not only to speak and write Greek, but even to perform divine service in that language: the Arabian language was then introduced into all the courts of justice and was even in general use among the people, till 1097. The Saracen oppression in all the countries of the East was so violent, that neither Theodore the Patriarch of Antioch, nor Politian of Alexandria, nor Elias of Jerusalem, could be present at the 7th Œcumenical Council held in Nicæa (783). They unanimously empowered the Priest-monk and Syncellus Thomas and the Priest-monk John to be present in their stead at this Council, but they themselves were obliged to share the persecution and sufferings of their oppressed flocks.

During the administration of Aloosh-el-Koordi, Christopher the 92nd Patriarch of Antioch suffered the death of a martyr from the elder Omar-Eben-Manech. His body, which had been thrown into a river, was found by the Christians and conveyed by night to a monastery near the city. After the expulsion of the Saracens, his successor Theodore transferred the body of his murdered predecessor Christopher to the cathedral church of Antioch.

Many were the evils that the Church of Antioch suffered from the infidels; but now new evils, not less heavy to be borne, came on them from their former western brethren, who had separated themselves from the primitive union. The Crusades began. Under pretext of delivering the Sepulchre of Christ, the Popes made use of these wars to extend their exterior power over the east and the west. They placed their own Patriarchs in Alexandria, Jerusalem, and Antioch. In this last city there have been seven popish Patriarchs: the first was Tarpento, the last was Christiano, killed in 1237 by the Saracens. Eugenius III. proclaimed publicly, that the war which was called holy, was of no use whatever, but was necessary to the Western Church merely in order that it might place its own bishops in the Eastern Churches.

It would be difficult to describe all the evils, which the eastern Christians suffered from the papal authority during one hundred and forty years—from 1095 to 1237. Gregory VII.'s proclamation is well known, viz. that every one who would not acknowledge the unlimited power of the Roman pontiff, should be looked upon as a heathen; without mercy were Patriarchs, Metropolitans, Archbishops and Bishops deprived of their places. Those who made any resistance were killed or burned in the most cruel manner. Monasteries and churches were given up to pillage; the sacred things which they contained were defiled. The orthodox Christians were persecuted, oppressed and despoiled of their possessions. Many relics of the martyrs and saints were transported from Syria to Rome. Whole libraries and the original canons and regulations of the local Councils were also transported to the West. The Eastern Church, which surrounds the Sepulchre of Christ, was deprived of all its treasures. The Latin crusaders accomplished what the infidel Saracens did not even attempt to do. All these shocking crimes of the crusaders are hid under the wily curtain of the western history.

In 1204 Innocent III. undertook to put down the Œcumenical Patriarch of Constantinople and to raise Thomas the Venetian to that see. The pretended holy troops which were then assembled in Venice, instead of sailing to Jerusalem, suddenly turned against Constantinople. The order was fulfilled without delay: the crusader took possession of Byzantium and defiled in every possible manner the sacred things therein. Pelagius the Pope's Legate obliged all to submit to the Pope: the monks and priests that showed any opposition were hanged; the warriors were allowed to pillage the churches and the monasteries; the nunneries were defiled and dishonoured.

The Latin Patriarch then residing in Antioch, as well as the other Bishops in all Syria, hearing of these proceedings of the Pope's Legate in Constantinople and of other Legates in Jerusalem, and on the Island of Cyprus, imitated them and renewed everywhere the oppression of the Orthodox clergy, forcing them to acknowledge the power of the Pope. The resisting Archimandrites, priest-monks and monks were burned. The papists in Antioch looked themselves after these funeral piles and were present till the flames had entirely consumed the bodies of the martyrs. The same was done in Jerusalem, and in the islands of Asia and of the Archipelago. Pope Gregory IX., who sent to Nicæa to the Patriarch Herman the ambassadors Hugo and Peter, Ammonius and Radulph, himself acknowledges these acts of violence, but he justifies the Pope, and showing surprise and a kind of pretended compassion, he lays all the blame on the unbridled fanaticism of his legates and warriors.

The annalists Manuel Malaksos and Choniates describe these violent proceedings of the Latins in Constantinople, when they took the capital. In the altar of the Sophia-Cathedral, they placed on an eminence a debauched woman and called her St Sophia; they divided the sacred vestments among themselves; clothed their concubines therein and led them about the city; they threw the church images on the ground, or sitting upon them played at cards. In one word, all the Orthodox Religion, from Byzantium to Antioch and Jerusalem, was defiled by the western crusaders. This is the principal reason why the Crusades had no success. The western historians pay no attention to these events, which throw an entirely new light on this whole epoch.

In 1237 the Saracens extirpated the Latins and again took possession of all Syria, Antioch, Jerusalem and all Palestine. The Caliphs again imposed their yoke on Antioch in the time of Ignatius the 112th Patriarch. The Pope's missionaries did not cease their operations in the East. By liberal bribes they induced the Saracens to appoint in every city elders from among the Jews, under whose power the Orthodox Christians suffered more than the ancient Israelites did from the Egyptians. The Patriarchal See was transferred from Antioch to Damascus.

From the year 1516, all Syria passed under the yoke of the Turkish power. In 1540, Pope Paul III. confirmed the order of the Jesuits. Then again members of this order were sent all over Syria to propagate the Roman Catholic religion. The Popes replaced their Jesuit missionaries by others; but from that time they have not ceased to act constantly in their own favour.

Such is the great struggle which our Orthodox Religion has had in Antioch and in other holy places of the East. During these misfortunes she had a constant support and consolation in her youngest sister the Russian Church. Let us now turn our attention to the relations which have existed from the earliest times between these two Churches.

They extend to the primitive time of the introduction of Christianity into Russia. Michael, the first Metropolitan, sent by the Byzantine Emperors to baptize Russia, was born in Syria, and was a pupil of John the 95th Patriarch of Antioch. To Michael are we indebted for the first planting of Christianity in our land, for the first monastery called St Michael's, with the gilt cupola; and for the first schools. Thus from the first commencement of Christianity in our country we see the connexion between the Church of Antioch and our own.

When Russia gained strength after having shaken off the ignominious yoke, our Czars did not cease to share their treasures with churches of the East, never forgetting the Church of Antioch. Thus the good and pious Theodore Ivanovitch, when rejoicing at the birth of a daughter in 1592, sent a liberal alms to the monasteries of Antioch.

Thus John the Terrible, doing penance for having killed his son, sent gifts to the Eastern Patriarchs, that they should pray for the rest of his child's soul. In 1580, Joachim the Patriarch of Antioch came to Moscow for alms; and the Czar first declared to him his desire to institute a Patriarchate in Russia.

In 1587 the Patriarchs of Constantinople and of Antioch sent for those of Jerusalem and Alexandria, and consulted together about establishing a Patriarchate in our native country.

In 1589 the institution was accomplished—and, in the order of the Patriarchs of the Eastern Church, that of Antioch is called the fourth, after the third, Patriarch of Moscow and of all the Russias. In the act of institution it was mentioned, that in Russia they were to pray for the Greek Patriarchs, that is, for all the Eastern ones; and that in Greece they should pray for ours; and our Church, at certain periods of every year, for example on the 5th of January, offers up prayers for the Patriarch of Antioch and for the others.

In the time of the Czar Alexis Michaelovitch, Macarius Patriarch of Antioch together with Paisius, Patriarch of Alexandria, came twice to Russia. He was a real zealot for the Orthodox Religion in the East, and achieved many great exploits. We shall communicate all that is known of him by the traditions of the Church of Antioch and by our historical documents.

Macarius was the 141st Patriarch of Antioch after the apostle St. Peter. He was born in the city of Aleppo; was married, had a son—and after his wife's death became a monk; in 1636 he was raised to be Archbishop of Aleppo, and in 1648 he rose to the dignity of Patriarch. He applied himself to his flock with all the zeal and self-denial of a true Christian pastor. The local authorities oppressed the orthodox Christians; the Patriarchal See was burdened with debts. Macarius, together with his son Paul, departed from Damascus to Constantinople, thence to Moldavia and Wallachia, in order to collect funds in behalf of the See of Antioch. On his return to Damascus he paid off part of the debts with the interest. Some time after he set off again to Erzerum and Achaltsik, belonging also to the Patriarchate of Antioch; and then through Georgia to Russia; how long he remained here is not mentioned in the Antioch History written in the Arabic language; but, on his return with his son to Damascus, he paid all the debts of the Patriarchal See, established schools, provided the churches and monasteries with surplices and vessels, strengthened his whole flock both by precept and example in the Orthodox Religion. During his first travels he translated from Greek into Arabic five, and during his second travels ten church-books, which before that time the common people did not understand, as they spoke no other language but Arabic. In Leipsic and Venice he printed the requisite number of these books and furnished therewith all the churches and monasteries of Antioch. From Erzerum, Achaltsik and other places he brought a quantity of different books and formed a very rich library at the Patriarchate. In 1672, to the great regret not only of the Orthodox Christians, but even of the Turks, Macarius died of poison by the artifices and envy of people belonging to another faith, and indignant at his zeal for the Eastern Orthodox Religion. (All the particulars of the life of this exemplary pastor of the Church were communicated to me by his Eminence Neophytus, Metropolitan of Heliopolis and Mount Libanus; and were by him extracted from an Arabic manuscript History of Antioch.)

To the traditions of the Antiochine Church let us add what is known out of our historical documents of the residence of the Patriarch Macarius in Russia. (This is taken from the Grecian affairs of the Moscow Archives, NN. 8, 9, 19. For communicating these curious documents I must return my sincerest thanks to Prince M. A. Obolensky, Chief of the Moscow Archives of Foreign Affairs.) From them it is evident that he twice visited our native country: the first time in 1655. In the number of persons who attended him is mentioned his son Paul the Archdeacon. The Czar gave him a triumphal reception, and made him rich presents. He received at that time a silver cup with a lid, weighing 8 pounds and 17 zolotniks; several velvet suits of cloths; satin; 140 sables of which 40 cost a hundred rubles each, and 80 cost fifty rubles each; in money two hundred rubles.

The second time, in 1667, the Patriarch Macarius came to Moscow together with Paisius, Patriarch of Alexandria, who is in the different documents called also Pope, on the occasion of the Trial of Nikon.

On the 16th of September, 1667, both the Patriarchs arrived in Simbirsk, and thence wrote a letter to the Czar for permission to continue their journey, which was hindered by false reports of the plague. On the 9th of October the Czar sent out to meet the Patriarchs, a colonel and the celebrated Artamon Sergaevitch Matveieff, chief of the Moscow Streltzi. A special ceremony was prescribed for this meeting, and Matveieff was ordered to show the Patriarchs the greatest respect and to honour them as he would a Patriarch of Moscow. Matveieff was to attend them all the way to Moscow.

Prince Prozorofsky was sent out to meet them near Moscow. In the city itself a triumphal procession accompanied them through the Spaski-gate to the Cathedral of the Assumption, thence they were brought to the place appointed for their residence. In the Patriarch of Antioch's retinue, which consisted of 15 persons, is mentioned that same Paul the Archdeacon, his son. On the 4th of November they were both triumphantly received by the Czar Alexis Michaelovitch. The Patriarch Macarius presented to the Czar these sacred gifts: a cross with part of the wood of the holy Cross and with the relics of the holy Apostle and Evangelist Luke, of the holy Apostle Andrew the First-called, and of others of the holy martyrs; to the Czarina Maria Ilinishna; the relics of the holy martyrs Eustathius, Placida, and Auxentius; besides this, to the Czar as well as to the Czarina, to the Czarevitch as well as to the Czarevnas, black incense, myrrh, manna and various eastern fruits. The Czar made the Patriarch still richer presents. It is pleasing to see by the above-mentioned evidence of the Antioch History, that the silver, velvet, satin, sables and money of the pious Russian Czar, went to pay off the debt of the Antioch See, and to establish orthodox schools in Antioch.

Both the Patriarchs then participated in the judgment of Nikon, which took place December 12th, 1667. By a letter of advertisement from the same date they gave an account of this affair to the other Eastern Patriarchs. In 1668, June 5th, the Patriarch Macarius departed after a solemn parting ceremony. In 1669, May 7th, he wrote from Iberia, to the Czar, begging him to forward without delay a passport for crossing the Sultan's dominions, without which he could not proceed. There are some fragments of incomplete papers which tell how the Khan of Shemakan oppressed the Patriarch on his way, and having taken from him by violence the Russian Czar's presents, paid him for them five thousand rubles only, instead of the eight which they were worth. (In London, in 1836 were published: The Travels of Macarius, in Arabic, translated by Balfour.)

After the violent death of Macarius, in the time of Cyril the 148th Patriarch, the Roman Catholics elected the pseudo-patriarch Maximus, who took away the treasures, surplices, books, and conveyed them to Mount Libanus. From this time, namely from 1720, the Roman Catholic Patriarchate continues to exist, and to persecute our orthodox one with violence.

In the 18th century lived the Russian (pilgrim) Basil Grigorovitch-Barskoi-Plaki-Alboff, born in Kief, a monk of Antioch. He has left us a detailed description of all his travels on foot. In 1728, he visited Damascus, where is at present the See of the Patriarch of Antioch. Sylvester then governed there, but retired to Constantinople on account of the disturbances caused by the Uniates. In 1734 Basil Gregorovitch returned again to Damascus, and was ordained a monk by the Patriarch Sylvester, who loved him as a father does his son. He described Damascus with its churches; the mosques which had formerly been Christian churches; the Monastery Say-de-nia famous for its thaumaturgical image of the Mother of God, painted by Ev. Luke; the cave of St Thecla, in which sleep the relics of this first martyr; Mount Libanus, which he traversed when it was covered with snow in 1734 in the month of August; the town of Heliopolis, which was once famous, but was then in ruins, as it is at present; and finally Antioch, the ancient abandoned seat of the Patriarch of Antioch, and rendered sacred by the first acts of the Apostles Peter and Paul. How affecting is his narration of his approach to this place! He travelled four days; what hardships he underwent; it was Autumn; cold winds blew; continual rains poured down; his road lay across high mountains; no villages; in the desert of Turcomania; great affliction weighed down the exhausted pilgrim. He crossed the mountains and approached the fields of Antioch; but all of a sudden he saw on the road in a mountain, a church which had been a Christian one, hewn out of the stone, and in ruins. Cut in the walls he read the Greek words : "Holy God," and saw a cross with this inscription : "the Cross raises those who fall." Having read this, he forgot all the sorrow and hardships he had endured on his journey; bowed to the holy cross, and went on his way rejoicing. He describes the dreadful state of oppressed Christianity in Antioch: he listened to the liturgy with them in a cave, where they concealed themselves from the malice of the Mahometans. The times of the primitive persecutions of Christianity were here represented in a lively manner to the devout Russian traveller.

All that this eye witness described above a hundred years ago, is still true. The holy place remains the same; oppressed Christianity suffers as before.

The cave, mentioned by Basil Gregorovitch, still exists at the distance of an hour and a half from Antioch. On Sundays and holidays the Christians still perform divine service in it. During the heat of the day, and for the whole night the Turkish shepherds drive their flocks into this cave. At the break of day the priest in plain clothes, for fear of the Turks, comes to it, and together with the orthodox Christians clears away all the filth, and performs divine service. When service is over, the cave again becomes the asylum of the Turkish shepherds.

In 1813, a pious person, Aboo-Sabbas by name, wished to build, at his own expense, a church in Antioch itself. He obtained from the Sultan a firman to this effect, and was about to set to work; but the mullah opposed it, and accused Aboo-Sabbas of having the intention to build not a temple but a fortress. The sovereign believed the mullah, and hanged the pious Christian for his godly intention, together with three priests and a deacon, who were also impeached by the mullah of evil designs against the Sultan's power. From that time divine service is performed, as before, in the cave of the Turkish shepherds.

We will now represent the existing state of the Antioch Patriarchate. It has under its jurisdiction 3 metropolitan-dioceses, eight bishops, and all in all 25,836 orthodox Christian families.

The Patriarchal Throne of Antioch, though reckoned, as formerly, in Antioch, remains in Damascus in the monastery of Pelementi (the Assumption of the Blessed Virgin). In all its cities there are reckoned 1400 orthodox families, 10 churches, 32 priests with the ecclesiastics belonging to them; 5 monasteries of which 4 are for men, containing 83 monks; and 1 for women which is called in Arabic Saï-de-naya (the consolation of all the afflicted), distant about 30 versts from Damascus, and containing 32 nuns. In Antioch were born St Beryllus, a disciple of the Apostle Peter; the martyr-bishops Babilas, Lucian, Theodoret; the Venerable Father Abraham, and Eustathius. In Damascus were born the Venerable Sophronius, Patriarch of Jerusalem, St John Damascene, St Peter, who was adopted by father St John Damascene.

Metropolitan dioceses. 1st *Aleppo.* Orthodox families 105, churches 1, priests with their clerks in all 4. Simeon the Stylite and his reverend mother Martha were born in Aleppo. The pillar on which Simeon did penance is situated in the mountains, at a distance of 4 hours from Antioch.

2nd *Heliopolis* [Baalbek], where was born, A.D. 160, the martyr-nun Eudosia, and *Mount Libanus.* In these places and their environs there are in all 896 orthodox families, 7 churches, 26 priests with their assistants.

3rd *Tyre and Sidon.* The Metropolitan of these towns has his residence in the villages Hasbeia and Rasheia. This diocese reckons in all 1200 orthodox families; and 29 churches, and 65 priests. The Roman Catholics have lately taken violent possession of half of one of these 29 churches at Sidon. Sidon was the birthplace of St Serapion.

Archbishoprics. 1st *Beirout.* In the city Beirout and its environs there are 6000 orthodox families, 7 monasteries, 70 churches, 230 priests with their assistants.

2nd *Seleucia.* Orthodox families 1070; churches 18; priests with their clergy 38. Here are the relics of St Thecla the first female-martyr, called Isapostolical.

3rd *Tripoli.* Orthodox families 2000, monasteries 4, monks 16, churches 23; priests besides their ecclesiastics 28.

4th *Arcadia.* In the environs 2100 orthodox families; monasteries 2, churches 50, priests, exclusive of other ecclesiastics, 68.

5th *Emesa* near Palmyra. Families 700, churches 4, priests 7. Here are the relics of St Julian.

6th *Epiphaneia.* Families 2060, churches 6, priests 15.

7th *Adana.* Families 1500, churches 7, priests 17.

8th *Laodiceia.* Families 2085, churches 30, priests besides their ecclesiastics 35.

In the beginning of the patriarchate of Methodius the present Patriarch, a school was established in Damascus, in which the orthodox Christians learn the Greek and Arabic languages. In Beirout a school has been established for orthodox Christians, in which they learn the Modern Greek, French, Italian, and Arabic languages, under the immediate inspection of the Patriarch, the Archbishop of Beirout and the Russian Consul-General.

There are in all 21 Roman Catholic monasteries, formerly belonging to the orthodox Christians; of which 17 are for men, containing 336 monks, and 4 for women, having 82 nuns. Roman Catholic schools and institutions, established long ago, 13; 2 printing presses; 6 houses of charity. Roman Catholic families, living in Syria, in all 9775.

The number of Maronites amounts to 15,860 families, living in Syria and on Mount Libanus. Maronite schools 4.

The Missionaries of the Roman propaganda use every possible means to add to their numbers; they establish schools, and printing-presses; the books printed therein are distributed gratis to every Syrian; they build alms-houses and hospitals; take churches and monasteries from the orthodox Christians; they persuade their adherents to have no communication with orthodox Christians, and to look upon them as worse than Jews and Mahometans; the latter, as masters of those parts, are liberally bribed to persecute and oppress the orthodox Christians; under colour of benefactions they are furnished with small sums at the Jewish interest of 10 per cent. a month; securing the loan by taking immoveable property as a pledge; their possessions are taken from them by force of law, and then the destitute person is left the choice either of remaining for ever without them, or of acknowledging the popish dogmas and thus receiving back his property. The persecutions exercised by the Pope's missionaries against the orthodox Christians are excused by their zeal for their order.—The Protestant missionaries, who come from England and even America, act also in their own interests.

Seeing the extreme misery of his flock and the rich means of the adversaries, Methodius the 151st Patriarch of Antioch, now residing in Damascus, has resolved to address a petition to the Russian Emperor, that he should permit the Church of Antioch to stretch out her hand to his pious nation with a blessing and a prayer for succour. The Emperor has consented, and Methodius the Patriarch has sent off to our capital, Neophytus the Metropolitan of Heliopolis and Mount Libanus, having furnished him with the following letter:

Methodius By the Grace of God Patriarch of Great Antioch.

Our humility, together with the Holy Council of Archbishops under the jurisdiction of our most holy Apostolical and Patriarchal See of Antioch, announces by this recommendatory letter, that in consequence of a proposition of the most holy Governing Synod of Russia, His Imperial Majesty the pious Sovereign of all the Russias,—may his Empire be invincible and glorious for ever,—moved by compassion, has been pleased to grant his Imperial and most prudent permission for the coming into his orthodox Russian Empire, of one of the Archbishops of our poor See of Antioch, with his brotherhood, for the purpose of collecting alms, in order to establish schools and printing presses; to restore in Damascus the church of our Father Nicolas Thaumaturgus who is among the saints, to repair other old churches and monasteries, and to erect indispensable public Christian edifices; wherefore in consequence of the decision of the council, ratified by us, we have appointed and despatched, as bearer of this letter, Neophytus the Metropolitan of Heliopolis and Mount Libanus, and our beloved brother in Christ; with him are sent the brethren, father Sophronius the most reverend Archimandrite of our See, Anthimus the Priest-monk, and Mr John Papandopolo, Secretary of our See.

The Apostolical See of Antioch has long suffered under the heavy yoke of infidel thraldom, from which during this long and bitter subjection, it has borne and still continues to bear such multiplied and heavy oppression as we cannot describe in words. During the time that creeds contrary to our orthodox Eastern church have been propagated and strengthened here, our blessed predecessors the Patriarch and Archbishops, as well as we ourselves and our Archbishops, have suffered and still suffer innumerable oppressions and persecutions in various forms. Our much oppressed See beholds around it a deplorable sight: at present the Roman Catholics are strengthening and extending their doctrines in Syria; they violently take the best monasteries and churches from the orthodox Christians; nor are the church sacristies and libraries of our See less exposed to their plunder; they even take the precious and sacred sacramental vessels and coverings, vestments and books, which have been preserved here from time immemorial.

Of the churches and monasteries which in former times served as asylums for our orthodox Christians, some have fallen into decay, others have been deserted, and those which still exist are deprived even of the common vessels and sacramental coverings; and the Christians for want of orderly schools, teachers, and other public institutions, are wallowing in the most pernicious ignorance and barbarism.

All these shocking evils proceed from the great want of means by which all might be rectified.

Having stated our condition as well as we could, we apply to all you orthodox inhabitants of the Russian Empire, that, moved by heartfelt pity and Christian compassion towards the shocking misfortunes of the most ancient See of Antioch, you would graciously receive our above mentioned deputed Archbishop and his fellow-travellers, and that you would be generously pleased to afford succour in so important and saving an action as that of supporting Orthodoxy in Syria, each according to his means, in order that we may be enabled to renew and repair the churches and monasteries which have decayed and been deserted, to establish printing presses, and to institute Christian schools for the education of the clergy and other orthodox Christians, that we may not appear in every respect the last among other nations.

And we, with our holy Archbishops, lifting up day and night our supplicatory hands to the gracious and bountiful God, will implore His boundless goodness, to grant you perfect health, constant prosperity, a long life, and all the blessings desired by your pious souls; the names of those who afford succour, names so sacred to us, will be inscribed in the churchbook of our Apostolical See, as an eternal memorial.

May God who is rich in goodness, write your names in heaven in the Divine book of eternal life; may He reward you for your benevolence, by His heavenly gifts and bounties; may He deem you worthy of a blessed death, granting you in Paradise His Kingdom of Heaven. May His grace and boundless goodness with the prayers and blessing of our humility be with you. Amen.

In the year of our Lord 1842, September.

(*Signed*) Methodius, Patriarch of Antioch, prays in Christ for you all.

Archbishops: METHODIUS of Emesa.
BENJAMIN of Beiroot.
JOANNIKIUS of Tripoli.
ARMEMIUS of Laodiceia.
ZACHARIAS of Arcadia.
Metropolitan: ISAIAH of Tyre and Sidon.
Archbishops: BARNABAS of Epiphaneia.
JACOB of Seleucia.

Let us here repeat the words of our Eastern guest, the representative of the Church of Antioch, words which have already been printed in the Moscow journals.

"God grant that the orthodox Christians of all the Russias may under the reign of our victorious and pious sovereign, the father of nations, be preserved in peace a long, long time—if there is nothing eternal on earth; and may they, as each is inclined, give a part of their superfluity to their foreign brethren, who have enlightened them with the light of Evangelical doctrine, whereupon is founded the power, glory, and peace of their dear fatherland."

Weak will be a word from me after these words. I shall think myself happy, if this information about the Church of Antioch, her origin, struggles with infidels, her relations with us, and her present condition, shall serve to excite sympathy in my fellow-countrymen, and Christian zeal to afford her affectionate succour in her great sufferings.

APPENDIX. III.

STATE OF THE PATRIARCHATE OF ANTIOCH IN 1850

(*Translated from the Russ*).

THE SYRIAN CHURCH.

THE Syrian Church which has suffered so much, had early experience of powerful enemies of Christianity, and carried on with them a continual, sharp and unequal struggle during the course of 18 centuries, and is still carrying on the same in our own time. She begat and nurtured numerous children, but the greater part of them have rejected her doctrines, her traditions and discipline, have separated from her and persist in their errors (viz. the Nestorians, Jacobites, Maronites and Uniats).

HIERARCHY.

The Orthodox Syrian Church is governed by the Patriarch of Antioch. According to the fixed rule of the Eastern Orthodox Catholic Church, he must be elected by the clergy and people, and must be a Syrian ecclesiastic. This rule was adhered to almost universally down to the beginning of the last century. But from that time he has been elected from the Greek clergy by the Patriarch of Constantinople and his Synod—in consequence of the growth of the Unia in Syria. In order to form a well-grounded judgment both of the right of the Great Church to elect the Patriarch of Antioch, and of the canonical limits of this right, it is necessary to take notice of the following events in the history of the Syrian Church.

§ 1.

In the middle of the fifth century, the Christians of Antioch and their Clergy, in place of the Patriarch Domnus, who had been expelled by Dioscorus, received Maximus who was chosen and consecrated for them by the Patriarch of Constantinople Anatolius, contrary to the canons then in force in the Œcumenical Church. The Pope of Rome Leo I. objected against this infringement of the canons, but ineffectually. In the time of the Emperor Zeno the successor of the Patriarchs Anatolius and Gennadius of Constantinople, ordained and sent to Antioch Kalandion: Pope Simplicius condemned him for this, but again without any result. In the reign of Justin there was sent from Constantinople an orthodox Patriarch named Paul, to take the place of Severus the heretical Patriarch of Antioch.

§ 2.

In the first half of the seventh century, when the Caliphs had become masters of Syria, the Patriarchs of Antioch Macedonius, George and Macarius, all three Monothelites, and Theophanes who was orthodox, were consecrated at Constantinople: from thence they governed their flock, and there they died. It is manifest that at that time necessity justified a departure from the canons.

§ 3.

After the death of Theophanes, who has been just mentioned, the Syrian Bishops elected from their own clergy Stephen, by birth and language a Syrian, and from that time the Patriarchs of Antioch were all in succession natives, till Antioch was taken from the Caliphs by Nicephorus Phocas, Zimisces and Basil. But after the union of this city to the Greek Empire, there were some Patriarchs who were consecrated at Constantinople, as Agapius, John, Elias and George. However, the inhabitants of Antioch themselves asked for these Patriarchs from the Emperors.

§ 4.

After the Crusades, from the thirteenth century to the eighteenth, the Patriarchs of Antioch were elected and consecrated by the Synod of the Syrian Bishops. It is true that in troubled times, when there were hierarchical schisms in the Syrian Church, some of the Patriarchs were consecrated at Constantinople. But this was done only upon requests made from Damascus.

§ 5.

From the beginning of the eighteenth century, which was marked by the grievous struggle of Orthodoxy against the Unia, they began to elect and to consecrate at Constantinople Patriarchs from the Greek clergy: but again this was not done arbitrarily, but on the request of the Syrian Bishops who could not agree among themselves in the election of Patriarchs on the spot. In this way it was, that the chair of Antioch was filled by Silvester, and after him by Philemon, and after him again by Daniel, etc.

From all these facts it appears, that the Church of Constantinople took part in the affairs of the See of Antioch for various reasons: but at the same time that it also preserved this See; and that it has a right to take part in the election of the Patriarch of Antioch, when the

Syrian Bishops themselves ask that this should be done; otherwise there would have been an infringement upon the independence of the Patriarchal Throne. The appointment of a successor to the Patriarch of Antioch by his own election or bequest, ought by no means to be admitted: for this is contrary to the Canons of the Church and to the customs of Syria, and may beget dissatisfaction among the Clergy and people.

The Patriarch of Antioch, besides those rights which are common to Bishops, has certain special prerogatives:

1. The right of calling local Synods for the settlement of good order in the Church, or for the cutting off of any unedifying customs among the people: so, for instance, in the second half of the sixteenth century, there was a Synod called by the Patriarch Joachim to limit the expense of the antenuptials, given by bridegrooms to maidens or widows for the wedding entertainment: and in this Synod it was enacted that the bridegroom should give, according to his condition, from 48 to 12 piastres; hereby an end was put to the abuse of fathers and mothers, who demanded from bridegrooms for their daughters considerable sums.

2. The Patriarch of Antioch is not the irresponsible judge of all Church matters, or manager of all the Church property: his power is limited by the constitutions of the Synod of Damascus, held under the Patriarch Philemon in (the year) A.D. 1766—67.

3. The Patriarch of Antioch has the right to punish the Christians who are subject to his jurisdiction with imprisonment, and by sending them to the galleys. But this right is now almost nominal. Any, who should be condemned to punishment, would immediately join the Unia, and, through the protection of the European Consuls, would escape the execution of their sentence. Hence the Patriarch can only address mild admonitions to offenders and seek their voluntary submission.

4. In civil suits he pronounces his sentence only when the plaintiff and the defendant are agreed to have recourse to his judgment. However, his sentence may be set aside by the Turkish authorities.

5. The patriarch of Antioch is independent of the Pashas and their tribunals: he is subject to the jurisdiction of the Porte alone; but in Ecclesiastical matters, he is judged by a Synod.

6. As the head of the orthodox people, he makes himself responsible for it towards the Turkish Government (that is for its obedience) and answers with his own liberty or his life in case of any popular agitation. Thus at the time of the Greek insurrection, A.D. 1826, the Patriarch Methodius was thrown into prison, and only on Easter day was allowed to celebrate the Liturgy: and after he had celebrated it, they took him back to prison. In A.D. 1845, when a league was made by the Druses of Anti-Libanus against the orthodox Christians of the village of Hasbeia in the

diocese of Tyre and Sidon, the Patriarch of Antioch pledged himself to the Pasha of Damascus for these Christians that they should not do any act of hostility against the Druses. The Christians obeyed the Patriarch, but the Druses carried into effect their treacherous plot and massacred 250 men, murdering also or dishonouring their wives and children.

7. The Patriarch of Antioch, in like manner, equally with the Pashas, has his representative (commissioner) at Constantinople, to attend to the affairs of his See. However, his requests go to the Porte through the Patriarch of Constantinople.

The place where the Patriarch resides at Damascus is not spacious, but yet not too confined: only the buildings upon it are inconveniently arranged. The house of the Patriarch is already old, and his officers, such as the Archimandrite his Vicar, two secretaries and the rest, live in narrow chambers on the flat roof of the house. The church, which is within the Patriarchate itself, is the only one for all the orthodox Christians of Damascus, and it is a very poor one. One of the side apses of this church, the altar of which is dedicated to Saint Nicolas, was renewed not many years ago with money collected at Moscow by the Metropolitan of Heliopolis.

The Patriarchate at Damascus has been reduced to poverty from the following causes:

(α) The property of the Church was partly carried away to the Lebanon by the Patriarch Seraphim who became a Uniat, and part of it was plundered by the relatives of the orthodox Patriarch Cyril after his death in A.D. 1720. (β) During the long-continued hierarchical divisions of the sixteenth and seventeenth centuries, which cost the Church so dear, both the Patriarchs and the Christians, especially those of Damascus, were ruined by extortions and incurred heavy debts. (γ) Excessive losses were sustained through the struggle which went on for more than a century between the Unia and Orthodoxy. (δ) Lastly, during those intestine divisions which marked the first half of our own century in Syria, the Christians were reduced to utter poverty. As for the revenues of the Patriarchate, they are poor enough.

The Bishops.

In the last century there were counted within the Patriarchate of Antioch 16 sees, but now there are only ten: for the see of Akkis (or Akhaltsikh) has been incorporated into the Russian Church, and the other five, viz., those of Heliopolis, of Amida in Mesopotamia, of Bostra and Palmyra in Arabia and of Theodosiopolis (Erzeroum) have ceased to exist, Orthodoxy having in those places become extinct. However, there are two titular Bishops, one of Heliopolis, who resides

APPENDIX. III.   217

at Moscow, and the other of Palmyra, who governs the monastery of Saint Spiridion.

Of the nine sees at present existing, one, that of Tyre and Sidon, has the rank of Metropolis, while all the rest are Archbishoprics: Exarchs in Syria there are none, and so all the Bishops address themselves officially to the Patriarch himself.

In Syria, as in all the East, from the time of the Apostles, it has been the rule to appoint as many Bishops as possible: each of them has a small flock; consequently he is able with greater convenience and facility, to guide it to everlasting salvation, calling by name each one of the sheep of Christ. All the families see their Bishop every year, not only in the church, but also in their houses, and if he has the gift of teaching or of piety, which is more eloquent than all sermons, he is then a pillar and support of Orthodoxy. The habit and the pleasure of seeing the Bishop in their houses, the respect felt for his rank, and hearty gratitude for his apostolical labours, cause the Orthodox to press closely around him; and it is only flattery, deceit and violence, or influences of corruption that can draw away from him weak souls. If the Bishops had not been numerous in Syria, Orthodoxy would long ago have died out there.

The rights and duties of the Syrian Bishops are nearly the same with those of their Patriarch. A Syrian Bishop, as a man of God, enlightens by the Word of God, sanctifies by the Sacraments and disciplines by Ecclesiastical Censures, the souls entrusted to him by the Lord. As a man of the people, he shares with the Orthodox people poverty, humiliation and persecution from misbelievers; he every year visits all the families, both rich and poor, and lives from their offerings: he blesses their marriages, their baptisms and their burials: his door is always open for all whoever they may be who come to him either for counsel, or for judgment or for protection, and at his hearth there is often prepared a hospitable entertainment both for rich and poor from the means afforded by their own freewill-offerings, made according to their ability.

From the beginning of the last century till now, the Patriarchs and some of the Bishops have been and are native Greeks: they have rendered the Syrian Church services of no small importance. They gave her peace, by putting an end to hierarchical divisions; they gave her independence, by breaking off her dangerous relations with Rome; they have established order in the monasteries, and defended them from being plundered by the Sheikhs and their relatives: they stopped the defection of the Arab Bishops to the Unia, and long kept the Uniats in fear by the voice of the whole Church and the Greek nation, and by their persevering instances with the Turkish government.

Monasteries.

Happily, there have been preserved in Syria some Patriarchal and Diocesan monasteries which maintain Orthodoxy. Of the first kind are the following:

1. *The Monastery of Saint George*—which is in the diocese Arki in the mountains of Akkara. It is not known when and by whom it was founded; but it was repaired in A.D. 1700 by the Patriarch of Antioch, Athanasius, and enlarged by additional buildings in the years 1837 and 1838. Of religious in this convent there are thirty persons, who are all Syrians. Among them there is no actual Hegumen, but his duties are performed by a monk selected by the Patriarch. The church is very small. This monastery has in its neighbourhood a good quantity of arable land, which is cultivated by the free peasants of two neighbouring villages according to a fixed rule of partnership, by which they are to be content with the fourth part of the produce. The live stock of the monastery is in a good condition. The monastery itself is surrounded by oliveyards and mulberry trees for silkworms. Of vineyards, too, there is a good number. This old monastery is regarded with pious devotion by the inhabitants of that region, whatever may be their religion; more especially by the Ansari, who are in the habit of dedicating their new-born children to Saint George, inscribing them as belonging to the monastery, and then, when they are to be married, redeeming them by a small offering of money or of something else in kind. This custom extends even to the cattle of the Ansari, in case of any of them being sick and recovering. As this monastery is situated on the high way between Aleppo and Tripoli, it serves as a halting-place for whole caravans, so that of barley alone it expends as much as 1500 tchetverts and a great quantity of wheat, buckwheat, oil, wine, etc. But these great outgoings are compensated with some small surplus by the voluntary offerings of the travellers. This explains how it comes to pass that the monastery keeps in its pay as many as forty servants. Besides this, the monks of Saint George every year collect alms in the neighbouring and more distant villages, and especially from the Ansari, who are not Christians. The Kings of Georgia were benefactors to the monastery of Saint George by offerings of church plate and vestments, and allowed the monks to collect alms in their dominions every three years.

2. *The Monastery of the Assumption of the Blessed Virgin*, called Belemend, from the name of its founder, perhaps the same as the Crusader Belmond (Boemond). This monastery is built on the first rise of the Lebanon, within sight of the Mediterranean Sea, and it is distant from Tripoli not more than a ride of two hours and a half on horseback. At the time of the Greek insurrection, it was entirely desolate; there

were no monks in it, the church was without windows, without a floor, without an iconostasis, and without sacred vestments, and it was more like a prison than a house of God. The property of the monastery was in disorder, and in the hands of strangers. The present Patriarch, Methodius, wishing to restore this monastery, made a happy choice of a Hegumen for it in the Priest-monk Athanasius, a native of Damascus. In the course of thirteen years (1830—1842) this Hegumen by his disinterested and diligent management, put into good order the old possessions of the monastery, and acquired for it new. With the revenues arising from these possessions, he repaired the church, and furnished it with sacred vessels, vestments and books; so that it became the very best in all Syria: he repaired the whole monastery, added new cells, and furnished them with everything that was necessary according to the custom of the place. There collected around him thirty-five monks, all natives, and lived according to the rules of a cœnobium. That is not all: pained to see Orthodoxy losing ground in Syria, loving his countrymen and lamenting their ignorance of their Faith, seeing examples of good management in the convents of the Maronites and Uniats, which diffused among the people a certain light of instruction and knowledge, the Hegumen Athanasius established in his monastery a school for monks, with a view to fitting them for the preaching of the Word of God, and for the holding of Episcopal Sees. Monks, young and old, were daily taught the Arabic and Greek languages and church-music, by teachers brought expressly for them from Tripoli and Damascus; while he himself, every day after the customary Services, taught them the truths of the Faith and rules of good living, by reading to them the Lives of the Saints, or the Works of the Fathers of the Church, in their native tongue. Within the monastery there reigned order, obedience to the Superior, piety and chastity, industry and knowledge. It was a hive of God, and the bees themselves were fed in it with the honey of the Word of God, and built honeycombs for others.

The Hegumen Athanasius twice threw himself at the feet of Ibrahim Pasha, and begged of him two favours for his convent, viz., that it should be freed from imposts, and that it should be secured in the possession of its mills, which the Prince of the Lebanon, the Emir Beshir, was seeking to appropriate.

After this Hegumen, who went away to Jerusalem in the quality of preacher, the best of the monks were dispersed; some to the monastery of Saint George, some to Mount Athos, some to Sidon; the remaining twenty-two live on, hoping for better days.

3. *The Monastery of the Prophet Saint Elias* on Mount Lebanon, at a distance of six hours' ride from Beyrout. It is not known when and by whom it was founded; but it was repaired and improved in the years 1842—43 by the Hegumen Macarius a Greek. The whole monastery is very small and confined. The church is small, but decent: the new

cells, on the second story, are good enough. The monks in all are eight, and there are as many servants.

4. *The Nunnery of the Nativity of the Blessed Virgin*, called Saidanaia, at the distance of six hours towards the north from Damascus. This is the oldest convent in Syria. It was founded by the Emperor Justinian I. in the fifth century. Its site is very picturesque. The convent occupies, and one may say crowns, the summit of a high and bare hill standing isolated like Mount Tabor. In this monastery the church is not small, but dark and poor: it needs to have its upper part rebuilt: behind the principal sanctuary there is a small oratory, in which there is a miraculous image of the Blessed Virgin. The cells, with the guest-chambers, are in all eighty, the nuns thirty-eight in number: they come hither from all the Syrian dioceses, and are admitted by the Patriarch, on the recommendation of the Bishops. After a probation from one to three years, they are tonsured. Their habit consists of a black gown (riasa), and their heads are covered with a long black handkerchief, so that nothing of the face is seen except the eyes. The nuns of the Saidanaia lead a strict and abstemious life: they eat no flesh meat; each one receives from the convent bread, tolokno (oats boiled, dried in the oven, and ground), olive oil, fuel, and materials for their clothes and shoes, which they have to make up for themselves. The old nuns communicate in the Holy Mysteries every Saturday: the younger ones once in the month. They go out from the convent only when they carry down from the mountain to the neighbouring cemetery any one of the sisters who may have died. They have no Superior, but the duty of overlooking them is committed by the Patriarch to some one of the nuns who is more devout and intelligent than the rest. As for the administration of the temporal affairs of the house, it is attended to by two trustees; one chosen from the Priests of the Convent, the other a Christian of consideration from Damascus or from the village below the monastery. It is their duty to provide the monastery with all that is necessary: they are changed every year, and render an account to the Patriarch of their income and expenses. The convent is maintained by the freewill offerings of pious visitors, especially of Christian women, who come there to pray before the miraculous image of the Blessed Virgin, and bring their sick in the hope of obtaining healing through her. Besides this in every diocese there are persons acting in behalf of this convent, who collect for it voluntary offerings; but of property in general, moveable or immoveable, it has very little.

The Saidanaia Convent is exceedingly venerated by all the orthodox Christians of Syria. In it maidens who are poor or left orphans, crippled or diseased, and old widows, find refuge from the temptations and afflictions of the world, and serve the Lord day and night in fasting and prayer: there the sick obtain healing. In this convent there are also some educated nuns, who teach the young novices and some girls from the village, to read and write. It is satisfactory to know that there is in the world a well-ordered Syro-Arab nunnery. It is a flower-garden, consecrated to the Most Holy Virgin Mary; it is a hospital for sinful souls; a salutary well-spring of grace; the light of the younger Christian maidens.

5. *The Monastery of Saint Thecla*, at six hours' distance from the Saidanaia tő the north, at the Uniat village of Malloolah. It is built under the brow of a high and naked rock, and it is literally an eagle's nest. Under the dark projection of the neighbouring rock, in a cave arranged as a chapel, hidden within the rock itself, are preserved the relics of Saint Thecla. But in the monastery there is a poor church, dedicated under the name of the Forerunner. The Christians, and even the Mussulmans, have the utmost faith in the relics of Saint Thecla, and often obtain, through them, miraculous healing. But, unhappily, the convent is ill kept: in it there lives only a Greek Hegumen with a Deacon and two novices, whom he sends out to collect alms. Ten years ago he made some guest-chambers for pilgrims: and now he is intending to rebuild and enlarge the church.

Besides the Patriarchal Monasteries, there are also some small diocesan houses.

The Archbishop of Arki has two small monasteries of Saint Dometius and of the Prophet Elias, with two monks, not far from the Patriarchal Monastery of Saint George. The first possesses a small piece of arable land, enough for one plough; the second has land enough for four ploughs. These lands have been purchased.

The Archbishop of Tripoli has five small monasteries, within a short distance from the town of Tripoli.

1. *Of Saint James the Persian*, on the first rise of the Lebanon, which was made out of a cemetery church, about the year 1600; in it there are three monks.

2. *Of the Entrance of Our Lady into the Temple*, called Natour, on the sea shore, with three monks.

3. *Of the Nativity of the Blessed Virgin*, called Keftine, upon the stream Kadisha: in it there are five monks.

4. *Of Saint Demetrius*, on the bank of the same stream, but much higher up than Keftine, with two monks.

5. *Of Saint George*, called Kapher. In it there is one monk.

The Archbishop of Beirout has six small monasteries: (1) *Of the Assumption*, called Khamatour, on the stream Abou-Ali, near Tripoli; (2) *Of the Assumption*, called Kiaftoun, on the stream Asphour; (3) *Of the Annunciation*, called Nourie, on the sea; (4) *Of Saint George*, called Kharph, on the Lebanon; (5) *Of the Archangels*, at Boukaata, and (6) A new Monastery *of Saint George* at Souk-el-Garda, also on the Lebanon.

All the diocesan monasteries are supported by small portions of land, vineyards, oliveyards, by mulberry trees, feeding silkworms, offerings from pilgrims, and collections of alms. They are nothing else than so many Episcopal Lodges.

Taken collectively, the Syrian Orthodox Monasteries render a great moral service to the Church. Besides that they make bad people to become good, and some even to become holy;—besides that they serve as a refuge for innocence, for poverty, for orphans, for the aged, and for crippled sufferers;—besides the consolations of grace;—besides charitable attendance and miraculous healings; they support, at least in some small degree, the poor Episcopal Sees, and the Schools for the people. One must not omit here to mention also this, that if, through the inscrutable dispositions of Divine Providence, Orthodoxy should extend itself over Syria, the Patriarchal Monastery of Saint George will diffuse the light of Christianity among the tribe of the Ansari, who cherish a profound veneration for this monastery; while the Monastery of Khamatour will serve to baptize the tribe of the Moutwali who bring their silk to that monastery, and ask the monks to baptize them. Actual baptism is not given to them, but they are only washed with water; for the Moutwali, when they get well, remain Mussulmans. These two monasteries must be considered as bright sparks, from which the light of Orthodoxy may be kindled over all Syria.

The tolerance of the Turkish government allows the monasteries to acquire property, to any extent that is desired, but exacts from them the taxes fixed by the laws,—which is quite equitable. The monasteries paid no tributes only during the time of the Egyptian rule in Syria, till the year 1840.

The Parish Clergy.

The mode of maintenance of the parish Clergy in Syria reminds one of the Apostolic times. There from the beginning it has been the custom that the priests should be chosen from amongst the people and by the people;—citizens, or villagers of some instruction, men of repute, married, already advanced in years, who have bred up their children, and govern well their own households. The Syrian Priest is not burdensome to the people, because he has his own house, his own property, his own children, who provide for him in his old age, being either cultivators of the land, or artizans. He is the first servant of the Christian community, who willingly conforms himself to its will, and with self-sacrifice serves it according to the Lord's command for its salvation. He is a Pastor, who cannot be either proud, or cold towards his flock; else they change him for another.

The election of Priests is not always made with unanimity. It sometimes happens, that the families which elect are divided into parties in the villages and in the towns which have any numerous population. In this case they have recourse to the decision of their Bishop, and then he has need to show his tact and discretion in reconciling or pacifying them.

Unhappily one excellent institution of the Eastern Church owing to circumstances is not carried out in Syria: there are not at present any preachers belonging to the different dioceses. At Constantinople, Smyrna, Jerusalem and other places there are such preachers; and their duty consists exclusively in this, that they preach everywhere, wherever they are sent, or wherever the Bishops take them. In this way in the East, according to a custom of ancient institution, those priests who teach are distinct from the parish priests: they do not perform the offices of the Church. The ground of this institution no doubt is the thought that it is not every one who is capable of teaching, since it is not every one that has the gift of eloquence, whereas every one can perform divine offices; since for this there is needed only faith, purity of life and use. In Syria there are no preachers, because there are there no spiritual schools.

To the honour of the parochial Clergy there, one must say that they are sober, disinterested, and humble, that they strictly adhere to the rites and discipline of the Church to the best of their understanding, and exert themselves to teach some of the village children how to read in the church, if, through the poverty of the parishes, there are no special teachers for them. These children, when they grow older, take the place of our sacristans and clerks.

Among the Syrian clergy at the present time there are some exemplary labourers in Christ's vineyard; viz.

1. The Vicar of the Patriarch, the Archimandrite Agathangelus, a Greek from Anatolia, a meek man, of practical experience, and knowing both the Turkish and Arabic languages.

2. Athanasius, late Hegumen of the Belemend Monastery, a man of dignity, of natural gifts, of an energetic character, a good preacher and a good manager.

3. The Hegumen of the Patriarchal monastery of Saint Elias, Macarius, a Greek. He enjoys the special favour of the present ruler of the Lebanon, the Emir Khaïdar, in consequence of his having concealed his wife and children from the Egyptians, when Ibrahim Pasha sent this Emir into banishment. The Hegumen intercedes with him for any orthodox Christians who have been wronged; he even screens those who have committed offences and saves them from revenge or punishment through the power of the Emir: and hence all the orthodox inhabitants of the Lebanon respect and love him.

4. The Hegumen of the monastery of Khamatour, Isaiah, a Greek, a man of eloquence, of sound judgment, well acquainted with the Arabic language and with the customs and affairs of Syria.

5. The parish priest at Damascus, Father Joseph, who has a numerous family, a native of the place, a devout man of great faith, humility, disinterestedness and patience: he has been a priest now 25 years. It was he who effectually assisted the Patriarch Methodius in opening and establishing the school for the people at Damascus, going round to the houses of the Christians, and exhorting them to send their children to the school. He himself teaches the grammar of the Arabic language, the reading of the Holy Scripture, logic and rhetoric to some select youths: employing himself in the school, he loses his parochial revenues. He is supported by his sons, who go out to work. Besides his school and parochial occupations, Father Joseph has translated our Catechism from the Greek into the Arabic language.

6. The parish priest at Tripoli, a married man, Father Spiridion, a native of the place, a disciple of Father Joseph, a man of gravity: he teaches the Arabic grammar in the people's school at Tripoli.

7. The confessor in the Archiepiscopal See of Beirout, a native, a devout old man: he is unceasingly working in the printing office, preparing manuscripts for the press and collating them with the publicly received church books.

Schools.

The sons of priests very seldom succeed to the calling of their fathers and for the most part remain seculars: hence in Syria there are no young clergy; nor ever have been, in consequence of the clergy being elective.

The Patriarch Methodius would have brought together twelve boys from different dioceses, and wished to prepare them for the service of the Church; but he abandoned this attempt for want of room, and of the means of educating them.

In Syria there might have been instituted popular schools in conformity with the orthodox constitutions of the Church in that region. There the clergy is elective; there are no sacristans and clerks: consequently all the people's schools must be catechetical; in them there must be taught to all the secular children reading and singing such as is used in the Church, the Catechism and Sacred History, in order that those who are chosen from them to be priests, may understand their Faith and may know how to behave themselves in the House of God.

In Syria the incapacity of village and town priests to preach the Word of God ought to be supplemented by the employment of diocesan preachers. This spiritual want calls for the institution of a special *School of Preachers* with a number of scholars proportioned to the number of the Episcopal Sees. This would not be one of our seminaries, nor one of our academies: no, this would be a nursery of young monks, who have already renounced the world and dedicated their life to God, to the Church and to science; and who in the sequel should serve as salt to the impoverished land and as the light of the world in the chairs of preachers and archbishops. Such a school was established in the monastery of Belemend.

At present there are in existence three people's schools—at Damascus, Beirout and Tripoli.

The school at Damascus was founded by the Patriarch Methodius at the Patriarchate, from a sum of money given as alms by the Emperor of Russia to the Chair of Antioch in pursuance of letters for the collection of alms granted in A.D. 1763 and A.D. 1839, and from means furnished by the Patriarch of Jerusalem and by private persons from Russia. It consists of two sections; a *primary* section, in which little boys are taught reading and writing after the old method (not the Lancasterian) by three Arab teachers: and a *grammatical* section in which are taught the Arabic, Turkish and Greek languages. The last of these is learnt by very few and very unwillingly, because the knowledge of it leads to as good as nothing at Damascus. The priest Joseph teaches to a few youths the elements of logic and rhetoric. According to his account there are some of the scholars who may become good masters for this school. In it there are in all 300 boys, who receive instruction: the pay of the teachers is obtained partly from the contributions of the Christians, partly from the revenues of the Patriarchate.

The people's school at Beirout was founded at the Archbishopric at the expense of the citizens and of the monasteries of the diocese of Beirout: and since A.D. 1841, it has been enlarged by help from our Government and from the treasury of the Holy Sepulchre. In this school there are the same two sections as in that of Damascus: but here some youths receive in addition some sort of cultivation by learning the Greek and Italian languages, and the first principles of Geography and Arithmetic. The scholars in A.D. 1843 were in number 200.

In Tripoli there was opened a people's school in A.D. 1841 at the Archiepiscopal residence, in a house belonging to the Holy Sepulchre, and it is maintained by grants from the Archbishop and from the treasury of the Church. It consists of two classes: a *primary* class in which the boys are taught to read, and a *grammatical* class, in which they write, and learn the elements of Arabic grammar.

In the harbour of Tripoli there is another elementary school in which seventy boys are taught reading and writing by a lay master. This school is kept near the church of Saint George in a small dark and narrow chamber. It is maintained by the town's people.

In the other towns and villages of Syria the Christian children are taught letters after the old method.

At Beirout there has long been an Arabic printing-press at the Archiepiscopal residence; but it remained completely neglected after the bombardment of this city by the Russians, in the latter part of the last century. In A.D. 1842 it was started again. Arabic type was obtained from France: a skilful superintendent of the press was engaged, and some thousands of copies of the Psalter and Missal were printed.

The Churches and the Orthodox People.

The Orthodox people in Syria are industrious, sober, temperate and religious. The mother, the priest, tradition and custom are the strict guardians of the Faith and of the rules of the Church in that country. In spite of their poverty, in spite of burdensome tributes and imposts, in spite of frequent wars, the Orthodox are forward to pay to their Bishops the fixed *pourie* (contribution); they make gifts to them and maintain the monasteries, the schools and the parish churches.

The Turkish government allows the Christians to repair and even to rebuild churches; but only in their former place and of their former size. This permission costs them very dear: for the Christians must get Mussulmans to bear testimony as to the place and size of the old church, exhibit this testimony to the Government and obtain from it permission to repair or to rebuild. It is only by this method that the work can be commenced. If anywhere there was no church at all before, and there is need to build one, in such a case they, in the first instance, fit up a house for prayer, and the Christians assemble in it for Divine Worship. Some years pass, and then they obtain from Mussulmans the necessary testimony and an act of the tribunal for the building of a church on the site of this house, on the ground that Divine Service had already been celebrated there.

In Syria the churches are sufficiently numerous: not only the towns and the greater villages, but almost every village, even the smallest, has its own church. And so it ought to be: for the villagers, if left without churches, are threatened by many spiritual dangers, as remissness in respect of prayer, indisposition towards confession and Communion, the probability of dying without receiving the Sacraments, indifference towards the Clergy whom they seldom see, the secret spread of heresies and schisms, etc. But when the churches are numerous, and when the priests are elective, not only are these dangers averted, but further the fervour and the consoling power of the Faith are maintained.

The churches in the Syrian towns are decent, in the villages they are poor enough. The number of extremely poor churches, or of churches which have been plundered by the Albanians and the Druses during the last troubles in the Lebanon, or have been ruined by earthquakes, or which have fallen in from time and want of repair, or which have never been completed or properly furnished, owing to the poverty of the parishioners, are as many as seventy in all the dioceses of the See of Antioch. There is need to restore and to furnish all these churches; there is need that we should assist in this work our fellow-Christians of Syria. France and Austria have sent large sums to the Maronites and Uniats who had suffered in the last civil feud on the Lebanon : shall orthodox Russia forget the Syrian people of her own Faith ? Moscow, that heart of Russia, has already welcomed the Metropolitan of Heliopolis coming to her in quest of alms.

In the Syrian churches on Sundays and festivals they make a collection of money on three plates ; and this collection goes to the sick and to the poor, for the purchase of oil and candles, and for the support of the clergy and teachers; according to the disposition made of it by the churchwardens, who are elected annually by the people and confirmed by the Bishop.

The Orthodox Syrians have some peculiar customs. They love to baptize infants on the day of the Theophany (Epiphany), and on the eve of the Festival of Saint John the Baptist. In their churches the women are separated from the men, and are hidden behind curtains and lattices. Instead of the Sacerdotal blessing which is usual among us the Priests lay their hands on the bowed heads of the Christians of both sexes and pronounce at the same time some prayer. When a Priest dies there is a general mourning for him. In Syria there are many poor, but the tributes due for them are paid by the rich.

In a word, in the Orthodox people of those parts, there is religious life, there is obedience to the hierarchical authority, even though exercised by strangers, zeal for the House of God, a desire to have their children instructed, devotions towards the monasteries, and brotherly love.

The Orthodox in Syria live among many tribes of different creeds on the south-eastern coast of Cilicia, in the maritime towns along the coast of Syria from Alexandretta to Tyre, on the mountains of Kelbie, Akkara, Lebanon and Antilibanus, in the broad valley of the Orontes, in the region around Damascus, and in the fertile plains of the Haurân.

Over all this extent, there are reckoned to be approximately of Orthodox inhabitants, beginning from the north and going southwards,

	In the Dioceses	Souls.
1.	Of Adana	1400
2.	Of Laodicea	4000
3.	Of Epiphania	4160
4.	Of Emessa	3200
5.	Of Arke	12,080
6.	Of Tripoli	7800
7.	Of Beirout	20,000
8.	Of Tyre and Sidon	5600
9.	Of Seleucia and Heliopolis	2800
10.	Of Antioch, Damascus and the Haurân, governed by the Patriarch himself	4800
11.	Of Aleppo	500

Total 66,340

This number is very small in relation to that of the rest of the races of different creeds which inhabit Syria, and of whom there are computed to be as many as 400,000 souls.

Moreover the Turkish government recognizes the Orthodox as a distinct nation, which has its own head in the person of the Patriarch of Antioch, and it regards this nation as having precedence over all the rest. The Orthodox are numerous only on the southern offshoots of the mountain range of Kelbie in the diocese of Arke. In the district of Khou of this diocese the administration was of old in the hands of the Orthodox family of the sheikhs Dergam. But the Egyptians, aiming at the suppression of all the local authorities, took advantage of the dissensions existing between the members of this family, and appointed a Moutselim to the above-mentioned district from among the Mussulmans. When the Egyptians were driven out of Syria (1840) the Sheikhs Dergam rendered the Turks services, in return for which the Seraskirs would have again committed the government to the senior representative of the Dergam family. But family dissensions broke out afresh, and the Pasha of Damascus sent thither a Moutselim from the Metwali who is not liked either by the Christians or by the Ansari. On the Lebanon itself the Orthodox are more warlike than either the Maronites or the Uniats. In the districts of Antilibanus in the villages Ras-Phokar, Khreba, Termimas, Khirbet-Merdg-Ayoun all the inhabitants are Orthodox. In time of feuds they commonly observe neutrality.

Approximate table of the Syrian population of other creeds.

	Souls.
Kourds	30,000
Turkomans	15,000
Arabs	4000
Ansari	70,000
Druses	70,000
Metwali (Shiite Mussulmans)	15,000
Sunnite Mussulmans (in the principality of the Lebanon alone)	4800
Maronites (in 17 Districts and cantons of the principality of the Lebanon)	120,677
Greek Uniats	36,735.

www.ingramcontent.com/pod-product-compliance
Lightning Source LLC
Chambersburg PA
CBHW062003220426
43662CB00010B/1214